HOW CAN YOU NOT HEAR THAT?

By TIM CAIN

D1528315

ISBN:
9798604887486

DEDICATION

To the lovely Mrs. Cain and her ongoing willingness to pretend she's hearing new things out of me.

CONTENTS

1 ... AND THIS IS MY SONG

Have you ever had someone approach you and insist they must immediately assault your senses with something (a song, a joke, a book, a movie)?

Yeah. If that was me, sorry. I don't do that as much as I used to.

You know why, though? Sometimes, when I've got that piece of music, it represents a moment that legitimately and irrevocably changed my life. And that's so joyous, I want to share it. For me, my behavior is no different than an addict in the middle of 12 steps who won't stop talking about it, someone recently converted to religion, or a person who's just fallen in love. My entire life is broken into moments defined by when they happened in relation to the music and art I was surrounded by at the time.

That's what you'll be reading here -- descriptions of the view from either side of those acquisitions, and into the pasts and futures of that point. I'm certain you'll find portions to which you relate.

The title of this book is "How Can You Not Hear That?"

If I had a dollar for every time I've said that to someone, I'd have retired long ago. If I had a penny for every time the thought has gone through my head, I'd own a plane. A nice one. With a pilot on-call.

But I've come to realize some people do not "hear that." They don't or can't listen for things in the manner I do. This is a flaw on no one's part. In fact, I suspect that as many times as people suggest they'd like to be able to hear in a specialized way, there are that many people who wish they were unable to hear in that specialized way.

So I invite you on a journey of a lifetime of music, music that's evoked reactions from me. You might share the memory and the reaction. You might not have understood people who reacted like I did, and perhaps I can enlighten you in some way.

In an entertaining way. This isn't a textbook, for crying out loud. Well, I'm not writing it as one anyway.

Through my life, I've had readers say to me, "I have no idea what you're talking about, but I love reading it." I don't think that's literal. What I think they mean is they just don't know anybody who thinks about this stuff the way I do, and they get something out of it. I hope that might be the case for you.

Or, as Shrevie says in Barry Levinson's film *Diner,* "Every one of my records means something! The label, the producer, the year it was made. Who was copying whose style... who's expanding on that, don't you understand? When I listen to my records they take me back to certain points in my life, OK? Just don't touch my records, ever!"

Or, there's this, told to Judd Apatow by Eddie Vedder: " ... we were playing a Kinks record and I said to my friend, 'Yeah, see the guitar tone, the distortion, the space in between,' and he was like, 'You know, some people don't listen to music like you. Some people just listen to it to enjoy it.' "

This is for people who might enjoy dipping a toe in that Eddie Vedder world. Please, allow me to sing you the song of my people.

Yeah yeah yeah.

2 SNIPPETS ONE

(In a day of social media, simple thoughts can be little more than words in the wind. The pages containing these bits is my way of preserving some of those of mine.)

I've got a lot to say to Roger Waters. He should call me.

**

A U2 cover. Please God, strike me deaf for five minutes.

**

Oh great. Androgynous guys playing hair metal. Glad these walls are brick. Easier to crack my skull.

**

"I want the songs to sound exactly like the originals," the paper quoted him as saying. You know what sounds even *more* like the originals? THE ORIGINALS.

**

And then some mornings you get to the office and think, "Oh, I am going to have to listen to a whole bunch of Buckethead today."

**

The "C-I-A" rhyme with "Maf-eye-a" in War's "Why Can't We Be Friends" is a vintage 70s lyric. Like McCartney writing "in this world in which we live in" or Steve Miller rhyming "Texas" and "facts is," not to mention "justice" and "taxes."

**

On the other hand, music has always been the way I spend my time, so it's also possible that the amount of time you spent mastering other life skills is time I spent parsing language on Graham Parker's "Squeezing Out Sparks."

3 FIRST AVENUE

My pattern for concert-going was established very early on.

The most important thing? Gotta get there early. Gotta get a seat. Gotta be sure we have the best eyeline possible. At least that's what I thought.

My concert-going friends were always very tolerant of this. Even if it meant hanging around for two hours before the show while nothing was happening.

There were plenty of good reasons we were early, whether my friends appreciated it or not. There was a whole lot happening. That doesn't diminish my concert-going friends' patience. But it wasn't, as it turns out, just specifically so Tim knew he had a place to sit.

The first time we got to a concert early enough to hear a soundcheck was Shriekback at First Avenue in Minneapolis in 1987. I was the first of a group of five or six, and I hushed the others as the band ran through a song I hadn't heard before. (And neither had most anyone else. They'd played it live for the first time the night before, we learned during our show.)

Then, as I leaned against the building near the front door, waiting to be allowed in for the show whose start was still hours away, out came the band members, one by one. Barry Andrews was first, all 5-foot-4 and no hair of him. He almost ran into me. There wasn't time for me to gather my thoughts enough to say anything intelligent or otherwise. Most of the band looked at those of us standing in line, bemused. Except the bass player, Dave Allen. He had one of the most perfect 100-yard stares I've seen.

I didn't always get to hear soundchecks, but I took advantage when the opportunity presented itself. I slipped into a St. Louis club, only because the door was open and no one stopped me. There was one guy behind the bar, and Moxy Fruvous doing its soundcheck. They were all business, working quickly to get levels where they wanted. They'd play only snippets of songs, but that was all they needed.

But then they started something that sounded … different. It was the first time I'd heard their cover of "Psycho Killer," which they were working into their set.

I knew enough to leap when opportunity presented itself. I found a pay phone in the back of the club, and called a friend and fellow Moxy Fruvous fan back home to share the experience. As the answering machine kicked in, I thought "perfect," and tried to subtly hold the phone to get the best possible sound.

You try to do something subtly next time you're in a room with six people, all of whom can clearly see one another.

The experience was made more perfect when my friend was unable to figure out what the distorted sound on the answering machine was.

Do you ever stop and take a look at how a stage is set up, and imagine what's going to happen when the space is filled with people? There are only two microphones, but you're sure at least three people sing. What kind of keyboard is that in the well? Will the drummer actually use all those toms? (Or conversely, how does he do what he does with just that setup?) Do the guitars look new, or road-worn? What could their appearance mean?

Look at the crowd. I'd look around a show's crowd and calculate myself as the oldest person there. At a Liz Phair show, desperate to find someone of my own generation, I approached one man and asked his age. "Do you think you're the oldest person here?" he said. "I'm almost certain of it," I said. "You're not," he responded, smiling.

"Were you alive when The Beatles broke up?" I asked. He wasn't.

Those are the kind of arguments you don't want to win.

On the other hand, at the first Tony Bennett show I attended, I was the youngest person in the audience by easily 20 years. (He hadn't been on "The Simpsons" yet.)

I got to the point where I'd look for band members wandering around before the show. I don't think I was ever a pest. I was harmless, and anxious to let people do their jobs.

Once in a rare while, I'd encounter someone *during* a show. I was in the rest room during a performance by the Frank Zappa tribute band Project Object. Someone was behind a closed toilet stall. I stood at the urinal in a

8

room that had little area for me and a sink, let alone for two people to maneuver.

The individual on the stool scat-sang along with a guitar solo, and sang pretty well. Just as I was thinking, "Am I in the can with Ike Willis singing? This is pretty cool," the toilet was flushed and Willis emerged from behind the door. I shifted my position at the urinal to allow access to the sink, and in the process blocked the door. I preserved restroom etiquette and kept from looking in his direction.

There was a pregnant pause, then he said, "Excuse me ..."

I moved aside as he walked out, thinking, "How about that ...?" I returned to the guy with whom I was attending the concert and said, "Hey, don't shake hands with Ike after the show."

My first trip to First Avenue was when it wasn't even called First Avenue. I hadn't been going to shows long. I had given up on live music before I even started. Most of the shows I attended had been in arenas, with between 8,000 and 13,000 of my closest friends. The last arena show I attended before deciding I was done was at the late and lamented Metropolitan Sports Center in Bloomington, Minn. Its site is a parking lot now.

In 1978, I saw Player open for Heart (on their "Dog and Butterfly" tour) at the Met. And as it happened – speaking of seeing musicians before the show – we arrived early enough for one of the guys in our group to spot and excitedly approach Heart guitar player Howard Leese as Leese was arriving for the show. Yeah, we probably got there early that night, too.

It was both a fantastic and depressing experience. Player came out and performed for exactly 45 minutes. Years later, I found out that was one of the final gigs for the original band. After a 30-minute break, Heart came on and played exactly 90 minutes. Everything was fine, but that was all. I wanted the unexpected out of my shows, and this one seemed programmed to the second.

I didn't go to another show for more than two years.

It was just a matter of time, though, before my introduction to that strange Midwest celebration of air guitar as art. It came at a time when I wasn't sure what kind of musical path I wanted to follow.

9

I wish I could say the air guitar competition I observed at Uncle Sam's in Minneapolis on July 23, 1981, helped me settle that decision at all. What it did, however, was show me how much diversity I wanted out of my music, and that variety was on display on the stage and in the audience throughout the evening. I was at the club to see Squeeze.

The world was changing. John Lennon was murdered in December 1980, and I wasn't sure I could enjoy music at all anymore. Six weeks after Lennon's murder – and it seemed far longer than that, like maybe forever – I saw Elvis Costello in concert for the first time. Squeeze was the opening act. The extent of my knowledge about Squeeze at the time was they had a name I made fun of regularly.

A couple of friends owned a record store in Rochester, Minnesota, and were far more aware of the music scene exploding around them than I was. The first time I was aware of The Replacements was seeing the autographed copy of *Sorry Ma, Forgot to Take Out the Trash* that they displayed at the front of the store. My thrill was them bringing in hundreds of import albums, and hundred of used albums with a variety I'd never thought possible.

I worked briefly at the store. When the part-time hours proved too difficult for me to manage along with my full-time work, I announced my decision to leave the record store. Because I had liberally taken advantage of the employee discount buying records, I had to work without pay for three weeks just so we'd be even. I'd left that job with lighter pockets but a better record collection.

John Lennon was murdered on a Monday. I lived in a fog the rest of the week. On the Saturday of that week, I wandered into the record store. My friends were at the front counter on the phone, and I waved and started my walk through the store.

Immediately, they were on either side of me, walking with my as I found my way to the new releases area. "You OK, buddy?" one asked. "You all right, Tim?" the other asked. "We were just trying to call you."

They were worried about how I was handling the news of Lennon's murder, certainly because when we met, I was the long-haired guy who bought all the Beatles imports. Their obvious concern for my well-being was touching. And they followed through with more a week later.

They were as aware of my worship of Elvis Costello as they were of my Beatles passion. Costello was going to play a Minneapolis theater in a few weeks time. We, they pronounced, were all going to go.

I wasn't sure what the make of the idea after the Heart/Player show. I'd decided live shows were too programmed for me. I was also in the middle of thinking that if John Lennon was dead, so was my interest in music. I agreed, though. I knew enough about Costello by that time to know his concerts could be kind of dangerous. He could annoy audiences as easily as entertain. I'd read about 30-minute sets with every song played double-time. I was aware of a man who seemed to have a contempt for a portion of his audience. His music was threatening, flying in the face of what was going on in popular culture. I'd read stories and interviews about his abbreviated shows, which would happen when the band was bored with the crowd or too wired on amphetamines. I confess here and elsewhere – I honestly didn't think New Wave bands were doing any drugs. I thought the frantic pace came naturally. That's the way my motor ran *without* any enhancement. I always thought, "Cocaine? Who needs anything to go faster?"

I didn't know what I was going to see, but I was fairly certain it wasn't going to be 45 minutes of an opening act, 30 minutes of switchover time, and 90 minutes of headliner.

All of that was a pathway to the first time I saw Squeeze.

During the leadup to that January show, the guys who'd procured the tickets for us (Bruce and Doug -- hi fellas, and thanks -- you changed my life) enticed me tantalizingly and regularly with tales of how much I'd be thrilled with the opening act. Their name: Squeeze.

I'd seen their records in the store Bruce and Doug ran. There were some punk bands whose names I loved. I thought Sex Pistols was a great name. The Dead Kennedys did not scandalize me at all until an older co-worker was so appalled to hear me say it out loud that I had to reevaulate what I thought about the name. Although I wasn't particularly interested in The Slits. Nor was I particularly interested in Human Sexual Response. at least until I heard "Land of the Glass Pinecones."

We got to the Costello show and found our sixth-row seats. Sitting beside us was a young man, maybe 20, wearing a knock-off version of a vintage Army helmet. He had also fashioned glasses frames for himself. Out of four or five pipe cleaners.

I thought maybe the Midwest didn't exactly get punk yet.

Squeeze came on. Each song was better than the previous one. Bruce had the seat in front of me. About halfway through Squeeze's set, he turned around with a look of unbridled joy on his face. As a joke, he held his nose, the classic indication that what you're listening to stinks. I laughed with delight. I'm pretty sure I also screamed "YEAH!!!" loud enough for the band to hear me.

That January 1981 show changed a lot of things for me. I was so entertained, the next day I ran to my record store and bought every Squeeze album and 45 I could find. I was almost more excited about Squeeze than I was about Costello, who to me at that time was the most important musician in the world. And just months later, Squeeze came back to Minneapolis and played Sam's (or, more correctly, Uncle Sam's), "a danceteria."

It remains one of the strangest concerts I've ever attended. We were there early and grabbed our seats on the floor. The first bit of "entertainment" was an air guitar competition. I did not realize it at the time, but apparently this was a big thing across the upper midwest for a little while.

The air guitar acts ran the gamut. There were four preppy-looking college-age kids, two men and two women, who lip-synced to Manhattan Transfer's "Operator," using hair brushes as their pretend microphones. A group of guys came out in worn leather and could well have been Graham Parker and The Rumour. I wasn't yet deeply familiar with the band (interesting, given how *Squeezing Out Sparks* eventually became one of my favorite albums).

There was a gangly Rastafarian-looking gent who took to the stage with a

12

broomstick. He mimed to The Clash's "Brand New Cadillac." And then some. About halfway through the song, he scampered to the back of the stage, then charged forward. When he reached the edge of the stage, he leaped onto the dance floor.

It was early in the evening, so there were just a few people on the floor. My memory wants to tell me the guy landed doing the splits. Common sense tells me that's unlikely. At any rate, he cut a mean rug on the floor. And some time later, I saw Shriekback's Lu (short for "lunatic" -- no lie) Edmonds do the same thing, except the dance floor held a crowd that somehow cleared room for him to land, and he stayed on the floor, playing maniacally as the crowd surrounded him.

But that was later.

There was something magical about that July night. Squeeze came out to a rapturous greeting. The recently released *East Side Story* was getting airplay, including the hit single "Tempted." That (to my disappointment, honestly) became their chance to feature keyboard player Paul Carrack. When Squeeze opened for Costello, the band featured Carrack on his hit from the previous decade, "How Long" by Ace. They did it spectacularly that one time I got to hear them do it.

East Side Story was in the midst of its climb to No. 44 on the Billboard album charts. But that felt like a No. 1 to those of us who'd grown to love the band. And I could easily count myself among that number just months after buying my first record by them.

The beauty of playing catchup at that time was the blessing of a relatively unlimited budget and a lot of time to listen to records. I would trawl through stacks and piles of imported 7-inch records, looking for that non-album track I hadn't heard. I then spent subsequent hours committing it to memory.

By the time Squeeze took the stage at Sam's, I honestly felt I knew their work as well as they did. When they played one of their most well-known songs -- "Pulling Mussels (From the Shell)," from their fantastic *Argybargy* (No. 117 on The Big List) -- I felt an indescribable thrill when dozens in the crowd sang along with the line "a Harold Robbins paperback." Later, when Chris Difford sang his "solo" on the bridge of "I Think I'm Go Go,"

13

he looked as sheepish at the applause he received as I was delighted by it.

Our side – the geeks, the pop music lovers, the ones who loved good song structure and beautiful harmonies – was going to win after all! An easy enough conclusion to come to when all that surrounds you is people who are on your side.

It didn't even bother me that much of the crowd looked like rejects from the quartet lip-syncing Manhattan Transfer. I was coming of age with my fellow late Baby Boomers. Punk didn't seem like my music, as much as I loved the energy. I was a middle class white kid in the upper midwest. I wasn't that angry. New Wave was the music that spoke to me. It was energetic and fun, and every once in a while -- like when Elvis Costello and his band would play for 45 minutes, then run off the stage while leaving all the guitars onstage feeding back, just to force the audience out -- it seemed a little dangerous.

Squeeze wasn't dangerous. But they were energetic. And drummer Gilson Lavis was, for a long time, the best drummer I saw play live. We all enjoyed ourselves, and why not. We laughed, we danced, we sang along, and we got to see an air-guitar act of guys with literal mops for hair and a pail for a drum do AC/DC's "Highway to Hell."

The same delight was present for the next show I saw there. The venue was now called First Avenue, and it was a few months away from being shut down for a time while Prince filmed parts of *Purple Rain* there. It's much smaller than it appears in the film, which I think is probably an "of course." But they sure found novel ways to film and a way to make the place look like a music fan's dream.

Marshall Crenshaw was a throwback to the early 1960s. modeling a pure pop style after The Beatles, but adding a little New Wave sensibility. Also, he wrote great songs. His first album (No. 20 on The Big List -- you'll get there) is a flawless collection, a dozen perfect songs. The expanded CD reissue adds another 10 indisposable songs. He had a run playing John Lennon in *Beatlemania*, so he knew how to handle a crowd. However many subsequent shows I saw him play, that one in 1982 set a standard that was never eclipsed. (Even years later in Chicago, where he played what I considered a perfect Marshall Crenshaw playlist, he was so uninspired, I just got depressed.)

14

Gone was that crazy attitude of my first visit, dismissed for a more serious and sincere take on edgy rock and roll. None of us were going to leave the show and go turn over cars.

It was going to take me some time to realize that Uncle Sam's had morphed into something more comprehensive than I could ever have imagined. Funk, punk, pop, and whatever the heck else was going to be popular with the First Avenue crowd was what was going to carry the day. Tina Turner played the place the same year as Crenshaw, at the start of the comeback that would result in 1984's *Private Dancer.*

That first night I saw Marshall Crenshaw proved to be memorable. Figures was the opening band. I was delighted because the lead singer smashed an acoustic guitar onstage. Sure, he changed out his gorgeous guitar out for a crappy acoustic as the song started. We knew they were near the end of their set, so we should have figured something was up.

Still, it was electrifying to be present and see an instrument destroyed. I've gone through assorted feelings about such destruction since. Right now, I'm inclined to think it's fine. But when I was 24, and had only seen the action on film, it made a statement. Even if that statement was nothing more than "I am going to wreck a crappy guitar."

Then came Crenshaw, who had little more to play than his first album and the handful of B-sides he'd written. The combo was my favorite Crenshaw stage band: his brother Robert playing drums, and the impossibly bouncy Chris Donato playing bass. That's not an exaggeration. Donato jumped in time throughout the show. Marshall was the star. It was impossible for me to take my eyes off Donato.

That show featured one of my favorite moments ever watching live music.

The set was striking even a novice listener like me as running without flaw/ But then the trio launched into a song. What emerged from the stage was a confusion of noise. The three stopped, looked at one another, and started again, this time perfectly.

Someone had messed up. Or two. Or all three. They were playing different songs.

Donato handled the aftermath wonderfully. As he continued to hop with each beat, he pulled his hand away from the bass a couple of times to put it over his mouth. The mugging made me think he was taking the blame for the mistake (even if wasn't his). That was a good thing considering Marshall was the star and Robert, who as far as I was concerned was holding the whole thing together, appeared as though he wanted to be anywhere else. He'd be willing to punch anyone who approached him.

Funny how I was able to build personalities for them within 30 minutes of seeing them onstage, eh?

Just a few weeks later, Dave Edmunds came to First Avenue. It was going to be my second attempt at seeing him. The first ended amid a series of concert defeats. I had tickets for an XTC show at the Guthrie Theatre in Minneapolis, a venue that means something to folks in Minnesota. (I saw Todd Rundgren do a one-person show there. I also saw Bobcat Goldthwait do a killer standup set there with Tom Arnold as the opening act. Before he was married to Roseanne Barr.) This was at the time Andy Partridge was severely afflicted with stage fright, so I got a refund. I turned that cash into a ticket for an Edmunds show at a Minneapolis theater. A friend and I approached the theater to find the doors locked and a sign indicating the show had been called off.

Yeah, that kind of stuff used to happen.

Edmunds' show was a strange one, at a strange time in his career. All of a sudden, he was kind of an MTV star maybe? Interestingly, I was far more disappointed at the current phase of Edmunds' career then compared with now. He's just put out *Information*. All of a sudden, the guy who worked to recreate Phil Spector's Wall of Sound style of recording, but played everything by himself, was awash in 1980s keyboards. Electric Light Orchestra's Jeff Lynne Jeff Lynne'd himself all over Dave Edmunds. This was the post-*Out of the Blue* Jeff Lynne, when style was of far more importance than substance. The lead single was "Slipping Away," another one of those Jeff Lynne songs that sounded just like Jeff Lynne felt like every song should sound like.

And don't get me wrong, because Electric Light Orchestra's *A New World Record* is one of my favorite albums, and Jeff Lynne has written some of my favorite songs, and if not for Jeff Lynne, there's a pretty good chance George Harrison would never agreed to go back into a recording studio

16

with Paul McCartney. (I'm pleased, as much as I don't like how much "Free as a Bird" sounds like a Jeff Lynne production. "Real Love" was my preference, though.) But by the time the 1980s arrived, Jeff Lynne's musical decisions and my musical choices were on diametrically opposed paths.

At least the title cut of *Information* sounded like a Dave Edmunds song. Sure, a Dave Edmunds song that Jeff Lynne heard and said, "Hey, I know how to fix this," and decided to roll in every cheap 1980s keyboard and play them all at once, and add drums that sounded like a sloppy marching band.

I'd never seen a stage performer use a pre-recorded tape during a performance. Granted, it's not like I was 25 and going to three shows a week since I was 15, but I was still stunned as I saw Edmunds' drummer slip on a pair of headphones so he could hear the click track and lead in to both "Slipping Away" and "Information." For crying out loud, The Beatles were still together when Dave Edmunds made his first record. He couldn't possibly think pre-recorded tracks were OK?

All this time later, I've sat through club shows with a dozen people were attending and sat and watched somebody else sing to a CD he or she had given the sound person. It wasn't even karaoke night.

My next visit to First Avenue was under significantly different circumstances. Squeeze, Crenshaw and Edmunds were decidedly pop. Maybe a side road off the mainstream. Certainly, every once in a while, they could connect with the general public. But they weren't Shriekback.

When I heard Shriekback songs pop up in Michael Mann's *Manhunter*, I about fell out of my chair. I grabbed Shriekback's first album, *Care*, as soon as I could find it. When I'd read about their "intricate rhythms and atmospherics," I was fascinated, and even more so when I actually heard it. This was also the time I was looking to expand from the Squeezes and Crenshaws of the world. There were other sounds out there, and I was starting to find them. A stunning dividing point for me was when I played the first 4AD Colourbox album and its crazy obnoxious guitar inserts and its dance fake drums pumped up version of "You Keep Me Hanging On" for a friend. I expected him to be as excited about the possibilities as me. He was appalled. A similar thing happened to me years later when I

17

expected everyone to be as excited about Babymetal as I was.

I wasn't going to abandon that stuff I loved. But, boy, there was so much going on out there. And I needed more than Springsteen, Madonna, Michael Jackson and Prince. I was young, and had a music-loving brain that needed to be fed.

Shriekback were the kings. And remain so to this day. Two of their albums, 1984's *Jam Science* and 1985's *Oil and Gold,* are in spots 37 and 40 on The Big List. The only other artists with two albums in my top 40 are Pink Floyd, The Beatles and Frank Zappa (three each), McCartney/Wings and Elvis Costello. Not only is that elite company, they're acts I suspect are at least passingly familiar to most people reading.

In the mid-1980s, my friends quickly tired of Shriekback. To this day, that reaction baffles me. On their first album, they had a song called "My Spine is the Bassline," and I found that wildly appropriate. From the second any of their more rhythm-based songs started, I was plugged in, and inevitably disappointed when the song would fade and end. I couldn't wait to see how the show played out, and neither could my college-age brother-in-law, who brought along some friends.

The collection of us wouldn't have looked out of place anywhere, wholesome white kids dressed like they were on a field trip to the mall, or a night of cautious drinking, or watching an episode of *Moonlighting.* I wasn't prepared for what I saw when I got inside.

It was like someone had posted signs advertising a Robert Smith lookalike contest. Goth, for me, was still a look that lived in large cities. This was my first exposure to it in person.

I found myself laughing.

I had a lot of anger in me, but I hadn't fought through a lot of hardships. I even landed a full-time job as a newspaper writer with just a little more than two years of community college education. I had a lot of luck. Looking through that prism, I wasn't sure exactly what the goth kids had to complain about. So just as I had done with the kid at the Elvis Costello with the homemade pipe cleaner glasses, I'm smiled with amusement as I looked at a collection of unisex Robert Smiths.

A woman in our group had a decidedly different reaction. She came back from the rest room horrified. "Two guys just came in the women's room and pissed in the sink!" she exclaimed. At the time -- as a younger man with a significantly larger bladder -- I thought, "That's what you get for using the bathroom at a rock club." Around this time, I'd discovered Robyn Hitchcock (much more on him in a bit here) and his pre-solo career band, The Soft Boys. They had a song called "Rock and Roll Toilet," which unfortunately and really for no good reason became a song that I immediately associated with her incident.

The song had more resonance for me a few years later when I was at the Metro in Chicago for a late-night Moxy Fruvous show. Manic Street Preachers played an early show at the club, and dozens of Fruheads lined up outside the club, providing a chance for a TV station to pick up some nice B footage for a feature they were doing on the band.

After an interminable wait, I really had to go to the bathroom. I went into the facilities at the Metro, and immediately found myself standing in a room-wide puddle of urine. I wasn't sure whether something had backed up, or if Manic Street Preacher fans decided there were no rules for bathroom use at a show. But that definitely was a rock and roll toilet.

I kept looking around at the crowd for the Shriekback show, thinking, "Is this really what these people think this music is all about?" Then the opening act made me think maybe they were right.

"Did he just sing 'I feel like a piece of burnt toast on a wire'?"

My brother-in-law Greg was even more baffled. He'd thought he'd heard something strange, but it wasn't until I asked him my question that the possibility of those words existing in the same space became a possibility.

The singer continued to angrily attack his guitar, and he strode purposefully to the microphone to continue the song, spitting out the lyrics.

"I'll be damned," I said to Greg. "He *did* sing 'I feel like a piece of burnt toast on a wire'."

I'd heard a few bands where two people stood on stage and played along with a tape playing the track of a third instrument. I've generally never liked the practice. Seeing James Taylor sing along with a tape of his pre-recorded harmony lines on *Saturday Night Live* felt unnatural. Seeing bands with pre-recorded drum or bass tracks, concentrating on playing along with the click track that existed for the person playing the track but not them, well that just felt sad.

"Aww. What's the matter? You can't find a couple of friends to fill out the other spots for you? That's kinda too bad. Do people just not like you?"

(Understand before I go further that I have a better idea now why it was that way then. And I understand how it is that way now. The point of this is how I took a huge step toward understanding it.)

"I feel like a piece of burnt toast on a wire"? The line killed my interest. I was just waiting for Shriekback. Who were wonderful. Spooky, dark, bleak, stage-commanding. Singer/keyboard player Barry Andrews, a tiny tiny man, was impossible large on stage. These guys meant it. They weren't angry, but they were earnest.

Kind of like me.

Older and wiser, for my second Shriekback show I was prepared for whatever kind of audience First Avenue was going to throw at me. I'd seen the poppy, the preppy, the college, the goth -- what new could it be prepared to show me? Of course, there was the Prince factor. While his existence hung over First Avenue like a disappointed expectation, it never bothered me that I wasn't in a shrine to Prince while I was in the place. To me, the place existed somehow outside his world. Of course, by this time, he was huge enough and unlikely to be in Minnesota, so I never saw him there and was never going to.

Before that second Shriekback show, a song was sneaked into the pre-show playlist. Part of the pre-show playlist was a video for Kate Bush's "Running Up That Hill," a song I already knew and loved. Only this time, they dropped a screen down in front of the stage like a curtain, and we watched Bush's ballet video for the song. It was my first experience like that, and I wasn't sure how I felt about it. As I watched the video, I thought, "Yes, this is about the Kate Bush-iest thing I've seen," and I couldn't keep my eyes off the screen

Immediately thereafter, as I was busy trying to process what I'd seen, what sounded like a guitar-and-voice demo started playing. In retrospect, people are surprised I didn't realize the performer. It was clear to me plenty of people know who it was, and were excited to hear it.

It turned out to be Prince's "The Cross," being played for the crowd well in advance of the release of the *Sign o the Times* album.

In my defense, I still maintain *Sign o the Times* sounds more like a collection of demos than a Prince album. I know they tried hard to make it sound that way. I still defy anyone to find me three songs in Prince's catalog that sound anything like "The Cross." Except for the vocal wash at the end, which I'm not convinced was on the end of the version I heard at First Avenue.

Oh, and Prince was allegedly in attendance to observe the reaction, I was told later.

A friend was pretty excited to be at the show. He shared my enthusiasm about Shriekback, but was a recent convert, and hadn't kept up with the releases as I had. So he was most excited about hearing "Lined Up." The only problem was, they hadn't played it the previous time. I figured it was some kind of statement of purpose: "You might know us for only this song, so we're not going to play it." I didn't expect Elvis Costello to play more than 45 minutes the first time I saw him. I didn't expect to ever hear Shriekback play "Lined Up" in concert.

I was wrong in both cases. To the delight of my friend -- and to the delight of the rest of our group, which got a particular kick out of me getting my come-uppance -- Shriekback opened with "Lined Up."

The show was top-notch. Andrews had even more command from the stage. Which I found more interesting as I surveyed the makeup of the crowd. It seemed to be mosh-pitters. I wasn't sure if they were there for the right show. A couple of things that happened that made me think maybe I was right. The show wasn't a loss. It was never going to be. It featured what continues to be one of the most exciting moments I've seen in person. This was the show where Lu Edmonds jumped from the stage onto the dance floor, and the crowd somehow parted to give him room to land. It also featured the story I tell most about concerts, and I'm not even sure why this one is so important.

Shriekback's big "hit" at the time was a song called "Nemesis." It was a big dumb rock song with big dumb chords and dumb loud drums, and I loved it. While I knew it wasn't representative of what they were as a band, that was the song I'd often pick to attempt to introduce people to them. It also featured the word "parthenogenesis," and you bet I looked it up. ("Reproduction from an ovum without fertilization." It's the "long ungainly scientific word" he mentions below.) Andrews himself said:

> "...my intention was to get a laugh—or at least an internal smirk— from the big—almost football crowd—chorus, the long ungainly scientific word, the huge daft power chords, and everything within this barmy context of 'let's examine the nature of morality'—like some philosophy professor who went to Vietnam and listened to a lot of Gary Glitter."

That's exactly how I'd describe some of the mosh-pitters, although the closest any of them got to Vietnam was watching *The Deer Hunter*. And they didn't help themselves as Shriekback went into "Nemesis." The key part of the song is the concluding line of the final verse. Andrews sings, "But I don't know, my dreams are visions/We could still end up with the great big fishes." In retrospect, Andrews' next move may have been a mockery of all of the BIG ROCK SHOWS that ever existed. After singing "my dreams are visions," he put the microphone into the crowd, right in one guy's face.

Mustering all he had within him, the audience member screamed "YAHYAHYAHYAH YAHYAH!"

Someone singing along with Devo's "Uncontrollable Urge" could have done no better.

It was a moment I've quoted incessantly since. Only a handful of people get it, and they are annoyed by it. But in the three-plus decades since, I've been known to randomly yell just as that audience member did:

"YAHYAHYAHYAH YAHYAH!"

Years after that show, I picked up a CD by a band called Editors. As I listened, I tried to figure out what I might have read that convinced me to pick it up. Back in 1987, the opening act at the Shriekback show was Comsat Angels. Although the openers were known as C.S. Angels, thanks to a threatened lawsuit from Communications Satellite Corporation. I dove into the used record bins, picked up a couple of Comsat Angels albums, and anticipated seeing them open.

I hoped their music would be better live than on record. They sounded thin on disc, which wasn't a surprise. A lot of bands sound thin on disc.

They came out and stunk the joint up. I wasn't intending to be funny, but set some folks in my seating area laughing when, as the band stretched out the end of one song with power chord after power chord, I said, "Enough already. Finish the song. Who do these guys think they are, Uriah Heep?"

(Note reference to third-level heavy metal band popular in the early 1970s.)

I'd never thought about Comsat Angels after that. Then I came across a story about Editors. Someone wrote they sounded a little like Comsat Angels.

"How on earth," I thought, "can anyone except me remember what Comsat Angels sounds like?"

I put it out of my mind. About six weeks later, I finally listened to Editors.

The disc annoyed me. It sounded a little like something, but I couldn't place it.

Finally I realized it.

"I'll be damned," I thought. "They *do* sound like Comsat Angels."

In the meantime, I'd developed an insanely intense desire to consume every piece of art Robyn Hitchcock produced.

1984 was as much in need of a shakeup of the popular music status quo as 1977 was. But by 1984, everything was just too big. So I had to go looking for it in the corners. I was fortunate enough to have some guidance along the way.

Look, it's not as though the songs at the top of the charts were BAD SONGS. Kenny Loggins, Phil Collins, the omnipresent Lionel Richie, they all had their gifts as songwriters. In fact, I always tend to think of 1984 as the year everything blew up for the 80s' pop's Big Three: Madonna, Prince and Springsteen. But if you look at the list of top singles from 1984, it's Richie who outpaces everyone with multiple entries.

I found it all growing remarkably safe. It wasn't as bad as some of the mainstream pop that came before. I never felt like writing, as I did about Annette Funicello's version of "Let's Twist Again," that "if this song had a video, it would be Miracle Whip being spread across Wonder bread." But I was in my mid-20s, and I wanted at least a little danger. I didn't want to be standing in line at the record store with my mother's peers as they bought Rod Stewart albums. Not to mention Cyndi Lauper, while insisting "She Bop" was just a cute and comic little song.

It was as though they'd never really *looked at* the video, which is as subtle as a sledgehammer, and brilliant. And a clever parody of/tribute to Madonna's "Dress You Up" video with the staircase at the end.

Had there been more Cyndi Laupers and fewer Lionel Richies, I might never have gone off searching. But had there been more Cyndi Laupers and fewer Lionel Richies, music wouldn't have had its 1980s explosion, either.

Trouser Press magazine had been my guide to the wonderful but hidden. Unfortunately, it dwindled and vanished by 1984. I still had my vintage copies, the ones I'd been buying (or had been sent with my subscription) for five years. So I mined those pages for more obscure things I'd missed or ignored earlier, and I was also armed with the periodic copies of *Buckettful of Brains* magazine, which exposed me to wonders like the Long Ryders, Green Pajamas, and (most significantly for the purpose of this part of the story) Robyn Hitchcock.

I picked up Hitchcock's *Gotta Let This Hen Out!* around the same time I was discovering Shriekback, Beat Rodeo and the 4AD label (particularly

Cocteau Twins, whose gorgeous *Treasure* is No. 66 on The Big List). To make an awkward connection, *Gotta Let This Hen Out!* was Hitchcock's *Kiss Alive!* -- a live album that served as an introductory best-of. (And they both shared odd exclamation points as part of their names.) I was taken first by the stranger elements like the a capella "Uncorrected Personality Traits" (which posited that Marilyn Monroe was a man) and "Brenda's Iron Sledge," in which number of people pile on a sled going down a hill, until it hits a tree ("and disintegrates").

I was immediately enraptured, and more so as I caught up with Hitchcock's history. On the album released just before the live recording *Gotta Let This Hen Out!,* Hitchcock sang about "The Man With the Lightbulb Head" and "My Wife and My Dead Wife." This was my kind of surrealism.

It's worth noting, I suppose, that "My Wife and My Dead Wife" followed "Brenda's Iron Sledge" on *Gotta Let This Hen Out!* The calm nature of the studio recording is jarring, and the same could be said for "Uncorrected Personality Traits" when I got around to finding the original version of that.

It's also worth noting, again I suppose, that the first compact disc I bought was Hitchcock's lovely *I Often Dream of Trains,* No. 58 on The Big List.

I was fortunate enough to have discovered Hitchcock at a time when he was scrambling in clubs all around the United States to make some kind of dent in our market. A friend and I learned that Hitchcock planned an in-store appearance at one of our favorite Minneapolis record stores, which sounded marvelous. An autograph *and* a bonus performance? Count me delighted.

I had built my Hitchcock selection significantly. I was acquiring live tapes of his performances (as I was wont to do at the time, via a pretty underground and sadly illegal community. I was picking up variations and re-releases of the Soft Boys, the band he led before becoming a solo artist. I wanted desperately to show Hitchcock I was a fan who knew his stuff. I was not a Timmy-come-lately. I also wanted his signature on something not everyone else owned.

I grabbed *Groovy Decay*, which all these years later is still in my top five of favorite Hitchcock albums.

As we jammed into line to have our mementos defaced on March 26, 1986, I looked with contempt upon the items my fellow fans brought. Just ahead of me in line, a guy pulled out a bank deposit slip. He shrugged, told Hitchcock that was all he had, and the artist proceeded to fill out the bank form and sign it.

Seconds later, the guy immediately ahead of me produced a light bulb from his pocket. (A reference, of course, to Hitchcock's song "The Man With the Lightbulb Head.") To my surprise and delight, Hitchcock took the light bulb nonchalantly, as though this was how he was confronted on a regular basis. (And what did I know? Maybe he did.) Hitchcock drew a little face on the bulb, and handed it back.

I approached the way Ralphie approaches Santa in "A Christmas Story." I knew actually seeing one of his own recordings would thrill him. My friend had a similar advantage because he had a record with him as well. But I was ahead in line.

Hitchcock grabbed my album and flipped it over a couple of times, looking at the front and back covers. Without saying anything, he took his gray marker and scratched out his eyes from the cover photo, scrawled the word "CRAP!" and emphatically underlined it.

I was stunned. It was definitely not the reception I expected or desired. I felt mocked, marginalized. My friend and I stood in the record store, which suddenly felt crowded and hostile. I turned and said I didn't really want to hang around for the in-store show. We dropped our records off at the car, and went to a newsstand to kill time before the show.

Even as we walked away from the record store, I said, "You remember what Tommy Smothers said when John Lennon was drunk and interrupted their show? That thing about being disappointed when someone you really admire turns out to be a jackass?"

I wasn't in the best of moods.

It may have been Hitchcock's way of dealing with an uncomfortable situation. In the ensuing years, I encountered any number of musicians who battled social discomfort. I also imagine my tendency to let my fanboy out a little sooner and more significantly than appropriate didn't help. In retrospect, it's easy to imagine that Hitchcock's Soft Boys bandmate Kimberly Rew was writing about Hitchcock's fragility with "Tourists of Insanity," a 2005 song I initially interpreted as being about tragic mental casualty Syd Barrett of Pink Floyd. It essentially discusses how people are glad to visit and be entertained or appalled by an artist's mental damage, but they don't want to be around to see how messy the aftermath becomes.

And somehow, Hitchcock changed my mind back within an hour of taking the stage. I wasn't sure whether his stage stories were prepared and memorized or extemporaneous. I'm still not. The times I've seen him and the dozens of shows I've listened to offer me no real solution. But experiencing them in the moment was thrilling.

The show was essentially a promotion for *Gotta Let This Hen Out!* At that point, I generally agreed with Hitchcock about his career highlights, so he easily won me back. But when he returned mere months later, we decided -- well, I guess it was me who decided -- against the pre-show record store appearance this time.

Early in the set, Hitchcock started telling a story full of non-sequiturs, one of the features from his shows that confounded and amazed me. I suppose I would have thought myself pretentious at the time to declare I loved the absurdist nature of his work.

That's also, as it turns out, one of the things I love about John "a soap impression of his wife which he ate and donated to the National Trust" -- which for the longest time I heard as the more hilarious "National Truss" -- Lennon. I heard some Beatles in Hitchcock's work, and he certainly had a Lennon-like voice, even though I suspect he'd have preferred to sound like Syd Barrett. The second show we saw was in advance of his *Element of Light* album, which I think I like specifically because it felt like a record he made for me at this exact time. I sure can't be objective about *Element of Light*. I admit I like it more than I should.

And one of the things I like is "Somewhere Apart." I've been known to describe as a little-known Lennon song, play it for people and have them

27

convinced I was telling the truth. I also did it with Electric Light Orchestra's "Can't Get It Out Of My Head" and The Hudson Brothers' "So You Are a Star." But what "Somewhere Apart" has that the other two do not is Hitchcock's lyrical ability. The standout lines for me from Hitchcock's song are "so give me fish eggs, and violins" and "I'm gonna burn your bongos tonight." That's absurd.

Hitchcock's introductory monologue was a complex story that wound into the absolutely terrifying plague story-song, "Lady Waters and the Hooded One."

My friend didn't share my enthusiasm for "Lady Waters and the Hooded One." He once noted something along the lines of "I could like Hitchcock a lot more if there were more songs like 'Acid Bird' and fewer like 'All the Monks and the Queen of France.' Has he ever written a song with that title?"

And then Hitchcock played another song, another one that would end up on his next studio album. He stood alone in the middle of the stage, single spotlight, the entire band offstage, and begin picking an introduction on his guitar.

The studio version adds a bass guitar and a percussion rhythm. It doesn't need it.

I wrote about the moment, along with the record store incident, 23 years later when writing about my favorite concert experiences.

**

We were hearing a song we'd never heard before.

We were in the midst of hundreds of people, many of whom had polished off one too many adult beverages and most of whom seemed uninterested in hearing any new material from the artist on stage.

Yet my friend Tom Weber and I found ourselves for all intents and purposes alone with Robyn Hitchcock as he played the unreleased and previously unheard (by us) song "Raymond Chandler Evening ."

28

As the song concluded, Tom and I exhaled and leaned back in our chairs. It was at that point we realized we'd both been leaning forward, elbows on our knees, straining to get closer to the stage, to attempt to inhabit what Hitchcock was singing.

We had been literally holding our breath. Time has stopped for us.

**

The concert was my favorite concert until 2010, when I saw the Roger Waters' "The Wall" in person.

Hitchcock played another song that always had my friend shaking his head, "Sounds Great When You're Dead." In an interview, Hitchcock discussed how great it would be to have a Walkman coffin that played heavy metal over and over. Again, the surrealism was delicious. And the song contains one of my favorite Hitchcock lines: "We're at our most together when we're at our most apart."

No one else in my world was writing stuff like that. Even Elvis Costello, I imagined, would listen to that line and think, "Whoa…" Hitchcock went into another world with his next song, another one new to us. He described what we quickly realized were images from gay magazines of the 1950s. In a bath together, men "cover each other with soap." In the forest, "they cover each other with leaves."

Frank Zappa said one of the reasons he wrote about the things he wrote about was because he thought they deserved to be preserved as much as other things he heard being preserved. I'd like to think Zappa heard "Ted Woody and Junior" and thought, "Glad somebody did that one."

(It's also worth noting that my friend's wife did not share the delight he and I had when I'd call their house and ask to speak with "Woody.")

It was a conflicting experience. A miserable face-to-face encounter, but a brilliant concert, far and away the best I'd seen. And, as noted, remained exactly that until a quarter-century later.

Not everyone shared my analysis of the record store incident. Immediately thereafter, The Lovely Mrs. Cain was laughing about it, and said, "It sounds exactly like something you'd do." I didn't grasp what she was saying. I could find people as appalled as I was, but I also came across too many who said, "That's kinda cool."

I continued to be a fan, and continued to read Hitchcock's interviews. It eventually became clear he was unhappy with something about *Groovy Decay*. It seemed to be dissatisfaction with the songs, the sound, the production, and even his relationship with his art. It was after the release of *Groovy Decay* that Hitchcock took all his unpublished paintings, drawings, lyrics and demos, shoved them in a trunk, took them to a beach and burned them.

At the time, it seemed to me a tragedy, and senseless destruction. It began in my head a debate that's rarely stopped since. What does an artist owe to the community they create? Anything? What does that artist owe to society? To posterity? To themselves?

My mind has flipped any number of times pondering those questions. At this point, I'm happy for Hitchcock, and sad for myself. There may have been something he burned that would have evoked something enjoyable to my experience. But if the decision freed Hitchcock's artist, fantastic for him. If *I Often Dream of Trains* was borne from the ashes on that beach, it was a worthy death in exchange for that work.

I've also slowly come around on Hitchcock's decision to deface my album cover. Maybe he signed it that way because he couldn't take it to a beach and burn it. While the memory of the experience still stings, maybe he didn't mean in as viciously as I took it. And at the very least, he gave me an experience and a memento shared with no one else.

It's an original Robyn Hitchcock piece of art.

My last show at First Avenue was a few months before I moved away from Minnesota. (I also moved in time to miss the next Hitchcock show at the venue by just a couple of weeks.) Fittingly, friends who had seen Hitchock and Shriekback with me were along as we attended one of the trio of "homecoming" shows Husker Du traditionally played. We had no idea that (a) they were on the verge of breaking up and (b) they were going to play their *Warehouse: Songs and Stories* album in full and in order.

But first, Peter Case went out and did an acoustic show that was ignored by about 90 percent of the audience. One friend got so frustrated with the crowd in the upper level at First Avenue that he got up and walked downstairs to join a handful of people actually paying attention to the singer.

In *Blender* magazine's 2007 issue, they had a "hot" list. One of the items *Blender* described as "hot" was bands performing full albums in concert. They mentioned Sonic Youth doing *Daydream Nation,* Ben Kweller doing *Sha Sha,* Lou Reed doing *Berlin* and Brian Wilson doing *SMiLE.*

I'd seen Wilson do *SMiLE* in total two years before that Blender list. I heard the Beatles tribute band Liverpool play *Sgt. Pepper's Lonely Hearts Club Band* beginning to end in order around the same time I saw the Wilson show. Zappa Plays Zappa did all of *Apostrophe (')* on one of its tours. Those experiences can be special.

But sometimes, it can be a disaster.

Husker Du traditionally played a trio of shows at First Avenue every year to mark the anniversary of their forming. In 1987, they'd released *Warehouse: Songs and Stories,* a two-album set crammed with 20 tunes. I viewed it as at best a sideways step from 1986's *Candy Apple Grey,* but it was still better than most of the stuff that was out there. The hometown shows always received positive reviews, and we were excited to be going.

The promise began to fade as the audience talked throughout Case's opening acoustic set. But the excitement of Husker Du's arrival re-raised our spirits. The band came out and played the first song off *Warehouse.* OK, not a great kickoff, but maybe a statement of purpose. Then they played the second song from *Warehouse.* Then the third. Then the fourth.

You get the idea. Before we realized it, we were knee-deep in *Warehouse,* and people were talking again, louder this time, to be heard over the sonic boom that was Husker Du in its prime.

Husker Du never found inspiration and connected with one another, let alone the audience. The response became more tepid with each song. After 25 minutes, conversations in the crowd were battling the band for sound

31

dominance.

One friend was so stuporized by the show that finally succumbed, head rolling back, face toward the ceiling. He was snoring. I was astonished. To me, it was the equivalent of watching someone taking a nap on a busy airplane runway. I never thought it possible for somebody to fall asleep with a band turned up to 11, but he proved me wrong. We kept an eye on him, only because he'd snapped his head back in his chair and was sleeping (and snoring) with his mouth open, and we were afraid a passerby might use his mouth for an ashtray.

A few weeks later, Husker Du announced it was splitting up and, having seen a show of band members barely interacting, it was hard to be surprised.

That's a lot of what First Avenue was to me. A place I grew up. I saw a whole lot of things I'd never seen before, and a whole lot of stuff I'd never see again. It was a good ol' rock and roll toilet.

4 SNIPPETS II

So today I learned I have an MP3 of the 12-inch mix of Toni Basil's "Mickey." The Spanish language version.

I swear, I have no idea how I got some of this stuff.

**

All right, everybody exhale – the first set of Police tour dates are available. Here's hoping Sting brings his lute.

**

"You could write a book about your experiences following these bands, too, you know. A series of personal essays. Put it on the list." -- Amy Hoak

**

There's no detail of my life I do not find endlessly fascinating.

**

So what purpose exactly is served by piping in Joy Division's "Love Will Tear Us Apart" at a retail location?

**

Boy, that Otis Redding was excitable, wasn't he?

**

And then there was that time I was driving in Ohio and saw an exit for Ashtabula and thought, "Wait, Dylan was singing about a real city?"

**

I'm fascinated to realize that while I consider Elton John and his artistry vital and a matter of course, to people born even 15 years later than me, his art really isn't important. He's just ubiquitous.

5 CONCERT STORIES

The editor of a specialty publication asked me to submit a list of my favorite concert performances. He requested five, I negotiated more. I'd already cut my list to 10 and didn't feel I could cut any further. As it was, I was saddened I didn't include my first concert, my first Elvis Costello show, and all the shows by a band I've seen more than 20 times, Moxy Fruvous.

All of these shows on this list have key selling points. Some were improbable double bills that wound up fantastic. In others, the acts took advantage of the settings, cavernous or intimate, to create memories that live on. One in particular would still resonate with me 30 years later.

1. Robyn Hitchcock, First Avenue, Minneapolis, 1986
For months afterward, I was still singing "Raymond Chandler Evening" and a few of the other new songs Hitchcock introduced. Later I found myself wondering if it had actually happened.

2. Shriekback, First Avenue, Minneapolis, 1985

Shriekback's dark, percussion-driven songs wouldn't be out of place today. They were decidedly futuristic 24 years ago. Imagine a short, bald lead singer, a shirtless bass player and a wild-haired lead guitarist who jumped off a four-foot stage onto the floor mid-solo. In those pre-wireless days, his guitar cord wound its way around the stage and into the crowd, which formed a circle around him as he soloed. A year later, they put on a different, yet just as mesmerizing, show in the same location.

3. Neil Young, St. Paul Civic Center, 1978
The *Rust Never Sleeps* tour was a trip through Young's career, with eight new songs. That included the majority of his to-be-released *Rust Never Sleeps* album, which remains one of my favorites. The show also featured an oversize set, "road-eyes" dressed like *Star Wars* Jawas characters, and the loudest sound I've heard at a show before or since.

My hearing was muffled for the next four days. That's rock 'n' roll. That's also the last concert I attended without ear protection.

4. Doug Stanhope, Pops, Sauget, Mo., 2005
It was just a standup comedy show, the way Facebook is just another website. Stanhope got up and did close to 30 minutes talking about his attempt to find a fresh salad somewhere in Sauget, and followed it with another 100 minutes of insightful and obscene and comical and offensive observations.

Around the 75-minute mark, I stopped laughing for a bit and just marveled at how I'd be willing to listen to this man talk as long as he wanted. As it turned out, that almost happened.

5. Jill Sobule, Blue Moon Coffeehouse, Bloomington, Ill., 2002
Sobule regularly delivers, combining storytelling with offbeat but still great pop and folk songs. This was the fifth time I had seen her in concert. This show stood out because it followed her *Underdog Victorious* album release. So I got to hear "Cinnamon Park" and "Strawberry Gloss." And, after a request yelled out from the audience by me, the breathtaking "Tel Aviv," in which Sobule assumes the persona of an underage prostitute. Five years later, after I recounted the moment to her in an interview, Sobule was moved to pull the song out and play it that evening at a California concert.

34

6. Squeeze, Sam's, Minneapolis, 1981
You've already read about this one in the chapter about First Avenue. "A Harold Robbins paperback!"

7. Barbara Bailey Hutchison, Richland Community College, Decatur, 2001
I've seen Hutchison a dozen times, and every show has been superb. But this was the first, and it was exceptional. I knew exactly zero of her songs. By the time the show was over, her melodies (and the melodies of others that she'd made her own) had burrowed into my head, and while I didn't realize it at the time, I'd made a musical friend and a friend friend. That's pretty special.

8. Jeff Healey Band/The Thieves, Mabel's, Champaign, 1989
I'd seen Healey play on *Late Night With David Letterman* in that crazy style of his, guitar laid across his lap. It was only with repeated viewings that it occurred to me that the guy who danced and skipped across the stage might be blind as well. Weeks later, his tour came to Champaign and was a must-see. The late Healey was one of the few with the nerve and the talent to attempt a Jimi Hendrix song ("Foxy Lady") and pull it off.

Opening act The Thieves (although I remember them being called "The Nashville Thieves") played sparkling, rocking pop. I finally acquired their (only) album, and it made my top 10 list for 1989. For a time, I even thought their performance was better than Healey's.

9. The Smithereens/Cindy Lee Berryhill, The Atrium, Springfield, 1992
Berryhill was a folkie favorite of mine from the early 1980s. I'd lost track of her, and was stunned when I saw her name on the poster as we approached the door. When I got inside, she was already onstage, doing wildly creative music. She was superb, and extremely polite to the handful of us stumbling over ourselves to praise her post-show.

As if that wasn't cool enough, The Smithereens came out and just wouldn't stop playing, and no one complained. In a show that was more hard rock than pop, the quartet showed they knew how to rock an audience.

10. Material Issue, Mabel's, Champaign, 1995
A beautiful audience sing-along with the conclusion of "Very First Lie." They concluded the show with The Sweet's "Ballroom Blitz" (after faking

starting the show with it). "Ballroom Blitz" concluded with a demolished drum kit, the first time in 18 years I'd seen that done in person.

(I updated this favorite concerts list a few years later, and that update remains accurate. The additions: Roger Waters' "The Wall," ScottTrade Arena, St. Louis, 2010, at No. 1 (yeah, you'll read a whole bunch more about this in a bit) and Rosanne Cash, Harris Theatre, Chicago, 2010, at No. 6.)

***

The best concerts sometimes provide the best stories, but not always ...

***

-- Robin Trower, St. Paul Civic Center, 1977

This is the best "just say no" story I can come up with.

As was the tradition at the time, I came prepared with some smoking material, something I was told was "pure Columbian." The guy sitting next to me asked if he could partake, and four of us -- we both had friends with us -- shared a joint.

(I understand how foreign and horrifying this might sound to a 21st-century reader. Trust me -- it was fine, regular and expected.)

Upon inhaling, the atmosphere in the room began to change for me, and not in a good way. Thirsty, I went to get something to drink. Those tending the soft drinks were clearly torturing me, as the soda was coming out of the fountain in slow motion.

This should have been a tip.

Another tip should have been suddenly finding myself with my cheek plastered against the wall. Only I wasn't against a wall – I was on the floor.

I somehow got our drinks and began making my way back to my seat. As if that wasn't difficult enough, I suddenly found myself being approached by a pair of St. Paul's Finest. I froze, and visions of police, handcuffs and

Midnight Express ran through my head. (Which was odd, because that movie didn't come out until the following year.)

I was convinced jail time was in my immediate future. I was done for.

Suddenly, as though walking on air, I breezed comfortably past the constables. I was safe. There was a higher power.

Two guys had picked me up off the floor and flung me toward the concourse wall and walked away without receiving any thanks.

I finally got back to my seat. The stranger sitting next to me, with whom I'd shared my "pure Columbian," was slumped in his chair, eyes rolled back in his head. "Hey," I said as I nudged him, "you're missing the show." "I know, man," he said. "It's just that the room keeps spinning."

I handed my friend his glass. He looked in it and said, "Was there supposed to be something in here?" There had been. But now I was wearing it.

-- Elvis Costello and Squeeze, Northrop Auditorium, Minneapolis, 1981

John Lennon had been murdered a month earlier, my dad had been killed in an accident four months earlier, and I didn't know if I cared about anything any more, much less rock music. Squeeze – whom I'd never heard, but had been assured I would love by the guy who procured me sixth-row tickets – came out, and I DID fall in love. (I went to the guy's record store the next day and dropped $35 on Squeeze records.)

And Costello came out and was amazing. When my procurer Bruce handed me tickets to the concert, they were in the sixth row. Jeez. Costello would be able to glare at me in person and even more intensely than he did on that *Saturday Night Live* appearance doing "Radio Radio" where the camera refused to blink. (And nothing else happened, because the director wasn't sure what to do, and allegedly was afraid of catching *SNL* producer Lorne Michaels on camera. An animated Michaels was charging around behind the cameras giving Costello the finger.)

Costello ran through hits old and new, and did a couple of cover versions to show he had more depth than most wanted to give him credit for. Patsy

Cline, Stevie Wonder, Sonny Boy Williamson. He served notice to me that he'd barely begun to explore the depth of his talent.

-- Cindy Lee Berryhill, Springfield, Illinois, 1992

Going with a friend to see The Smithereens, we got into the place and saw a poster for the show. I said, "Cindy Lee Berryhill is opening?" I spent a little time educating him about Berryhill, who had two albums out at the time but was playing a whole bunch of stuff I didn't know.

It turned out to be material from a new album. My friend bought a copy, and while The Smithereens were setting up, he found his way to the artist to have Berryhill sign it. I hung back. They were talking, and my friend said, "I didn't even know who you were, but my friend here was telling me about you." I shook her hand and introduced myself and told her how much I liked her previous two albums and was looking forward to hearing the new one.

She gave me a hell of a hug, and kissed me on the cheek. It was one of two times I was kissed by a performer, with Jill Sobule being the other.

Well, and Steven Tyler, but that doesn't really count, and it's another story.
-- Moxy Fruvous, The Galaxy, St. Louis, 1997

I saw this band more than 20 times in a three-year stretch, and this was one of the greatest shows. Most memorable because they had a technical breakdown mid-set, and immediately went into an acoustic guitar-and-vocals-only version of The Beatles' "Please Please Me," explaining that if there's ever a problem during a show, they do a Beatles song and everything is all right.

How could I not love that?

A couple of years later, the lovely Mrs. Cain and myself (with a few friends in tow at each date) did a three-show Fruvous run -- two in Chicago, and one in Madison. Somewhere along the way, the lovely Mrs. Cain and I got into a discussion about Moxy Fruvous' set lists.

One of the reasons I loved following the band around was the constant changes in the set list. They'd never do the same set twice, they improvised at least one song a night, and there were always surprises. Still, I thought I could predict many of the songs they'd play.

Through a lengthy discussion, we settled on a wager. I would submit a list of 20 songs, and if the band played 15 of them, I'd earn a t-shirt. I liked my odds. The band often played 25 or 30 songs in concert.

The first night of the wager, five of their first seven songs were on my list. Then things went south, and the count ended at 12. The following night, in Madison, they played 13 off my list.

After the show, I ran into Moxy Fruvous' drummer. As we talked, I told him about the wager, and he asked the lovely Mrs. Cain if he could see the list. He looked at it, and said, "Yeah, this one was on the original list. We were gonna play that. Oh, I took that off at the last minute." And so on. It was killing me.

The drummer turned to the lovely Mrs. Cain and said, "Does he get the t-shirt?" She said, "No. He didn't get 15." The drummer said, "Awww, come on!"

She was undeterred. If, she said, I could get the other three members of the group to say the same thing to her, she'd reconsider.

It was late. We had miles to go. I was t-shirt-less.

(As you read this, understand, yes, I know Jian Ghomesi was the drummer for Moxy Fruvous. I am aware of and condemn the assaults made by the former Canadian radio personality. I will add that as I experienced and even as I wrote these pieces, I was unaware. Feel free to judge me. That's OK.)

-- Ditty Bops, Steppenwolf Theatre, Chicago, 2007

Something keeps me returning to live music performances, in spite of the irritations, such as driving, uncomfortable seats (if there are any present), performers failing to start on time, and the late hours one must keep to attend the real quality shows.

For this show, I was reminded of one of those reasons.

A friend and I went to the Steppenwolf Theatre in Chicago to see The Ditty Bops, a band whose second album, *Moon Over the Freeway* was seventh on my 2006 top 10 list.

It was the second time I saw them, and the setlist didn't have much overlap with the previous show, which was good.

I'd not previously heard "Sister Kate," a true jitterbug/swing-style tune off their first album. The crowd appeared to include a number of Ditty Bops veterans, as audience members were mouthing words and eagerly anticipating -- something. That was "Sister Kate," and an invitation to "get up and dance."

Immediately, a half-dozen audience members leaped on the stage and began doing interpretive dance. (Hey, as long as the kids enjoy themselves, who am I to complain?) Before long, the stage was packed with about three dozen respectful dancers, who may have been dancing for themselves or for the audience. It didn't really matter. It was pretty joyful, and extremely entertaining.

It also reminded me of a 1997 show at Foellinger Auditorium in Urbana. Better Than Ezra, touring behind the *Friction, Baby* album, was at the top of its game, and had a rapt audience. The band seemed to be enjoying itself, and vamped through an encore (including playing a snippet of their *Schoolhouse Rocks Rocks* contribution, "Conjunction Junction").

Singer Kevin Griffin invited the audience on stage, which seemed as much of a joke as the Al Green cover he'd tossed in earlier in the set. But people took him up on it.

Foellinger holds hundreds of people, and while the show wasn't a sellout, by the time everyone interested in getting on the stage was there, probably close to 200 people were standing onstage with the trio. People clustered around the band members -- I saw one guy intently talking to the drummer as the band continued to play -- and the performers eventually got to the point where not only could those of us left in the audience not see them, they couldn't see one another.

40

They began talking to one another via their onstage microphones, and there must have been some signal between the three that I couldn't pick up on, because suddenly, the band broke into the brief instrumental from *Friction, Baby,* "At CH.Degaulle, etc." -- the same song they played to open the show.

-- 1978, Nazareth/Sammy Hagar, Austin, Minn.

I knew who Sammy Hagar was at this time, believe it or not. But I knew him as the guitar player from Montrose. I was interested in what he was capable of doing.

The pre-concert experience was one of the most frightening I've had, and I wasn't that surprised when more than a year later, 11 people died in a crush in Cincinnati trying to get into a general admission concert by The Who. This Nazareth show was general admission, and the crush of people trying to get in (to a hockey arena considerably smaller than the Cincinnati Coliseum) was awesome and scary.

Unfortunately, Hagar was scary as well. He took a crowd primed for a show and essentially put them in a stupor with a combination of mediocre songs and awful sound. (After that, one friend in attendance and I regularly did our version of "Sammy Hagar blues" for one another, screeching like tortured cats. It was a response to Hagar saying, "We're going to play some blues for you now," then producing a loud, wrong-key note, complete with some wailing feedback.)

Hagar quickly went from bad to worse. And I'm not proud of this, but I booed. I've walked out on a bunch of acts in my time going to shows, but I've only booed twice -- at Hagar, and at T Bone Burnett. (I'm especially not proud of booing T Bone, but he was really, really bad, and extremely poorly matched in opening for The Who.) (Also, I thought Flock of Seagulls was really horrible, and I walked out on a band called Satchel after their guitarist spent a song giving someone the finger. I assumed it was at the audience, and I wanted to remove my offensive presence.)

I wasn't the only one booing in Hagar's direction. There were probably 2,000 people in attendance, and easily three-quarters of the room was as unimpressed with Hagar as I was. He completed a song, screamed petulantly into the mike, "You fuckers went to sleep tonight, Austin, that's

41

what you fuckers did!"

Oh great. Sammy Hagar sucks, and suddenly it's *my* fault?

A crescendo of "boo"s rained down on the stage. My group sat in the back and giggled, and we laughed even harder as a handful of folks in the front -- maybe a half-dozen -- held up lit lighters, the then-universal sign to encourage an act to come back on stage.

Sammy didn't really grasp it, though. He came back out, pointed to the front row and yelled, "The matches have it! We're doing another one!"

The "boo"s doubled in volume. "Oh, gaaawwwwd, no!" one of my friends yelled. I laughed.

Hagar completed the song, bowed his head and walked to the mike and thanked the audience, and told us he hoped to see us again soon.

The fake sincerity made it pretty clear that he had been told backstage to straighten up his act and apologize to the audience. And it made it much easier to think Van Halen was right when they canned him many years later.

**

There are some habits some folks have at music shows that are just bad form. Some of this came back into my mind after spending 20 hours at shows one weekend.

Whatever most of us say, some of that bad behavior will never be stopped. But if I can reach even two or three people with this, it may delay my implementation of the Web site I-hate-your-stupid-band-and-I-hate-your-stupid-fans.com.

* Keep your mouth shut. If you need to socialize, step outside, go to the bar, go to the back of the room - whatever. Just let those of us who want to listen to the music do so without the lingering details of what you did at work today.

* They're on stage with very loud monitors, and there are bright lights in their faces. They can't see or hear 15 feet in front of them. They can't hear you screaming 100 feet away. But I can. And I don't want to.

42

* They're not going to forget to play their "hit." Don't start yelling for it after the first song.

* Most important, if your favorite band is early or in the middle of the bill, don't resume your conversations after they're done. We were quiet for them and you. Now you be quiet for us.

These rules can work at shows of any size. But somehow, I get the feeling I might be preaching to the choir.

There are also favors that the band should do for the audience.

Especially if you are the opening act, get a set list. Put it together now. It's not like it's a secret that you're going to be playing the gig. List your best 90 minutes, and if you get to the gig site and you're only allowed 45 minutes, you can cut your list in half.

At any rate, having an idea of what you're doing on stage isn't just courteous, it's professional. Believe me, there's nothing -- no Dr. Phil episode, no Cameron Crowe movie, no U2 album -- more boring than watching people discuss what to play next.

Play SOMETHING!

I've been subjected to watching clearly uninterested parties shuffle through five- and six-minute songs, then light cigarettes on stage and discuss for two or three minutes what to play next.

My rear end was turning more numb with every drag off the Marlboro.

It's SHOW business, guys. If you're bored on stage, imagine how boring it is to watch you.

By contrast, I was fortunate enough to see The Clumsy Lovers. I had high expectations, but they were entertaining, gave every indication they were enjoying themselves, and even did a couple of things I could never have imagined.

I'd seen a note on their MySpace page (how old is this story anyway?) by someone complimenting them on violin player Andrea Lewis "coming up out of the crowd." I had no idea what that meant, and put it out of my head.

As the band played its last song, Lewis darted off the stage, to my confusion. From my vantage point at the back of the room, I saw her take a seat at the bar. I had no idea what was going on, and turned my attention back to the stage. In just a minute or so, something caught the corner of my eye. It was Lewis getting up from her barstool and jumping on the bar to walk along it and play another amazing violin solo.

THAT'S entertainment. And it was probably part of the setlist, too.

**

I was getting ready to leave for my annual weekend in Chicago attending International Pop Overthrow, a 16-day, 150-band festival of power pop music performers. (Mary Huhn of the New York Post said IPO is "like speed-dating for the rock 'n' roll set," which is a pretty good description.)

I've fallen in love with bands and people at IPO. I've also suffered through bands I've never heard of, which is the danger of seven- and eight-performer bills. (The advantage is if the performer stinks, they're only on stage for 25 or 30 minutes.)

As I was leaving, I said to The Lovely Mrs. Cain, "I'll give you a call over the weekend, probably to complain about the city or the lousy bands."

She laughed, then said, "Just remember, that can change in a moment."

She'd already experienced that a couple of years previous. I got lost trying to find a venue (these shows take place not in arenas but in clubs that are essentially storefronts), a delightful adventure that featured me turning the wrong way down one-way streets not once but twice.

(I wanted to print up a bumper sticker that said "I'm not as stupid as I drive" and slap it on the back of my car. Or my forehead.)

Once I found the venue, I sat through the worst batch of IPO performers I'd encountered before or since. Four hours of uninterrupted and unforgivable awfulness.

Angry about that and still stinging from my driving incompetence, I called the lovely Mrs. Cain and, like a petulant 8-year-old (and with no irony intended), I said, "I hate this city and I just want to come home right now."

She suggested I return to my hotel room, watch the Sunday night baseball game on ESPN, and return home in the morning.

I demurred. The reason I had picked the weekend I was there was to see a particular band, which was playing that night.

I returned to the tiny club and sat alone at a table in the back. During another lousy act, a guy came up and asked to look at my program. He scanned it and turned to another guy and said, "We're up after these guys," and handed me back my program.

I did a double-take and said, "Are you guys The Tearaways?" When they said yes, I said, "I'm here to see you guys!"

We began to chat. They asked where I'd heard of them (I couldn't answer any better then than I can now), what songs I liked, what other bands I liked. Their road manager came over and as he was told my story ("This guy drove three hours to see us!"), he excitedly said, "We're playing this set for YOU!" He brought over a t-shirt and a copy of one of the band's CDs that I didn't have, and gave them to me. (Guilt-filled, I later gave their merchandise guy a twenty. These guys had come from southern California. They didn't need to be giving stuff away.)

They played a killer set, then two other band members came over because they had to talk to the guy who drove three hours to see them.

It all changed in a moment.

6 SNIPPETS III

I'm pretty sure I like Kaiser Chiefs because they're everything I loved about Franz Ferdinand before Franz Ferdinand went and did whatever Franz Ferdinand went and did.

**

Sting, Stipe, Bono -- how is it possible that none of them disappeared up their own backsides?

**

"It's OK. Go. Do the thing you have to do, Figure out which song you need to listen to, and listen to it 97 times and love every second of it."

**

Just listened to John Lennon's "Love" and realized Robyn Hitchcock owes about the entirety of the *I Often Dream of Trains* album to its existence.

**

There aren't many albums that say "Christmas" to me more than The Rolling Stones' *Let It Bleed.*

**

Foellinger Auditorium in Urbana is the place expectations go to die.

**

I just feel fortunate that I lived to experience the day when I could listen to Donovan's "Season of the Witch" a dozen straight times without taking my hand out of the bag of Fritos.

I know I could do it before, if I had the 45 and an automatic return turntable. The point is that it was a really big bag of Fritos.

**

Liz Phair is my co-pilot.

7 ROGER WATERS' 'THE WALL,' THE ALBUM, THE STAGE SHOW, THE MOVIE, THE REVISED STAGE SHOW, THE MERCHANDISING

At intermission of my first "Wall" concert, two 20-somethings sitting in front of me excitedly turned around, eager to share their experiences and feelings. They'd been hugging one another and hooting and pumping their fists as their favorite songs came up, as the incredible spectacle unfolded before them.

My concentration was focused on the names and pictures being projected on the just-completed wall. I hadn't been expecting the up-to-date anti-war message present in Act One (and about to be amped up for the first half of Act Two).

The one-sided exchange was the female of the couple raving about how amazing the show was. I was still trying to process things. I was surprised by a current and relevant message. I'd considered the possibility that it would be at best a last-gasp spectacle of 1970s and 80s arena rock excess, and I was good with that going in.

All of a sudden, it was all different. My brain was scrambled.

And here was an enthusiastic college-age woman, bedecked in some kind of headband antennae and enough glitter to keep a manufacturing company in business for a month. She determined we were going to have a conversation.

"Did you like that?" she said.

"I think it may have been the greatest hour of a concert I've ever seen," I said.

When Grandpa, who's clearly been to his share of shows and someone else's as well, makes that kind of declaration, the youngsters sometimes sit up and take notice.

"Do you have anybody here with you?"

Now, I don't know what prompted this question. To this day, I find it one of the more curious concert interactions I've had. And I wasn't prepared for the truthfulness of my answer.

"Nope," I said. "This is my thing. For 30 years, I've wondered what this show was. I didn't want to share it with anyone, I don't want to listen to what anybody else thinks, I want to watch it and process it. There is no one I know who has the feelings about this work that I do. And the guy who wrote the thing just spent an hour changing some of those feelings.

"This is my story."

The album has sold millions of copies. Millions have watched the film, repeatedly. The live show has been seen by a few hundred thousand. Yet, I can't think of many other pieces of art that I find so strikingly personal for myself.

I was surprised by the brief entirety of her sole sincere response.

"I think that's so cool."

"Nah," I said. "I can think of a half-dozen people who would like to see this, and who would enjoy it as much as I am. I could have asked a couple of them to come along. I'm really being selfish. This is a dick move."

Her eyes locked with mine, and she slowly shook her head.

"It's not 'a dick move'," she said. "It's really special."

**

I've almost always found myself in Roger Waters' corner.

Waters is the bass player for Pink Floyd, and became its key songwriter and singer after the departure from the band of original singer/songwriter Syd Barrett. (The whole story is more complex than that simple sentence makes it, but for the sake of brevity, go with me. I have a point.)

You're forgiven if you don't know Waters' name. Pink Floyd was Syd and Roger and Nick and Richard, and then Dave replaced Syd. It's not exactly John, Paul, George and Ringo.

For me, Pink Floyd *was* Roger Waters, with a dollop of Dave Gilmour added in. So when Gilmour continued Pink Floyd in the 1980s after Waters declared it a dead beast, I was confused, and after listening to *A Momentary Lapse of Reason,* I shared Waters' outrage that there was an attempt to continue use of the band's name without him.

But Waters could be petty. He threatened to sue promoters and venues who used the Floyd name on a subsequent tour by the Gilmour-led band. He bad-mouthed Gilmour, perhaps frustrated that his solo efforts received less attention and acclaim compared with the faux-Floyd releases and tours.

Let me be clear as well that I realize I'm in a minority. Most Floyd fans embrace the work of both men, or prefer Gilmour to Waters. I'm not being contrary - I just prefer Waters' vision, and to me, Gilmour was a jukebox. (No, I didn't like the Gilmour-led, Waters-less Pink Floyd release *The Division Bell* either. Yes, I understand many people liked it a lot.)

After almost a quarter-century of acrimony, Waters and Gilmour somewhat resolved their differences in 2005 when the four "classic" Floyd members reunited for Live 8 and played a 23-minute set.

For me, it was nice to see the mates somewhat reconciled – they still couldn't resist taking snide, very English little swipes at one another. But Waters was in such awful voice that I consider him what he had considered Pink Floyd 25 years earlier – a spent force.

And that was fine. By 2005, Waters was 62, and there was no reason for him to perform like he had earlier in his life, let alone expect him to. So when Waters toured two years later and played his version of the legendary Floyd album *Dark Side of the Moon,* I was happy for him and glad I knew people who enjoyed the show. But I didn't need to see a pantomime Floyd and a guy with a bad voice.

Yet hearing in 2010 that Waters was planning to launch a tour of *The Wall* was intriguing. It's always been my favorite work of his.

I feel no need to delve into the specifics of *The Wall* album. You know what it is, or if you don't, nothing I can write about that recording and that concept will help you get a better handle on it. A crude sentence about the album would describe it as "a rock star deals with his daddy issues by writing a 90-minute opera about how tough he's had it in his life." Again, it's more complex than that, and Waters made it even more complex when he decided to mount a huge tour of the album three decades after its release.

The Wall was only staged a handful of times by Pink Floyd in 1980 and 1981. If you wanted to know what the staging looked like, you could find out, but it was via stories, a handful of photos and some poorly shot video tapes.

But most of us who wanted to see the production could only imagine the surround sound for which Pink Floyd was famous, what the plane was, how much the wall built during the show actually obscured the band from the audience.

So Waters' decision to launch an arena tour of *The Wall* gave thousands, including a large audience not even born when Waters conceived the original album, the chance "to go to the show," as he sings two different times during the production.

I wasn't sure I wanted to see the 2010 show, even though the staging of it sounded fascinating. Waters' voice quality concerned me, especially with *The Wall,* because it's singing intensive. Three things – well, four – changed my mind.

1. *Rolling Stone*'s story on the behind-the-scenes workings of the production revealed Waters was working out physically and working with a voice coach so he could do the entire show.

2. The Associated Press story about the first night of the tour indicated the best seats in the arenas might be at the back, to experience the entire grandeur.

50

3. A friend's review from an early show, which he called one of the best he'd ever seen.

4. The Minnesota Twins' failure to win a playoff game, which left my budget free for a Waters ticket.

As he started that 2010 show, Waters seemed far more comfortable in his skin than he did years earlier, when his goal was apparently being the world's most disgusted curmudgeon. He accepted what he'd accomplished, and appeared comfortable with his audience's appreciation of his work. He appeared comfortable with his audience, period.

All that would have been enough, I wasn't expecting the best show I've seen in my life. But that's what I got.

Many of the stage set pieces from 30 years previous remained in place, but others were updated with 21st century technology. The show made me appreciate what Waters and Pink Floyd attempted and accomplished in 1980-81, and being in the middle of it 30 years later overwhelmed me.

As I will shout from mountain tops if needed, this was far and away the greatest spectacle I've ever, ever, ever seen.

Arriving in the ScottTrade Arena in St. Louis, and working my way to my aisle seat (SCORE!), I was taken aback to see the wall – which would eventually grow to about 20 feet high and span the width of the arena – was already started on both edges of the stage. The pieces of YouTube video at which I'd allowed myself to sneak a peek didn't show that detail.

Nor was I aware of the "homeless" man who appeared about 10 minutes before the show started. He was pushing a shopping cart around on the floor of the arena, and he had to get fairly close to me before I saw his sign didn't just say "Homeless need money." Additional printing on his sign said "for booze and hookers."

I knew the show would start with fireworks and a blast of sound, but when it did, I immediately understood what the difference would be between watching video and the experience I was about to have. Dimensions. It wasn't the smell of cannabis – if anyone was smoking in the place, they were doing it away from me. And it wasn't the volume – Neil Young on his *Rust Never Sleeps* tour and Frank Zappa tribute band Project/Object had both previously assaulted me in considerably louder fashion.

The Wall has always been anti-war. It was also clearly personal to Waters, whose father was killed in World War II. Waters' willingness to open up the concept of *The Wall* to include everyone while reducing (but not eliminating) the personal aspects made it a more powerful piece.

Oh, Eric Waters is still omnipresent. If we as an audience knew anything, we understood the inspiration of the piece to be Roger Waters' father. A photo of Eric Waters in his Army uniform was among the first projections on a huge circle screen at the back of the stage.

But that picture was rapidly followed by a number of other images. Men and women of all ages, shapes, colors and nationalities appear in the circle, and then are "transferred" via technological magic to the wall being built as the show progresses, forming a photographic human wall of war dead. (Via the Internet, Waters solicited photos of loved ones lost to war.)

The walls we form around ourselves are not simply because of what's done to us, but also the things we miss out on – for example, when loved ones are taken in the cruelest way possible.

It was a theme the 2010 presentation of *The Wall* returned to often, even showing the pictures during intermission on the completely built wall.

Somehow, Waters took the arena experience and made it more like a theater. Since we were dwarfed by the wall along with him, he seemed somehow closer to us. The flying pig that appeared in the second act and the plane that crashed into the wall with a fiery propane explosion at the show's start all added to the dimensionality.

It was simple, clever, and effective.

One of the themes from the original album, concert presentation and film that was carried over is one that's always alternately fascinated and troubled me: The potential fascistic nature of rock shows. It's been an ongoing theme throughout the history of rock music, explored in film by some and in conversation by artists, observers and audience alike, some more intelligently than others.

Waters' vision of this has always been one of my favorite parts of *The Wall*. Artist Gerald Scarfe's animated marching hammers have always been the iconic image of the piece, even more so than the wall itself.

So by the time of "Bring the Boys Back Home" midway through the second act, my defenses were already down. Then images of war's devastation and malnourished children were projected along with U.S. President (and World War II general) Dwight Eisenhower's words, "Every gun that is made, every warship launched, every rocket fired signifies, in the final sense, a theft from those who hunger and are not fed, those who are cold and not clothed."

Well, that wrecked me. I haven't been able to tell people about the moment without choking back tears or just flat out crying. Maybe I'm just soft, but I don't remember ever experiencing anything like that after seeing something, except maybe the end of *Field of Dreams*. (Another "lost daddy" story. Hmmmm ….)

After singing the final line, Waters turned to face the wall with arms outstretched, looking up at the words "Bring the boys back home." Very theatrical, very effective.

Waters' presentation in the new production dramatically altered a couple of other songs as well. "Mother," the concluding song to the first side of the Pink Floyd album, has always been a love song/complaint about an over-protective parent. And while the mother marionette glared out at the audience from the back left of the stage, the images elsewhere made the song more about governmental/Big Brother-style protection. And in one of my favorite moments – however juvenile or obvious you might find it – when Waters got to the line "Mother, should I trust the government?" animated "Pink Floyd"-style lettering, huge on the right side of the wall, spelled out (in perfect rhythm) "No fucking way."

**

When talking with a younger friend about Van Morrison's *Moondance* album, I said side one is arguably the greatest album side in history.

"What's a 'side'?" my friend responded.

The first half of Act Two in *The Wall* – from "Hey You" through "Comfortably Numb" – that is a "side." And it too may be the greatest side in album history.

The problem is, *The Wall* Side Three is difficult to identify as a "side." It's bookended by two of Pink Floyd's greatest songs. "Comfortably Numb" is certainly one of my five favorite songs, maybe one of my top three. I love the album, and have lived with it for decades. There are 30-cut albums (like The Beatles' *White Album*) that I can recite in order, or in backward order or, given a little time, in alphabetical order.

I can come up with the songs that populate the "middle" of Side Three, but only after some thought, and I'm not certain I can get them in order. They flow perfectly together within the work. But for much of my purpose, those songs have always been a postlude to "Hey You" and a prelude to "Comfortably Numb."

So perhaps I was most susceptible in this specific area of the work. The stage production raises the stakes of those songs. "Is There Anybody Out There?" originally had struck me as another version of the rumbly, grumbly, synthesizer-air ride siren noise that concluded "Welcome to the Machine," or Waters' version of Frank Zappa's "Who Are the Brain Police?" Instead, I came to realize and hear it as a fragile and beautifully crafted piece of music, an antidote to the haunting "Hey You," a song that's even more haunting in a different and equally appreciable way.

Then comes the stretch where Waters takes your thinking and feeling and all of your intense emotions, and he twists them out and wrings them dry. Repeatedly.

"Bring the Boys Back Home" always seemed wholly out of place in *The Wall*. If it's a flashback, or a hallucination, it doesn't work like that for me. It always felt like a piece Waters had and wanted to cram in somewhere. It belongs more on Side One, where Pink realizes his father's death, rather than being a scene in which Pink seeks in vain for his father as the trains return. Or something. It was always the pothole on the road I had to drive through as slowly as possible in order to get to "Comfortably Numb."

With the stage production, that changed. I was shaken by footage of the shocked pre-teen girl wearing the peace-sign earrings, overwhelmed by the surprise presence of her soldier father. Then it got worse.

I was unaware of Dwight Eisenhower's 1953 Chance for Peace speech. When I saw the "every gun" quote, Eisenhower elevated on my list of favorite presidents.

It was depressing to realize nothing had changed from what Eisenhower had observed 50 years earlier.

And after all that, I get "Comfortably Numb"?

By the way, there are people who maintain the song's first guitar solo in the best guitar solo in history. It's not even the best solo in the song. Waters was correct in his 21st century *Wall*-staging decision to not change a note, to treat the solos as classical music compositions to be reproduced, not "improved upon."

**

Almost every concert I attend, a song about which I've previously been ambivalent jumps out. With *The Wall,* it was "You Better Run." A moderate hit single as a follow-up to "Another Brick in the Wall Part Two," and the closest thing to disco Pink Floyd ever recorded, it always struck me as a space-holder on the album, something that gave us a little room between the fascism of "In the Flesh" and the absolution of "The Trial."

Even the film used very British images of skinhead violence, a concept most Americans were at best familiar with through reading.

But in the live show, Waters opened my eyes to the song. His use of "enforced recreation," the armbands with the hammers logo, the military stances taken by the backup singers – well, it wasn't exactly subtle, and even someone who is sometimes as oblivious to symbolism as I am could pick this one up.

Waters gave the crowd a cross-armed salute (a physical replication of the hammers). Many in the crowd gave the salute back. In rhythm to the song, Waters and the backup singers clapped their hands over their heads, with Waters exhorting the crowd, "Come on! Enjoy yourselves!" It was an order, not a suggestion.

Many in the crowd clapped as Waters encouraged with "That's better!" I and many others refused to clap along. My interpretation is mirroring Waters is exactly what we were *not* supposed to do.

I'd love to know how Waters felt about his audience at that moment.

And "Run Like Hell" was disturbing, the most troubling (and, frankly, among the most effective) moments of the show. Almost a full-on attack on Apple and all of its iProgeny, Waters appropriates the iPod/iPod typography and market-clever capitalization style and spins it back at the audience. So line drawings of sheep, Mao, Hitler and BinLaden, among others, in a black-on-red motif are jarred with white wires and earbuds leading to their heads.

Along with the images are words like "iLead," "iProtect," "iFollow" (beside pictures of sheep), "iBelieve," "iPaint" (alongside Hitler), "iLearn" and "iPay" (beside gravestones).

You know, sometimes you just want to go to a show and toss back a couple of adult beverages and hear some songs you like. And that certainly was the case for a number of people in the audience of the show I attended.

But I'd also like to believe Waters did what he did with the production to make us think a little bit about what we were seeing and hearing.

**

Two years after that arena tour, Waters took the production on a tour of stadiums. I abhor stadium shows, even more than I abhor arena shows. The

56

first two shows I attended in my life were in professional hockey arenas, but when I finally grew comfortable going to smaller venues, I didn't want to see anyone in anything larger than, say, a 4,000-seat theater, and I'd prefer a club.

But the *Wall* tour was coming to Wrigley Field in Chicago.

One of the themes in *The Wall* is the inhuman nature of stadium shows, how everyone becomes a part of some faceless blob, and the only way to get through to the blob is to blow something up in front of them.

The chance to see a production of an anti-stadium rock opera inside a stadium was virtually irony too delicious to resist. And in another nod to Wrigley Field history, I was just two rows back and a few seats to the right of the "Bartman" seat, the seat occupied by the Cubs fan whose life was ruined in the aftermath of him reaching for a foul ball in a playoff game.

I was so amazed at Waters' ability to sing "The Trial" that it took me some time to realize he wasn't lip-syncing to the Floyd recording. The only reason I realized he was singing live was his inexplicable decision to change the girlfriend/wife's voice to one with a horrific French accent. In interviews, Waters said he changed things about the show every night. He pondered what went right and wrong, and considered adding things. I thought, "I'll believe that when I see it." The pinpoint use of animation calls for click tracks for the performers, so how much can he truly change?

More than I expected, as it turned out. And in other cases, maybe it wasn't so much Waters and *The Wall* that changed, but my perspective.

The flag-bearers at the start of the Wrigley show were not goose stepping on catwalks like they did in 2010. The plane that crashed into the wall seemed smaller. But was that fact, or was everything dwarfed by the enormity of the wall itself, more than two times the width of what I'd seen in St. Louis?

One piece had been added to the show, an addendum to "Another Brick in the Wall (Part 2)" (maybe better known as the hit single version of the song). Waters played acoustic guitar and gently sang the chorus to the song again, and devoted the bit to Jean Charles de Menezes. (de Menezes was a

Brazilian man shot in the head seven times in July 2005 by London police on a London subway after he was misidentified as one of the fugitives involved in failed bombing attempts. The death resulted in extensive public debate about British "shoot-to-kill" anti-terrorist policies.)

Another thing I noticed as new was pointed references in the animation on the wall during "Run Like Hell" to both George Orwell's *1984* and Franz Kafka's *In the Penal Colony*. These references may have been in place earlier, and I just missed them. It was a multi-media presentation unparalleled in its scope, and anyone who tells you they were able to grasp it all even in a couple of viewings is either a liar or a microprocessing unit.

If an artist is going to go to the trouble of inserting these references - and give the audience credit for the capability of understanding them - doesn't the audience owe the artist the courtesy of consideration of the reason for that placement? In other words, this is clearly serious business to Roger Waters. The least I can do is treat it as such.

At the first *Wall* show, I found myself getting more and more tense and involved throughout Side Three. By "Comfortably Numb," I realized there had been a gradual increase in volume, a touch that increased the intensity I was feeling. I was prepared by the second show, and put in earplugs at the end of "Bring the Boys Back Home." (This also gave me the chance to surreptitiously wipe away a couple of pools of tears.)

I found myself so emotionally taken with the Eisenhower speech moment at Wrigley that I was crying and shaking to the concern of those around me. I had to assure one man I was all right, and another slapped me on the back and said, "You a vet, man? Yeah, this is tough." That kind of brought me back to reality, as I said, "No." "Oh," he responded. "Then you got a kid over there. Yeah, I hope he comes back all right."

Not that either, but thanks.

**

Then came the kind-of-documentary film about the tour.

The Wall presentations as album, brief Pink Floyd show, film and even

Berlin concert were collaborative efforts. The album was a band/producer work. The show was a combined effort of cast and crew. The film was headed by a strong-willed director. All of the works were composed by the creative bulldozer whose efforts in the 1970s were responsible for chart success, 20 million albums sold, and an artistic respect unsullied by thoughts of "If everyone likes this, it can't be so good." That Waters might have, by this time, been one the most disagreeable humans in history does not enter into the equation.

Even the Berlin production of *The Wall* seemed more gimmick than art, with its guest performances and improbable nature. The production only existed because Waters had (jokingly, I'd thought) said he'd remount the show when the Berlin Wall fell.

But by the time the 21st century *Wall* was being presented to a wild- and wide-eyed little Timmy Cain in St. Louis, everything we were seeing was Waters' idea. It was *Roger Waters' 'The Wall'*. Everything but Waters was relatively faceless, and certainly allowed no personality.

That was and is fine. As presented, the story of *The Wall* is one that Waters has to tell us. Fascinating that a story that touched so many millions so deeply was changed ever-so-slightly, and we as an audience certainly needed Roger Waters there as a guide. Had the story changed so completely? (Well, yes, kind of at first, and then wholly, definitely and mind-blowingly.) If it could be changed that way, did we need Waters there, or could it have been presented by a faceless theater company with an attractive leading man? (Well, yes, it could have been. That would have been an interpretation that had occurred to apparently exactly no one for the 30 years after *The Wall* was released.) So whose interpretation was it? And whose voice and face did we need to ground us in the knowledge that this was the same story?

(The answer, by the way, is that big-nosed bloke in his late 60s, the guy playing bass for half the show.)

Waters' name is all over the credits of the film. Producing, directing, writing, every place a key creative name can be placed, Waters' name is there. As it should be. Waters spent too much of his creative life sharing too much credit. I've liked enough of his stuff for enough of my life to come to a singular conclusion: Roger Waters is the creative force behind Pink Floyd, and the only reason any of what they produced has any lasting artistic merit or quality. Disagree with me on that one? You're a big David Gilmour fan? That's cool. Nothing Gilmour's Pink Floyd produced ever had a bit of resonance with me. Heck, I even think *The Final Cut* is largely a crap album, rescued with a couple of decent songs tossed away while Roger Waters looked ahead to his next career step, without Pink Floyd.

So this is no complaint or indictment of Waters stamping his name all over the 21st century tour, or the documentary. But it's intended as a reminder. It's touching and heartbreaking on the surface, yes, to see Waters tear up while sitting in his car and reading the letter Waters' mother received during World War II, the letter that assured her that her husband (and Roger's father) had been killed in battle. The reaction may have been genuine, yes, but there are at least four different camera angles, and he (as writer/actor/producer) had to consent to showing his emotions to us in that manner. The same reminder is important when pondering Waters' presence at the memorial at the battle site, or the shot of Waters with his family, pointing out the marker for his grandfather.

And if I'm going to criticize him for those conceits, I also have to praise him for an even greater conceit. On his way to the Battle of Anzio memorial, he drinks and tells a bartender who doesn't understand English the story of the battle. A fantastic metaphor for both walls dividing us, and the uselessness of war.

"Everything has a meaning," film co-director Sean Evans said. "He's not into pretty pictures just for the sake of pretty pictures."

One of Waters' complaints while sifting through footage of the shows was seeing the number of mobile devices in the crowd. He was baffled about how the crowd could get anything from his show when those cameras were just adding more bricks in the wall separating the audience from the performer.

But at those arena shows, a pre-show announcement didn't discourage fans from using photographic equipment. The announcement merely and smartly asked that flash functions be shut off. My enjoyable memories of my arena show were enhanced by me locating full-length video from shows around the country.

Seeing the film, however, one can understand the complaints. In shots taken from overhead about halfway back from the stage, we see a sea of smartphones aloft. The light is distracting from the light onstage on which we should be focused.

That sea of smartphones was present at both shows I attended. (The pre-show announcement about photography being OK was not repeated at Wrigley, however.) The lights from the phones were not a distraction in person, however. It didn't even bother me from people around me, and I'm certain I wasn't bothering anyone taking the hundreds of photos I took.

I understand Waters' frustration at creating a bigger-than-life spectacle and watching an audience look at it through tiny smartphone screens. During the Wrigley show, I snapped about 350 shots. About half of them were totally useless. But that still left a lot of images I at least considered decent.

I mentioned the 350 number to one friend, who said, "Did you see the show at all?" And I didn't understand the question. It turned out my friend thought I had a camera pressed against my face for the entire show. In fact, what I did (for the most part) both shows was hold my smartphone near my body and just punch the trigger when something caught my eye. That's why there were so many useless photos.

So while I understood Waters' frustration at mounting this huge production and watching an audience reduce it to 2x3-inch memories on a video screen, it's also to his credit that he's created something that people want to capture and treasure.

I didn't even have my hands in the air as often as those around me (many of whom were also taking photos) who pumped their fists in the air with every new song. In some cases, I had to think, "You guys knew this song was coming next, didn't you?"

That's Waters' issues with his audience in a microcosm. It's part of what sparked creation of *The Wall*. Waters had both the fortune and displeasure of having his fragile art be loved by millions. He might have preferred to perform "Pigs on the Wing" in a coffeehouse in front of a few dozen quiet and attentive listeners. But that wouldn't accommodate the giant flying pig, so Pink Floyd had to play arenas like the one in Montreal, where Waters lost his temper with the crowd on the band's *Animals* tour, the event that became the conception of the *Wall* concept.

So often, Waters seems of two minds about his audience. He loves them, wants to communicate with them, wants to commune with them. At the same time, the faceless and fascistic nature of huge rock shows makes everything faceless – faceless performers heading a spectacle for a faceless crowd.

The Wall The Film shows some of that. The camera drifts by crowd members in slow-motion, making both poetry and mockery of fans' delight at seeing Waters, or hearing their favorite song, or being present. Images of hundreds of people feeling that warm thrill of confusion, that space cadet glow.

Waters also takes advantage of those fans. A group wears "Pink masks." He uses fans' enthusiasm to turn the rock-as-fascist-spectacle back on its head. He puts on his Nazi gear and hoists his hands above his head, wrists crossed in submission. It's not an accident that Waters demands the audience participate. Waters himself, like the corporations and organizations he satires elsewhere in *The Wall,* is a brand name demanding fealty.

**

There are several things that turn up repeatedly in Frank Zappa songs. Dogs (specifically poodles), vacuum cleaners and chrome pop up in various contexts, along with a series of fictional characters created by Zappa. He called the practice "conceptual continuity," choosing to advance the theory that the entirety of his art – recorded work, writings, live performances, even interviews – were all parts of a bigger whole. Zappa never really gave a meaning for the practice, or any reason for its importance. But it's part of his art. Waters has shown a similar interest in deeper meaning.

Pink Floyd's *The Dark Side of the Moon* begins and ends with a simulated heartbeat. The album is infinite, a Mobius in its very existence. I had three copies of the album in high school to better show how the front and back prism/heartrate monitor covers connected, conceivably infinitely.

Until it became the stuff of Internet shared knowledge, I was unaware of "… where we came in" being the first sounds on *The Wall,* and "Isn't this …" being the final sounds. It's a nice loop.

The same loop is created with the documentary, which starts in what appears to be an underground parking garage. Waters says, "Where we came in." And the final sound, as Waters has departed the stage and is about to get into transportation, he says, "Isn't this …" One of the people at the film pointed it out to me. I was astonished, both that it was there and that I, now fully aware of the Easter egg on the album, missed it in the film.

Improbably, this made me ponder a position flip on the great *Dark Side of Oz* debate. The theory states Pink Floyd's *The Dark Side of the Moon* is intended to sync up with the film *The Wizard of Oz.* I've always found this to be a steaming, albeit extremely amusing, pile of dog doo. The band members and even engineer Alan Parsons have denied the connection. I've always believed the denials. If you've done something that clever, why would you not brag about it?

The flip side of the argument maintains that Floyd had no idea *Dark Side* was going to become one of the all-time album standards. How or why could they have? And they wouldn't have had the resources to accomplish the syncing task.

The beginning and ending of the documentary have me wondering about Roger Waters and his own conceptual continuity, and whether *Dark Side of Oz* might actually exist.

Had I been directing *Roger Waters The Wall* The Film, I would have made different decisions. In a couple of points (specifically during "Run Like Hell"), a number of Apple-related "I"-phrases pop up on the wall projection. ("iProtect," "iBuy," "iDecide"). In performance, these appearances are numbing. The world being created within the piece is increasingly frightening. We've been observed by drones, a huge inflatable pig is floating above the crowd, and these new words are taking us into a new world.

These are not shown nearly enough in the film for my satisfaction. In the most puzzling decision, most of the flower clip from "What Shall We Do Now" is shown, but there's a cutaway from the video before the climactic violation. Why?

The scenes of the things happening onstage that I couldn't see or never considered while sitting in the crowd bring a new appreciation to the technical nature of the work. I couldn't count how many times I saw two- or three-step stairs, leading up and down the assorted levels of the set. The costume changes are more apparent. I had no idea how much Waters actually plays bass during the show.

Maybe one of the main points of the documentary is intended as peeks behind the curtain. We're shown how it begins and ends offstage, Musicians get close-ups. Most intriguing for me were the overhead shots, pointed from along the wall down toward those on the stage.

Those overhead shots don't give away all the secrets. I'd like to have seen more of the cherry pickers that put a singer and guitar soloist perched above the wall.

But I guess I have to give Roger Waters credit for one thing above all else. He knows how to tell the story way better than most of the rest of us do.

The top ticket price for the Steely Dan show is $232, at which point I assume they change the chorus in "Peg" to whatever one-syllable name you request.

**

Oh, for fuck's sake. Why do I have a disco instrumental of "Baby Face"?

**

Anytime I go down a YouTube rabbit hole, I end up hearing "Year of the Cat" at some point.

**

In retrospect, several of the plots on *The Monkees* TV show are trite, ridiculous, silly, or needlessly complex. Surprised I didn't realize this sooner.

**

You kids have fun, and let me know if the t-shirts are more than $75, OK?

**

Is there a more placid opening to a really great album than "Daniel" opening "Don't Shoot Me I'm Only the Piano Player"?
Why no, Tim, I don't think there is. Good question though.

**

So I'm hearing Bob Dylan's "Tangled Up In Blue" at Walmart? What's this supposed to do, increase my despair?

**

Why do I have Duran Duran's "Girls on Film" in any form, let alone an MP3 on my "long faves" playlist?

**

Van Morrison's "Moondance" makes the entirety of Al Jarreau's career redundant. Not the album. Just the song.

9 "THE ABBEY ROAD MEDLEY"

(Just as the second side of The Beatles *Abbey Road* consists of a series of pieces joined together, you can view this as the same.)

||*| 'Just think, Tim'

There are plenty of good reasons to get tired of performers or individual songs. Maybe you had that friend who was convinced you would love U2 or Bruce Springsteen or Frank Zappa if you just allowed them to give you a two-hour guided tour.

"HOW COULD YOU NOT HEAR THAT?"

Of course, it almost never worked.

There were people who heard The Beach Boys for the first time in decades when *Cocktail* came out and for the ensuing six months, America was tortured with "Kokomo."

By that time, I'd tired of trying to convince people that The Beach Boys were more than their older brother's *Endless Summer* 8-track tape. I couldn't get people to understand the beauty of "Wouldn't It Be Nice," let alone the entirety of the *Pet Sounds* album from which it came. (I eventually realized that until you've had your heart shattered, you're not really going to be able to understand *Pet Sounds*.)

But I never gave up trying to blaze a musical trail for my reluctant friends, willing or otherwise.

Sometimes, I wasn't interested in giving those reluctant friends the tour. They were just going on the trip, like it or not. They might have been hearing anything, even something for which they'd already repeatedly and repeated expressed their distaste. Honestly, I was just trying to open up another part of the world to them. I'd seen what kind of joy could result.

In my teens, I was particularly susceptible to peer pressure. I learned what happened when I confessed to liking the Carpenters more than The Doors or T. Rex. But I still liked some Carpenters songs a lot more than Doors or

T. Rex songs, and vice versa. I just let my friends or my peer group or magazine reviewers convince me of what to think. Sometimes, there were sad outcomes for me.

Hurricane Smith's 1972 hit single "Oh, Babe, What Would You Say?" always put an annoying halt to whatever groove I was in while listening to the radio. The song didn't fit. The strings were too loud. Damn, the saxophone was loud. And him singing this thing that sounded like it was written in the 1920s with that awful nasal sound of his? Well, turn up The Raspberries or The Moody Blues or something and drown out that shit.

And then it popped up decades later, and I thought, "That's really quite beautiful." There are still plenty of people my age who despise it. I regularly work to prevent myself from trying to convince them otherwise.

A few years after Smith's hit, George Benson was suddenly on every radio station I tuned to. I wasn't happy. While I begrudgingly respected his style, I didn't care for it.

Then, in another of those random play occurrences -- only a few days after I heard Hurricane Smith's song for the first time in years -- Benson's "Give Me the Night" came on. Had someone pressed me, I might have said that was the hit of his that annoyed me the most. I just had foul memories of it. But this time around, I heard the beauty in the song, appreciated the tasteful guitar, and realized it was a far better production (by Quincy Jones) than I ever could have realized

I was describing all of this to a friend, who responded, "Just think, Tim -- someday that's exactly what you'll be saying about 'Kokomo'."

||*| Paisley Park is in your mind

"Pilgrimages are important."

— a friend after hearing about my plans to tour Paisley Park

Being able to view in person even a piece of Prince's Paisley Park estate is a treasure. If you think you want to go, you definitely should.

But if you think you might be troubled by parts of the experience, you

67

probably will be.

Prince died on April 21, 2016, at his home in Chanhassen, Minn. It was quickly converted to a tribute site/museum, and doors were opened to fans and the curious.

The potential emotional issues don't detract from the content of the tour. And by all means, don't skimp, go with the more expensive expanded tour. It's worth it.

The dichotomy of the experience in the suburban complex just outside Minneapolis can be as enigmatic as Prince the performer, Prince the personality and Prince the human being.

While it's worthwhile just to visit, it's also worthwhile to analyze from the points of view of both the analytical devotee and the passionate fanatic.

IT'S ALL TOO BEAUTIFUL

Security seems omnipresent, from the purple-drenched entryway with ticket windows to the ceilings. Cellphones go in magnetically sealed pouches carried with the tourist. But they're unavailable while in the complex. No selfies at Paisley Park. At least not until you're walking out.

In the email sent with tickets are instructions that warn you can't arrive more than 20 minutes before your tour, and you must leave within 20 minutes of your tour's conclusion. A solitary security person (sitting in a pickup on the below-zero day of my tour) guards access to the narrow road to the small parking lot (no more than 40 cars) outside the entrance.

WHAT'S THAT UP THERE?

The tour begins in the first floor of a four-story atrium. On a cloud-free day, the sun illuminates a huge sitting room. The pyramid at the apex glowed purple when Prince was in residence. Two large purple couches frame an oversized rendering of Prince's unisex symbol in tile on the floor. We're told this was kind of a hangout room. When visitors came, this is where they were generally received by Prince.

The guide then directs your eyes up to the second story of the room, to what appears to be a plexiglass area of sorts, featuring a good-sized box and something else, from which my eyeline was blocked.

It turns out to be a re-creation of the building in which we're standing. And the box? "Those are his ashes," we're told. "This is where we prefer people pay their respects."

The fanatic in me says: Excellent. I was hoping they'd offer something like this. Paying respects. Like at Elvis Presley's gravesite in the backyard of Graceland.

The devotee in me says: Oh, seriously? Come on. Is this the place? Amid this opulence? Oh, it seems they think it's the place. Look on the tables next to the couches. They already have Kleenex conveniently placed for us.

In reality: Overwhelmed by what felt like a tacky tribute, it didn't make me shed any tears. That happened a couple of times later in the tour.

DO I BELIEVE A WORD OF WHAT I'M TOLD HERE?

We're told that with a few insignificant changes, the area we're touring is just as it was when Prince resided in it. It's made painfully clear we will not approach the second floor, the area where Prince died. The presence of security seemed to confirm that anyone who made any kind of dash toward the stairs would be brought down short of their goal and banished. It's clear by the presence of security that contingencies for this possibility exist.

The company that runs Graceland is also in charge at Paisley Park. In both buildings, the residents died on the second floor. In both buildings, you will in no way be allowed to even approach the stairs leading up.

Prince seems omnipresent as well. As the tour starts, you walk under a fresco featuring Prince's eyes, looking troublingly similar to the image at the start of the "When Doves Cry" video. Tour guides said Prince used this symbol as a caution to visitors: His eyes and ears were everywhere.

The fanatic in me says: Fascinating. They're showing us what he did with his environment. This is how it was when he was receiving people here. It's like I'm Prince's guest.

The devotee in me says: I'm on board with the whole camera thing. But why make a point of indicating tourists are being recorded? Most of the time in public anymore, I see the cameras. I assume I'm on film. Is this a double warning? And why are the security guys everywhere, and extremely polite, but certainly not engaging?

In reality: Everyone who was wearing Paisley Park clothing was almost unnervingly polite. As much as the presence of Prince's remains troubled me, the remainder of the tour was tasteful. I don't want to see where the man passed. I was hopeful it was inaccessible, and glad to find that was the case.

HOW MUCH MONEY IS INVESTED HERE?

Every corner you turn, there's something that seems priceless. Guitars designed specifically for certain periods in Prince's life are on display, apparently put in storage 20 and 30 years ago for this very purpose. Prince's tours featured different looks with each album. A pair of guitars exclusive to the "Gold Experience" tour caught my eye and delighted me. Multiple working studios include more modern recording equipment than some retail stores. (On some tours, you get to record in one, if you wish.) I lost track of the number of instruments I saw that appeared to have been played yesterday.

The tour concludes in the 12,500-square foot soundstage room. It's large enough to hold six stages. They're barely equipped, with just a pair of guitars and amplifiers and a set of drums on each. Naturally, each stage features matching sets of instruments from different tours. The room also holds a pair of cars.

And that's just for the recording part of what this section of Paisley Park represents. Dozens, if not hundreds, of pianos and guitars, largely custom designed.

The fanatic in me says: How fantastic to be able to see these things you can't possibly see anyplace else. A whole room along with the additional display materials elsewhere seemed like a lot of space to devote to *Purple Rain,* but hey, I got to see motorcycles from both that and *Graffiti Bridge.*

The devotee in me says: So why do they show us the soundstage room, and make a point of mentioning the custom piano sitting conspicuously in the corner? "It was delivered here the week he died. He never got to play it." Do they really have to remind us of his death at inopportune moments?

In retrospect: The complex Prince wanted to include a storage space for his recorded archives. He saved all manner of formats, going back to Beta video tapes. We were taken to Prince's video editing bay. The room featured space for at least a dozen people to comfortably sit. There, we viewed a montage of previously unseen Prince video allegedly uncovered in those archives. When they showed a 60-second film of a live acoustic version of "I Could Never Take the Place of Your Man," tears welled in my eyes, and I had to turn my back briefly on the tour guide and my fellow tourists. They left me plenty of space.

HAVEN'T I BEEN HERE BEFORE?

The soundstage area is where the theatrical performance film of *Sign o' the Times* was shot. Filmmaker Kevin Smith talked about the atrium and the soundstage area in *An Evening With Kevin Smith*. During a half-hour story about an aborted documentary he was filming for Prince, Smith detailed Prince's other-worldly nature and pronouncements. Smith's stories essentially confirmed others' stories about Prince's devotion to his muse and his disregard of anything that didn't fit within his vision of his world. Charlie Murphy gave birth to a Prince basketball legend with his "True Hollywood Stories" tale about Prince on *Chappelle's Show*. (Remember "Game, blouses"? The line was uttered on my tour. By the tour guide.)

For some of us, having those portraits in sound and vision have already helped us form a 3-D mental image of locations. You don't have to have seen the "TV Room" or the "Jungle Room" at Graceland to be aware of their existence. But it's different when you see them in person. You feel like you might have been there already.

Speaking of been there already …

Everyone from Minnesota has at least three Prince stories about how they were justthisfar from one another.

I thought of First Avenue on the Paisley Park tour as we walked through a space that was essentially a nightclub, replete with booth and tables, swinging doors, a stage and a full-service kitchen. The room felt eerily like a miniaturized version of First Avenue, only 20 miles or so southwest from it. The tour guide brought the thought to completion when pointing out the iron work in the room was modeled on the iron work at First Avenue.

The fanatic in me says: This was even more fantastic than I could have imagined. All of these rooms are spectacular.

The devotee in me says: If you can do it, it's great. But who would ever have imagined a little First Avenue inside this huge building?

In retrospect: How huge is Paisley Park? Combine almost any of the two rooms in this building, and you have more square footage than my entire house. That's not true of Graceland.

WHAT'S THIS COOL STUFF?

I know people who have won Grammy Awards. I've held them. Both the trophies and the winners. They're cool, but there are a bunch of them out there.

But how many people do you know who have won an MTV Video Music Award? Have you ever seen one of those trophies? Ever been in the same room as a genuine Academy Award?

My answer to the latter two questions is now "yes." The Academy Award is in the room devoted to *Purple Rain.* Speaking of other cool stuff in there, among the other items on display are Prince's purple velour jacket, his motorcycle, and a bound hardcover copy of the movie script, with Prince's name embossed, and a purple bookmark.

This room was the second place I lost my composure. There have always regularly been times when listening to Prince where I've been taken by surprise. I've heard either musical or vocal treats I hadn't noticed previously. I've had entire songs whose meaning and significance have changed for me over time.

The most wonderful thing about music is it can always take you by surprise in ways you never could have anticipated.

So while I watched the clips collage from *Purple Rain* played on two big screens positioned on the wall across from one another, I was overwhelmed by the clip of "Darling Nikki." It really is a stunning performance, and

Prince is clearly in the moment. It would have been reasonable at the time to think of that performance as once-in-a-lifetime. We didn't know until much later that it was actually closer to a once-in-an-evening type of performance as his reputation grew.

As the other two people on my tour wandered away, I was able to gather myself, and think about the Video Music Awards statue. It really is a stupid-looking off-balance astronaut. And it really looks as cheap behind glass as it does on television.

But it appears perfectly normal on display alongside Grammys, Soul Train Awards, BET Awards and Golden Globes.

Amid the opulence, it's easy to lose track of Prince the musician, or at least get lost in the music of his youth. Even the platinum and gold discs on display everywhere are inevitably for music released in the previous century.

Later, I was thrilled when we were led into a studio where Prince had recently worked, recording what was to be an album for the Blue Note jazz music label. We were played a track from the unreleased album, a four-minute instrumental that would fit perfectly as a solos section in a later-period Steely Dan album. Steely Dan and Prince are two of my favorite performers. The music was fine by me.

But they didn't show us everything. They didn't show us the basketball court where Charlie Murphy lived his famous story, although we were assured it was there. According to Murphy's story, he and his crowd played basketball against Prince and his associates. Prince and crew were wearing their stage clothes, complete with heels. Prince's team demolished Murphy and crew, and Prince made them pancakes.

I can't believe I didn't hear that story from a fellow Minnesotan years earlier.

They didn't tell us whether the ping-pong table on which they insisted we play was the same one on which Prince famously humiliated Michael Jackson. There's a Prince legend that says when the two met at Paisley Park in the 1980s, Prince mocked Jackson and played a little rough in an impromptu ping pong showdown.

Our guide insisted we play ping-pong just so we could say we played on Prince's table.

The fanatic in me says: Everything about this tour is likable. When else would you ever get to see any of this stuff, let alone all of it in one location?

The devotee in me says: Hurry up and release that Blue Note album. And honestly, there's nothing that stops me from *saying* I played ping pong on Prince's table.

In retrospect: Even if you regard the collection of awards somewhat pedestrian and straight-forward, they're still presented tastefully, and I suspect if I went through the tour again, I'd see things I missed this time around.

THAT'S JUST ME

As I said at the start, if you think you want to go, you definitely should. The absence of your own photographic evidence of the experience shouldn't be regarded as a negative. Prince always wanted people in the moment. Even in death, he holds some control over that.

Our guide asked if I'd ever seen Prince perform in concert. I said, "No, for the same reason I never wanted to see Paul McCartney in concert. I don't want to hear the big song. I don't need to hear Paul McCartney sing 'Hey Jude' in person. (I'm thrilled that those who do still have the opportunity.)

"Prince would never have played the show I wanted to hear.

"I didn't care to ever hear 'Purple Rain' live, and I knew I'd have to sit through it, audience singalong and all. The idea made me nauseous."

But that's just me.

||*| I was a lackey for MTV

It was the summer of 1986, and I happened to answer the phone at home on a weekday afternoon. (I worked at an afternoon paper, which meant plenty of early mornings and plenty of late evenings, but the afternoons were often free.) I answered a few perfunctory demographic questions, and was asked if I'd like to participate in a survey about videos on MTV.

Take an opportunity to influence the medium that was homogenizing music? How could I resist?

I can't remember the time commitment. It was six or eight weeks, enough for me to think, "Maybe I should have asked about this before I agreed to do it." A guy would call me every week, play a 15-second snippet from a song, and ask me to rate the video on a scale of 1 to 5, or "haven't seen it." I wound up getting asked about 30 or 40 songs in every call.

I remember the time of year specifically because of one song, The Bangles' "If She Knew What She Wants." I had a crush on Susannah Hoffs (what guy didn't in 1986?) and a fervent hope that The Bangles and their Beatle-y sound would bring more of that style to the mainstream. The Prince-penned "Manic Monday" reached No. 2 on the charts, stopped short of No. 1 only by Prince's own "Kiss."

But Prince's song also robbed the Bangles of the Beatle-style charm I adored.

I got comfortable enough with the guy conducting the survey that by the third or fourth time he called, when the "If She Knew What She Wants" snippet came up, I suggested they change the network to "Bangles TV" and put that clip in permanent rotation.

If the goal was to encourage me to watch more MTV, it worked. I hadn't watched that much of it for years, since it had been added to my cable lineup. I hated a lot of what I saw on MTV, and I'd turned away. By this time, I was listening to Robyn Hitchcock and Beat Rodeo and Smithereens, and wondering why I wasn't seeing *them* on MTV.

But by participating in the survey, I was doing my job for my generation.

By the time we got to the end of my term, my caller seemed as weary of me as I was of rating. One thing had kept me going through the final weeks, though. I was certain I'd be offered some kind of reward for participating. I hoped for at least a t-shirt, although if they'd offered to send Martha Quinn to the house for a weekend, I'd have suffered through that. (She's a pixie, y'know.)

Nothing. Nothing more, that is, than a curt "goodbye."

It's been years since MTV has been interested in my opinion about anything, almost as many years as it's been since they truly were a music video network. But there was a time when they followed the lead of radio stations and actually surveyed their listeners.

How old does this make me feel? About as old as when I talk to new reporters about carrying my suitcased typewriter when I was in high school.

||*| John Cage

As my "bucket list" came up in discussion, I told a friend about my desire to perform a John Cage composition -- 4'33" -- with any symphony that will have me.

She was not aware of Cage. So as others scattered, knowing the stories I was about to tell, she settled in to hear John Cage tales.

I watched her face for reaction, the same way I do anytime I'm talking with people about unlikely or improbable or non-traditional art. It used to be so I could judge them, and judge them as inferior if they did not share my enthusiasm.

But now, when I talk about John Lennon's "Revolution 9" or "Nutopian National Anthem," or Frank Zappa, or The Residents, or anyone who does things outside the lines, I no longer make that judgment. It's just not that person's choice of art.

But she was receptive, which got me even more excited, and prompted me to go find the following column for her. It was published in the Decatur (Ill.) Herald & Review in Aug. 2004. It's one of the five best columns I've written.

*** Decatur Herald & Review, August 2004 ***

So how's your work of art coming along today?

What's that? You don't have a work of art? Well, maybe you do, but just don't realize it.

(In that day's paper) we have a story about a church in Germany where, last month, two notes were added to an organ that is playing a John Cage composition, "Organ2/ASLSP" or "Organ squared/As slow as possible."

The composition is designed to last 639 years. Started on Sept. 5, 2001 (the 89th anniversary of the birth of the controversial composer, who died in 1992), the first 18 months of the "performance" was silence. (As originally performed, the composition lasted about 20 minutes.)

For many people, their feeling about Cage's art gives insight to how they feel about more liberal interpretations of what art can be. To some of us, Cage's compositional concepts are revolutionary, freeing music from artificial restraints and making clear over and over that music is all around us — it's just a matter of realizing it and experiencing it.

For others, Cage's work is that of a pretentious poseur who simply sold some gullible over-thinkers a bill of goods and gave him a reputation he didn't deserve.

Some of Cage's work eludes me, but "Organ2/ASLSP" is as fascinating as some of his other offbeat work, taking existing appliances or spaces and making them become something else altogether.

Cage's ideas are not the exclusive domain of the classical music field. Frank Zappa used Cage-like concepts extensively, most notably on his *Joe's Garage* albums, where most of the guitar solos were taken from concert tapes Zappa had recorded. The solo from the performance would be dropped into a studio recording done by Zappa's band.

John Lennon lifted a live BBC Radio performance of "King Lear" and placed it into "I Am the Walrus" when doing the final mixdown.

Cage's composition "Imaginary Landscape No. 4" was written for 12 radio receivers. Cage's score indicated how the radio "players" should tune the radios and change their volumes, giving structure to each performance, but because of the nature of radio, each performance of the piece was unique.

Cage's most controversial piece, "4'33"," is essentially four minutes and 33 seconds of silence, but again, each performance is unique because while the performer is not playing an instrument, there is still ambient noise, be it breathing, feet shuffling, coughing, or whatever else is brought into the performance.

Accepting this as art and composition can lead to a revolutionary breakthrough — the realization that we can all be artists.

Zappa wrote about it in a way most understandable to me in *The Real Frank Zappa Book,* saying in effect that to create a piece of art, you only need to worry about the frame — that is, where the art begins and ends. ("Don't worry about whether it's good or bad," Zappa wrote. "There are plenty of people around willing to tell you that.")

You can live your life as a performance art piece, and all you need to do is decide when it begins, and at some point determine the piece has concluded. You can compose a song by deciding whatever noises you make beginning at a certain point and the song ends whenever you decide. (Making the decision to not follow Cage's lead and end your song in less time than 639 years would probably be a good idea, however.)

Want to write something, but think you "don't know how to write"? Maybe it's in your power to create a new kind of communication. (Do you think graphic novels have been around forever?) Painting? Drawing? Everybody can paint. Everybody can draw. It's how we start communicating. It's only aging that makes us think we're not "good enough" to continue.

If it's something from which you draw pleasure, why stop just because you're not "good enough"? At almost every life endeavor, you improve with practice.

(An office discussion about this topic often dead-ends, however, with dance. You might lack traditional skills at drawing or singing, and you're not going to do much harm to anyone. Really bad dancers — like yours truly — can hurt themselves AND others. It's a conundrum we need to work around, or at least accept for the time being.)

Is Cage's "Organ2/ASLSP" art? How can it not be? Is it a pointless intellectual exercise? Possibly.

No one reading this will be around to hear the conclusion of the performance. The world may end before the performance does.

But in the meantime, it's an ongoing work of art, one that can be experienced by millions who wander into a German church. It's got me trying to figure out where the heck Halberstadt, Germany, is (it's not far from Berlin) and how the heck to get there. And there's no hurry. (And don't worry — no dancing, either.)

If nothing else, "Organ2/ASLSP" shows us the only limit to our capability to produce art is the limit of our imagination.

||*| Grand Funk Railroad's "Gimme Shelter"

Look, you don't like Grand Funk Railroad's version of "Gimme Shelter," and I get that. There's a style of elegance and seduction in the Rolling Stones' version, especially when Mick Jagger's vocals suggest violence in kissing when he and Merry Clayton turn "It's just a shot away" at the song's close to "It's just a kiss away".

In Grand Funk Railroad's version, it's a straight-ahead kick in the guts and in the nuts. From the start, the music is more foreboding, letting you know something serious is going on.

The Rolling Stones invite you in. Grand Funk Railroad knocks you on the head, drags you in and pummels you with the terror. By halfway through, the screeching guitar amid the wall of noise from bass and drums are joined by the jungle-like thumping of a tom-tom.

When Grand Funk's version reaches what should be its conclusion, the band busts out the cacophony of noise that marked the end of every 1970s concert metal jam performance. *Then* there's another 100 seconds of playing.

Sound hideous? If you think so, you clearly were not a teenage boy in the mid-1970s. For my entire life, I've been reading criticisms of Grand Funk Railroad. And the criticisms are bitching because the band was unapologetically what they were -- loud, musically crude and quite willing to cater to their audience. They were proud of being popular.

As my musical tastes were forming, I'd read criticisms of their performances and wondered why so many people seemed to like this band when the writer did not. I loved the "Mark, Don and Mel" mythologizing, in which manager Terry Knight claimed the Grand Funk Railroad's members were famous enough to require just one name, like Napoleon, Jesus, Mao and Twiggy. (Knight, of course, was a silly man). I loved the silver coin-shaped die-cut cover of *E Pluribus Funk.* I treasured my gold-color vinyl versions of *We're An American Band*, album and 45, proof that I had bought the records early in their production run.

And let's face it: To me, they just sounded *cool.* Always did.

Do I understand the criticisms? Sure. What the people just a little older than me hated about Grand Funk Railroad was pretty much what I came to hate a few years later as REO Speedwagon and Journey drifted away from what they were to what they became. I thought there was something genuine early on with Journey and REO, but grew disappointed as they became more obvious. People who hated Grand Funk Railroad never saw anything genuine in the band. (A lot of them couldn't even be touched by something as amazing as "I'm Your Captain/Closer to Home.")

Still, I'll bet even a lot of them would like to hear Mick Jagger sing over the Grand Funk Railroad musical track of "Gimme Shelter."

||*| The Association

Movie producers are missing the boat by not using an easily identifiable music act in films.

I've never liked the practice of using popular music as a shortcut to identify time periods in films. We've all seen the classic moments punctuated by music key to the era, locking us in to a specific point in time. The soundtracks to *Forrest Gump* and *The Big Chill* are perfect examples of skimming from the 1960s for shortcuts in storytelling, allowing the music to make up for the imperfections in the stories.

The miracle is that both of those soundtracks, even the expanded versions, managed somehow to avoid including "Incense and Peppermints" OR "All Along the Watchtower."

But if filmmakers are looking for an untapped area that can easily identify the era, they need to dig into the catalog of the band The Association.

In 1967 and 1968, The Association were at their peak. The drove the sunshine pop movement, best defined as love songs with quiet, gentle arrangements and pleasant harmony vocals. While The Association were the early kings of the genre, it eventually grew to be owned by The Carpenters. The Association's songs defined their time so completely, they would never fit in any other era.

The big hits: "Windy," "Cherish," "Along Comes Mary" and "Never My Love." All solid. Forced to choose a favorite, I'm not sure I could separate "Windy" and "Along Comes Mary."

I don't recall hearing any of these songs in films, connected with their eras or otherwise. I can't imagine movie-makers haven't imagined using them in some way. Picture the potential movie-ending freakout – like in a *Shrek* film, or mimicking the conclusion of *The 40-Year-Old Virgin* - that could be accomplished with "Windy."

My suspicion is either those who own the rights to the songs are asking for too much money, or the rights are of questionable enough ownership that it's easier to avoid a potential legal wrangle and just pick a Creedence Clearwater Revival song.

But hearing one of those Association songs by the original artist in a period film? That might open up as many ears as the *Guardians of the Galaxy* soundtrack did.

||*| Oh hell yes am I watching this

I came across a documentary on Amazon Prime, and decided to share some thoughts on social media. Here is the transcript. In what I find slightly more delightful, looking up the documentary, I saw the title on the photo/poster said *The Beach Boys and the Satan*.

81

1 p.m.: A "documentary" titled *The Beach Boys and Satan*? Oh hell yes am I watching this.

1:03: Holy crap. Within three minutes, we've got a clip of the start of the robbery scene from *Pulp Fiction*.

1:06 Minute six: 90 seconds from the film *The Girls on the Beach*

1:07 Oh holy shit, the late Kim Fowley, at least 70 years old in this clip, is singing some kind of folksy blues thing.

1:08 Don Was? What the hell?

1:09 Lots of fun vintage clips of the Boys. Satan is still hiding.

1:10 Mike Kelly from Destroy All Monsters? Seriously, does any person reading this have any idea who Mike Kelly is?

1:11 Chris Darrow. Seriously. I had to Google the guy myself. And these guys are talking about psychedelics, and there's no Beach Boys music post-*Pet Sounds* yet.

1:13: Performance clip of "Sloop John B" I've never seen. Live. Looks like 1967. Carl's wearing a scarf. Damn, I need to find this full clip.

1:14 DON WAS IS TALKING WHILE A GUY IS CLEANING HIS FUCKING POOL.

1:17 Brian Wilson singing "Love and Mercy" (1988). Why? Who can tell.

1:18 Wouldn't it be great if the guy cleaning Don Was' pool was Kim Fowley?

1:20 Clips from Brian's 1976 birthday party. This film is, to be charitable, indirect, random and baffling.

1:23 Oh man, you can always win me back showing the clip of Ronnie Spector singing "Be My Baby."

1:26 If douchebags had currency, Mike Love's face would be on it.

1:28 They're talking about *Pet Sound*s over background music of

"Vegetables." I think they just threw song clips in the air, and however they came down was how they got put in the film.

1:29 Now Dennis is dead. It's 1983.

1:30 Not any longer.

1:31 The FULL CLIP of the *Inside Pop* "Surf's Up" performance?

1:34 Janis Joplin. Goddammit.

1:35 Oh ... Hendrix and Brian Jones too. It's the dead people parade. Must not be any public domain footage of Morrison available.

1:39 Kim Fowley is singing about Charlie Manson. Maybe Charlie is Satan. I can buy that. We're 39 minutes in. Stuff is happening.

1:41 *Lucifer Rising* clip. Yes, *Lucifer Rising*. The Kenneth Anger film.

1:42 This is trippier than if you combined *The Apple* and the 70s version of *Phantom at the Opera*.

1:44 Ahhh. So The Beatles had it easy because there were four of them, and Brian Wilson worked solo. Making your case by trashing The Beatles is a fool's game, and a pathetic argument.

1:46 Oh no ... the bit where they made Brian surf for the '76 TV special. This always makes me sad.

1:48 OK. Sharon Tate's murder. We had to know this one was coming.

1:51 We're eight minutes from the conclusion. It's going to take a lot of magic to tie this into even a sloppy package.

1:52 Kenneth Anger is an interesting artist, but why the hell is he in this?

1:53 Get this: A guy says the demonization of Charles Manson as a mystical and powerful Svengali was a plot by the government to help strengthen Christianity.

1:53: My head hurts.

1:54 Another Charles Manson verse from Kim Fowley.

1:58 If I have to guess at the point of your documentary, you have not succeeded. So I guess Satan was Manson. And the walrus was Paul.

2:01 p.m. One friend responded, "I feel like this was sent to you by the film gods for your bday." In the middle of everything, one friend posted, "Oh Tim, please stop watching."

||*| *Captain EO* rerelease

(November 2011)

What do you think about Michael Jackson these days?

Do you think of him as an artist at all? Or has the freak show that always surrounded his existence obliterated any consideration of the man as a songwriter, singer, dancer, performer?

Jackson was back in the news when a jury found Dr. Conrad Murray guilty of involuntary manslaughter in Jackson's June 2009 death. The same week, for the first time in 24 years, I saw *Captain EO,* the Disney/Jackson 17-minute 3D film attraction. Disney last year brought the film out of storage for the first time since mothballing it in 1994.

(I always wanted to use the word "mothballing.")

Jackson in 1987 at this time was at the height of his fame, with the world anxious for any kind of follow-up music to *Thriller*. My companions were more interested in jungle cruises and the Matterhorn, and tolerated my desire to see Jackson's show.

With the second viewing, my reaction was almost exactly the same. I was annoyed with Jackson interacting with the too-cute and unfunny Muppet creations. (Oh, hey, there's a sloppy and clumsy elephant. And there's some annoying winged creature that hovers in front of you in *three dimensions!*)

But I was taken - both times - by the music. I'm not a huge fan of dance. I mean, I admire it and like watching it, but I don't know enough about it to be an intense a fan as I am of other art forms. So when Jackson dances, I'm amazed, but I wonder if I'm amazed by an amazing performance or by the equivalent of a warmup exercise.

But I know the music, and while the two *EO* songs aren't among Jackson's greatest, they're both still good. And they reminded me that there was a time when the only thing I knew or cared about Michael Jackson was good and interesting music.

I don't know how much of Jackson's music remains relevant to people today. There was a Cirque du Soleil show based on Jackson's music touring the country, eventually landing (as everything seems to) in Las Vegas. I'd like to think more people are interested in the music than the freak show. I wish I had any feel about whether that was true.

||*| *Elvis at Stax: Deluxe Edition*

Here's the beginner's version of Elvis Presley's career:

He breaks through to popularity, then goes into the Army, effectively killing the musical and societal revolution he sparked. He left the Army, started making mediocre movies, and despite a handful of returns to form, he doesn't matter again until his American Sound Studios recordings (including "Suspicious Minds" and "In the Ghetto") and television comeback special. Then he goes to Las Vegas, sinking all credibility with youth, and dies long before his time

The only problem is, every once in a while, evidence comes up that discredits the beginner's version.

One of those pieces of evidence is the three-disc set, *Elvis at Stax: Deluxe Edition.* The set collects in one location a number of previous releases, and features 28 songs and 27 outtakes/alternate versions.

Here's the thing. These sessions took place 40 years ago at the legendary soul and R&B studio in Memphis where some of pop music's greatest hits were recorded. Presley went in as a 38-year-old man - ancient by the pop music standard of the day - and recorded material that could have produced the greatest album of his career, and what certainly would have been in the

85

conversation for best album of the year.

Of course, the same could have been said about what happened four years earlier, with the American Sound Studios sessions. And it can reasonably be argued that those stunning recordings are the greatest of Presley's career. I love the Sun sessions collections from the very start of his career, but the Presley album I return to most is *The Memphis Record,* a collection of those 1969 sessions.

The dichotomy of Presley's career and life was the split between the R&B-loving revolutionary and the Southern gentleman who sang gospel, between the hip-swiveling rocker and the smoldering ballad singer. There was no interest on the part of anyone - not his people, not his record company - of building a career for Elvis Presley. So there was never a concern about helping him release and market a fantastic album. RCA would sell its Elvis singles, and they could probably predict within 1,000 how many copies each album would sell, such would be the consistency of Presley's audience.

So Presley was never really an album artist in his lifetime. It was the concert recordings - especially from the 1970s - that exploded on the charts.

But of 28 songs recorded at Stax in 1973, six made the Billboard singles charts. Maybe a couple of them shouldn't have, but the majority were great songs that hold up today. Just, for whatever reason, they didn't resound with the public the way "Suspicious Minds" or "Burnin' Love" did.

But if those six songs had come out as part of one album, and Presley/RCA kept out some of Presley's tendency toward treacle, that Stax album might have battled Lynyrd Skynyrd's *Pronounced,* Wings' *Band on the Run,* Elton John's *Goodbye Yellow Brick Road,* Led Zeppelin's *Houses of the Holy* and Pink Floyd's *Dark Side of the Moon* for the spot of most legendary album of 1973.

(And the comment about Presley's treacle is an observation, not a complaint. Treacle was always a huge part of Presley's repertoire. Complaining about it would be like complaining about British hard rock and metal bands doing sub-standard 12-bar blues - it happened all the time, and you had to just accept it as part of the package.)

Exhibit one: "Promised Land." This song alone gives a person enough evidence that Presley was the greatest Chuck Berry cover artist ever. If you've heard "Brown-Eyed Handsome Man" or (especially) "Too Much Monkey Business," you've heard Presley doing Berry great. But to hear "Promised Land" is to hear transcendence.

Extension of the point as found in film: The submission of the best 90 seconds from the first *Men In Black* film, in a scene that also includes the film's best line.

Exhibit two: "Raised on Rock." Written by Mark James, who also wrote "Suspicious Minds," Presley/RCA thought highly enough of the song to make it the title cut of a batch of the songs released on album. Interestingly, it was the only song of our three examples released on the album. *Promised Land* was eventually released in 1975, as the title track to its own album. Also on that album ...

Exhibit three: "If You Talk In Your Sleep." This is the revelation of the Stax set. Presley's final released was drenched in horns and strings, and made the Billboard top 20. But another version included on the new set is "take 5" of the song. It's filthy in a brilliant way. The band is slinky as it works around its arrangement, and Presley smolders in a way that's almost embarrassing in its intensity and intimacy. It's fantastic, at once reminding the listener what Presley was, and what he could almost be seemingly at will later in his life. If only he'd wanted to more often.

One final personal note:

No one can ever convince me that Peter Frampton didn't listen to "Thinking About You" dozens of times before writing "Baby, I Love Your Way."

||*| "It all sounds the same to me."

(2013)

A friend recently sent me a text that filled me with pride and enjoyment and yeah, probably more than a little bit of hubris. The text said, "Promise me you'll never stop giving me beautiful music." I'd given the friend a CD with a pile of MP3s, and that friend sent me that text – one of the coolest messages I've received in my life – in response to one of the albums on the CD.

That same friend, though, has never said anything positive or made any inquiries at the many power pop songs and the occasional album I've pushed her way. Finally, as I pressed for her impressions of the music, she finally said – and couched it, because she feared I'd be hurt or disappointed by the response – "Tim, it all sounds the same to me."

Well, of course it does.

That's the one issue with the genre that I fully accept. I've often said that while I'm excited that I've lived through as many popular music style shifts as I have, and I'm thrilled to be able so readily and quickly to access things I've never previously heard, I'd still have been perfectly content if music had stopped evolving in early 1967. If all I had to listen to was British pop rock from the early 1960s, I could live with that quite comfortably.

And in many ways, that's what the best of power pop does for me – allows me to live musically in that period, and still have a cell phone, a microwave and thousands of songs on my iPod. (Yes, I still have and use an iPod.)

It's not fair to people reading what I write. They develop different expectations than they should for the music I love, the music that may sound all the same to them. And it's unfair to the artists, who in my world deserve a much larger audience. And even me calling an album the best I've heard all year doesn't help a suffering musician who still ends up with boxes of CDs in storage, representing a drain of funds and hundreds of people who didn't listen to their album, even though they probably should have.

It used to frustrate me that bands I loved were not as successful as the popular bands of the day. I've reached the point where I realize my tastes go where they go. I'm surprised when I like something in the mainstream, because I know my tastes – while drawn to what I consider well-crafted and thoughtful music – simply don't often mesh with most of the rest of the people still listening to music.

I'm good with that. As long as people are enjoying and embracing art in some form, I'm pleased.

||*| Jason Isbell

(July 2013)

Jason Isbell has met the most fascinating people in the world. Or else he has a brilliant imagination.

Maybe it's a combination. But Isbell consistently writes songs about real people, songs that turn into miniature movies in your head. He creates vivid images with words, images impossible to resist or erase.

Several years ago, Grammy-winning folk singer Barbara Bailey Hutchison and I were having an email conversation of the merits of Joni Mitchell's songwriting versus Carole King's songwriting. Hutchison wrote, "I love the way (Joni Mitchell) finds a unique and new way to say something ordinary. In 'A Case of You,' she writes 'I met a woman, she had a mouth like yours, she knew your life. She knew your devils and your deeds.' Carole would have written, 'I met your mother...' (Okay, an exaggeration maybe, but you get the idea.)"

One is not by definition better than or preferable to the other. But when a person finds what they like, they can come up with a pretty precise way to detail what they like.

In 1977, Griel Marcus wrote a sentence that's been imprinted on my brain since. Criticizing generalizations in a song lyric by Randy Newman, Marcus wrote, "Where is Newman's eye for the specific, the eye that picked out the little fat man next to Calvin Coolidge in 'Louisiana 1927'?"

What that observation said to me, even though Marcus was talking about one of the better songs on the album, was the pointed eye can tell you things you'll never otherwise realize.

In 2007, Jason Isbell released a song called "Dress Blues." After time spent listening to it incessantly, friends were peppered with emails asking for an interpretation. I was trying so hard to determine whether it was a pro- or anti-war song — eventually determining it was, in fact, neither — the true appeal of the song was obscured.

It was Isbell's beautiful, image-evoking lyrics that locked me in. Isbell writes of a place with "Flags on the side of the highway and Scripture on grocery store signs," where people are "drinkin' sweet tea in Styrofoam cups," and at the scene of a funeral of a serviceman, "nobody showed up to protest, just sniffle and stare."

In 2004, the band Drive-By Truckers released an Isbell song that was equally pointed in its observations. Written in the voice of a father talking and giving advice to his young-adult son, "Outfit" fits a book's worth of material into its four-minute running time.

The father talks about the car in which the young man was conceived ("a Mustang, a 302 Mach One in green"). He describes his "careers" in a foundry, as a janitor and time wasted at a technical school. He's now working as a painter for his own father, but warns his son "don't let me catch you in Kendale with a bucket of wealthy man's paint." (I've never figured out whether Kendale is a neighborhood or a city, and I never figured it mattered.)

But the key pieces of advice the father passes on are practical:

Don't call what you're wearing an outfit.
Don't ever say your car is broke.
Have fun, but stay clear of the needle.
Don't sing with a fake British accent.
Don't act like your family's a joke.

Those are five pretty good pieces of advice right there.

Isbell's *Southeastern* fits with what has been the pattern for my appreciation of Drive-By Truckers' and Isbell's own solo albums: Like one, be disappointed by the next. *Southeastern* is an uptick, marked by

Isbell's pointed lyrics and fantastic storytelling.

Like the guy who gets punched out in a bar after suggesting to someone, "two kinds of men in this world and you're neither of them," and during his subsequent drive home, "she asked if I had considered the prospect of living alone." Or even the incomplete (or believe-it-or-not) story of the song that starts with the chorus: "Don't want to die in a Super 8 motel, just because somebody's evening didn't go so well."

Southeastern is a fine album. And it reaches the levels of "Dress Blues" and "Outfit" with "Elephant," a beautiful set of lyrics wherein you don't even know what the song's about until it's halfway over.

Two people with a history — of friendship, but apparently not of sex — sit together in a bar. It's not until after the first chorus that we're told she has "sharecropper eyes and her hair almost all gone" and "when she was drunk she made cancer jokes."

Ohhh. That elephant.

As the song continues, the woman has lost her voice, which is just as well, because neither of them wish to talk as they "try to ignore the elephant somehow."

By the end, where Isbell says "I buried her a thousand times" and "there's one thing that's real clear to me, no one dies with dignity," it defies logic that a human hearing the song could not be touched in some fashion.

Sometimes, I'll wonder whether well-written lyrics have a spot in music anymore. That's not pining for any kind of real or imagined "old days." It's an appealing style and trait for me, and the number of people willing to put the effort into the wordcraft seem few and far between, that's all.

And it's a huge part of the reason Jason Isbell's work is so inspiring.

||*| Alan Douglas

There was always something about the Jimi Hendrix recordings that came out after his 1970 death that just didn't sound right to me.

It wasn't until years later, when archived live recordings began to be issued, where I felt Hendrix's legacy was being represented properly.

So I was one of those who objected to Alan Douglas' work. Douglas was responsible for much of the early Hendrix posthumous releases.

Let's immediately give Douglas credit where it is due. He was by many accounts stubborn and dictatorial as a producer, but he also did remarkable work as a United Artists Records jazz producer, helming albums by such legends as Art Blakey, Charles Mingus, Herbie Mann, Bill Evans, Max Roach and Duke Ellington. He published works by Timothy Leary and Lenny Bruce.

But it's the Hendrix connection that makes his name (and his infamy). In 1974, Douglas acquired the rights to more than 1,000 hours of tapes recorded but unreleased during Hendrix's lifetime. He was in charge of two albums, *Crash Landing* and *Midnight Lightning,* which included re-recordings of the rhythm tracks behind Hendrix.

The result, ultimately, for me and others was a bizarre feel of something not quite right, some things out of place. I had a similar feeling listening to Buddy Holly acoustic tracks with additional musicians' work grafted on. It felt like it was music made by people not even in the same room as one another. As it turned out, they all weren't even on the same plane of existence as one another.

I didn't like Douglas' work, but it didn't bother me, because the original Hendrix recordings were still in my life. And when the live shows eventually began to leak out, that was the time to get excited. His Woodstock set remains a personal favorite and go-to.

And Douglas never felt the need to apologize. He felt he was doing what Hendrix would have done. After *Crash Landing* was released, he said, "I did what I had to do and it sold 2 million copies."

And maybe *Crash Landing* was exactly was Hendrix would have done. We'll never know. But given the changes Hendrix went through from the

Experience to Band of Gypsies to Gypsy Sun and Rainbows (his Woodstock group), *Crash Landing* didn't sound like the kind of evolution to which Hendrix listeners had been accustomed. Maybe had Hendrix lived, that's exactly what he would have wanted. It seemed and seems improbable.

Even as one argues against Douglas' artistic decisions, it's important to notice that Hendrix's recorded legacy was sliced, diced and pureed largely beyond recognition by any number of other companies and individuals. Hendrix's albums are Elvis Presley-like in that many should come equipped with "buyer beware" stickers.

It also fascinates me that I'm unable to find any photographs of Douglas and Hendrix together.

(AFTERWORD: This was published after Douglas' death in 2014. I received an email from someone with an email at the Hendrix Foundation's address thanking me for writing this. All I thought I was doing was pointing out that I didn't care for Douglas' posthumous releases, and apparently I stepped into some kind of debate in that community. I was just as quickly dismissed from the discussion, perhaps because I've also confessed to liking Hanson.)

||*| Doug Fieger

(2010)

Obituaries, if papers even choose to run them, will note one accomplishment for Doug Fieger, who died from brain cancer complications at age 57.

Fieger will be remembered as the singer of "My Sharona," which exploded in 1979 amid an overabundance of mediocre disco music and sat at No. 1 for six weeks.

And as far as some people are concerned, that was that. The one-hit wonders whose song results in shrieks of recognition and nostalgia when it pops up in unlikely places.

The band was plenty more, as fans more intense than I will remind you.

The Knack put out a half-dozen albums, Fieger released music with the band Sky before The Knack, and put out a solo album. He continued to release music well into his last decade. He'd even rebounded from a lung cancer battle, losing half a lung, but continuing to perform.

It's difficult to remember now how fresh The Knack sounded flying out of my stereo system in Rochester, Minn., in 1979, amid all that disco music. It's also difficult to remember the severity of the backlash after a combination of factors.

1) Fieger declined to do any interviews when *Get The Knack,* the band's first album, was blazing to No. 1 (where it stayed for five weeks) and selling two million copies in the U.S. In retrospect, his attempt to build a mystery around the band along with his realization that he wasn't required to talk - and he probably didn't have much to say given that the group had put out a total of 41 minutes of music - was a legitimate decision, if not a wise one.

2) People were genuinely offended by "Good Girls Don't" (whose chorus consisted of those three words, plus "... but I do"). I suppose I understand that, but it was hearing "Good Girls Don't" that made me buy the "Get The Knack" album. I still think it's a great song.

3) The Knack reportedly turned down larger financial offers so they could be on the same record label as The Beatles, Capitol, and also demanded to have their album pressed with the famous "rainbow label," just like The Beatles' original releases. There was a backlash over this, along with the group's "uniform" of white shirts and black pants. (Somehow, this all seemed incredibly important at the time. There was even a "Nuke The Knack" "movement.")

So The Knack probably didn't deserve to sell two million copies of their debut, and they probably didn't deserve a No. 1 single either. But neither did they deserve the backlash that helped splinter them.

Fieger persevered, and the fact remains, he wrote some great songs. I'd probably feel compelled to mention his death even if all he'd ever done was write "Oh Tara," which I consider one of the most beautiful pop songs I've ever heard.

||*| **And I don't know if I'm ever coming home**

Let's start this story at the end, so you're not wondering whether it's happy or sad -- the guy came back in one piece. He's still alive. I see him on Facebook. He looks better than I do.

OK. That's out of the way.

Thanks to its presence in a series of eBay ads, "Daydream Believer" was on my mind a lot. There's a pretty vivid picture in my mind linked with the song, and it involves an uncle and the Vietnam War.

That war was pretty much a constant of my childhood, but it was just pictures on a (mostly black-and-white) television set until my uncle was drafted in 1967. Then the war became up close and personal and really scary. (And maybe it helped that I was starting to comprehend what was going on there.)

My mother was the oldest sibling, and she and the oldest son and both of their families and some other people I should probably remember but don't drove 90 minutes from southeastern Minnesota to the Minneapolis Airport to send my uncle off as he began his trip halfway around the world.

I don't remember much about being at the airport except for being numb. For some reason, I understood there was a chance I'd never see the guy again.

The reason I associate The Monkees' song with the war came on the trip home. My uncle's daughter, a year younger than me, and I sat in the back of his station wagon and looked out the back window, pretending to be disc jockeys as our parents played the AM radio extra-loud for us so we could hear it in the back. (Which, in retrospect, was an incredibly neat, nice, cool and hip thing for them to have done.) While the DJ prattled and commercials ran between songs, my cousin and I did our own radio broadcast, with the focus of my comments being about the multiple colors in the sky as the sun set.

95

(I was always strangely fascinated by sunsets, which either represents an early appreciation for beauty or that I grew up in a really boring town. Maybe both. Maybe neither.)

At some point, "Daydream Believer" -- which we'd been hearing on the radio all day and all month -- came on the radio, and my cousin and I sang along with it at the top of our lungs, the way only 8- and 7-year-olds can. (And miraculously enough, our parents *still* didn't turn off the radio.)

I won't pretend I realized it at the time. Looking back, I realized it all locked in at that point. My uncle getting on a plane (and we didn't know if he was ever comin' home, to paraphrase another Monkees song), the sunset, the singing, the song -- it's been there ever since.

He mailed us regularly when he was in country. I would hold and look in fascination at the blue-tinged envelope and the tinted stationery, his surprisingly neat handwriting assuring my mother/his oldest sister that he was well. In some ways, it felt as though he never left.

There was a lot of growing up between the airport and his return, let alone his return and today. But curiously enough, the vivid memory hasn't spoiled the song for me. I like it. It's not my favorite Monkees song (that's "I'm a Believer," with "Goin' Down" and "Tapioca Tundra" right behind), but I don't despise it, either.

Hearing it just brings an odd rush, a refusal to believe it all could have taken place a half-century ago, and a small bit of melancholy for a world I came from but can't even really claim I know anymore. If I ever did.

||*| Davy Jones

Davy Jones never broke the top 50 with a song under his own name.

He never appeared on a top 10 television show.

He never starred in a hit movie.

Yet upon the news of his death at age 66, millions of people were saddened. And they didn't need to think about or be reminded of any of his accomplishments. It was enough that he was "Davy Jones."

How many people become such icons with so little of our traditional concrete examples of success?

The Monkees' career, for all intents and purposes, ran 18 months.

The singles chart success of the band for which Jones sang (and in whose television show he co-starred) started in Sept. 1966, and their last top 15 single was released in March 1968. But what a stretch. Three number one singles. Three more top 10 singles.

Four No. 1 multi-platinum albums, when multi-platinum was more rare than it became.

And a legend was launched. Jones appeared as himself on "The Brady Bunch" television show in 1971. "Girl," the song Jones sang in the episode, did not chart at all. But millions still remember it, as the show popped up regularly in syndication. Jones reprised the gag 24 years later in *The Brady Bunch Movie.*

That doesn't happen. It would be like a villain from the *Batman* TV series showing up as the same character in a *Batman* movie starring Michael Keaton or Christian Bale.

Jones was able to pull it off.

There's a simple explanation for everything to do with Jones and the affection for him.

Americans love people who work hard. They enjoy seeing people do things they enjoy, particularly if they do those things well. And Jones was talented, talented in a way we didn't see much in his prime, and that we see even less now.

He was a true triple threat, an actor-singer-dancer, and to boot, he was a good-looking guy who gave the appearance of a genuinely likable personality.

Jones was something that just doesn't exist much any more. He was a showman. And he was a showman for 50 years. He appeared on the same

Ed Sullivan Show episode as The Beatles when The Beatles made their American TV prime time debut in 1964. At that time, Jones was in the cast of the Broadway musical *Oliver!* and he sang a pair of songs, as many as John Lennon did that night. (And Lennon had to share the lead of "I Want to Hold Your Hand" with Paul McCartney.)

Jones never seemed to buy into being in one of the world's biggest acts in the mid-1960s. Sure, he put on the costume – he indulged in his substances, and he groomed his Beatle-cut just so, and when the time came, he wore beads and held incense just like everyone else. But Jones was never a hippie. He was wearing a costume, putting on a show, and loving it. His job was to entertain, not change the world. And that's what he did his entire life.

On one hand, it's amazing in a sad way that for more than 40 years, Jones was able to live off name recognition for something he did for a brief stretch in the mid-1960s. Maybe he aspired to more.

But on the other hand, it's amazing Jones maintained goodwill with so many for so long. He remains mentioned regularly as an all-time favorite top teen idols, four decades after he was a teen idol. And unlike many of his teen idol peers, Jones never made pains to distance himself from that persona. He always embraced it. He appreciated his fans, the pleasure they derived from his work, and he always seemed to appreciate the chance to entertain.

There are considerably worse legacies one could leave.

||*| Tiny Tim

There aren't many songs that make me as inherently sad as Daryl Hall and John Oates' "You Make My Dreams."

The song came out during the brief period of time that I worked in a record store. I worked there long enough to develop the equivalent of about two weeks' pay of debt to the store itself. It was one of those indie-style store that just about every town had two or three of in my early adulthood. Their prices were lower than the mall's store, the selection was cooler, and employees got a discount.

Before long, I owed my soul -- or at least the entirety of a single paycheck -

- to the company store. I decided to quit while I was behind only a bit.

I had plenty of amusing times, even in the brief stretch I worked there. I passed an impromptu quiz from one of the owners to name 50 jazz albums in the store, because he wanted to have a jazz album sale. But he didn't want me looking through the stacks of records. He wanted them recalled from memory.

Fortunately, he allowed multiple albums from one act, as long as I could remember the name of the album. Bob James seemed to have about a dozen albums in our stacks at the time, and I could at least describe the different covers, so he gave me credit for those.

I briefly had my access to the store's stereo system revoked. One of the owners first suggested there was more music in the store than *The Records,* the fantastic debut album by the British power pop band. While I understood his point, there was nothing else I wanted to hear. He strongly suggested something closer to the top of the charts. (Which, honestly, would have been just about anything at that point.) I ended up refusing, and he stripped me of access to the player until circumstances forced otherwise. That moment came soon enough.

I loved the swag the store would get. The offerings were generally cheap and silly, but they were also often unique. I'd wear the button or a series of pins or a cap, and have fun pretending that I was working. What work? I was working in a record store. I'd done radio in college, and I was getting paid what felt like an obscene amount of money to write about high school sports for a daily newspaper. For me, it was the same as it would have felt for most kids if they could have been a professional athlete, a fireman and an astronaut all at the same time.

One day, I put on a pin that said, "Ask me why my heart's on fire." A woman came in, saw the pin and said, "OK, I'll play. Why is your heart on fire?" I responded, "If you buy the new Randy Meisner album, I'll tell you."

Meisner's first post-Eagles solo album, *One More Song,* was getting a bit of a push from the record company. The first song on the album was "Hearts on Fire."

The woman said, "I already have the album. That's why I asked why your heart was on fire."

I wasn't going to make a sale, but I was going to make a memory. I took off the pin and handed it to her. She appeared surprised. I said, "It's going to mean more to you than anyone else who comes through the door today."

And if I didn't make a memory for her, at least I made one for myself.

I made another memory the day this cute girl walked in. She was blonde, attractive and about 4-foot-8 in heels. Some might have considered the manner in which she was dressed as trashy. I'd seen people walk into class at college looking worse.

I readily confess to being a little too helpful with her. In my defense, she earned it with the smile and personality she was laying on me. I thought I caught the other guys working snickering at me, but I figured it was something stupid they'd have plenty of time to give me grief about later.

I had no idea how accurate that was.

The wee lass asked about good new music to dance to. I pointed her toward the obvious at the time -- Diana Ross' "Upside Down" and Paul Simon's "Late in the Evening" among them -- but she was looking for something newer. I saw a 45 of "She's So Cold" by The Rolling Stones, played a snippet of it, and she demanded the disc immediately. With the distance I was from my co-workers, they couldn't stop me from putting discs on the turntable. I also suppose they were more forgiving since I was playing current hits of the day and not a two-year-old album that was barely released in the United States, and with different mixes, so shoddy was the effort.

She was also excited as I talked about Diana Ross' "I'm Coming Out" and Stevie Wonder's "Master Blaster." (I never thought of "Whip It" at the time -- I was always stunned when Devo was popular.)

She grabbed a half-dozen 45s, stood on her tip-toes, kissed me on the cheek, whispered "Thank you" and went off to pay for her acquisitions.

After she left, one of the guys turned to me with a smirk and said, "Chasing after the stripper, are we?"

"Was she a stripper?"

The record store was on the same block as a "gentlemen's club," which was downtown, just around the corner from the post office and the library, and across the street from a relatively fancy restaurant that was packed every noon hour. This bit of geography didn't seem to strike anyone in Medical Mecca Rochester, Minn., as out of the ordinary.

(The restaurant was the site of one of the greatest stories I heard. I wasn't witness to it, but a female reporter at the paper talked about going to lunch at the fancy restaurant with a male reporter. The guy forgot his wallet, but didn't realize that until after the meal was over. Seeking an exit, he stood up, glared at the woman and with a combination of befuddlement and outrage, exclaimed, "Fifty dollars?", flung his cloth napkin on the table, and stomped out. As the woman told me and others the story, she detailed her humiliation and irritation at having to pay for the meal after apparently being quite publicly outed as a prostitute.)

The presence of the strip club was just another thing in my life at the time. I honestly never went in.

But what I did in helping that young woman find her music was the only reason I was any kind of good employee for that record store. I could win people over with my enthusiasm.

Some time later, two fat guys and a freak walked in. That's not the start to a lame joke. It's a description of two overweight slick gangster management types straight out of central casting (one of them had a shirt open too much, overflowing gray chest hair and a coke spoon dangling around his neck), and Herbert Khaury.

Tiny Tim.

Tim was, of course, well past his prime by then. But when could you not have said that about Tim when America got sick of his schtick?

He was carrying the grocery bag which held his ukulele, but it held all kinds of other stuff. The only reason I knew that was because of what ended up happening. He was wearing what I think of as his traditional garb -- a white dress shirt, badly wrinkled, and a matching plaid jacket and pants that were probably 30 years old, and looked every bit of it.

The "managers" cornered the store owner for some discussion, and Tim, seeming a little lost, turned to me and asked, "Do you know what the kids are listening to?"

Where do you point Tiny Tim in 1981 when he asks what "the kids" are listening to? Especially when the kids were listening to so much weird stuff. He seemed to know and tolerate the hits of the day (like "Bette Davis Eyes" and Neil Diamond's "America") but wanted something that sounded fresher.

I'd been a fan of Daryl Hall and John Oates from the time I heard "Sara Smile," and I thought they'd done nothing but get better since. (I eventually changed my mind back to marking the "silver" album as their high point. I'm not even sure "Sara Smile" is in my top five favorite songs on the album.) I championed their work to anyone who would listen, and here I had a captive audience.

I pulled the 7-inch 45 RPM record of "You Make My Dreams Come True" out of the stack of discs that were just kind of around for the moment -- the single hadn't really hit the charts yet. And Tim loved it. I tried to throw a couple of other songs his way. I was enthralled with Terri Gibbs' "Somebody's Knockin'," taken by a sound that came along every once in a while, but was really striking when done right. (I felt the same way eight years later, when Alannah Myles' "Black Velvet" came out.) I tried Abba's "Super Trooper." But Tim kept demanding a return of Hall and Oates.

For one of those all-to-rare moments in life, I felt truly musically connected to Tiny Tim. He wasn't a freak show in his late 40s, and I wasn't a tubby dweeb who didn't know as much about music as he thought he did. We were two pals sharing a love of a song.

The reverie was broken up by one of the managers, who was talk-singing alternate lyrics for the song as a "suggestion" to Tim, although to what end I could not imagine, nor did I want to. My memory has probably tainted the moment, but my memory is of Tim being immediately deflated and dutifully following the man away.

But he bought "You Make My Dreams" *and* "Super Trooper," he opened the grocery bag and tossed the records in, and I saw a bunch of stuff, nothing that registered in any way, I was trying to process everything I'd just experienced.

And that might have been my last exposure to Tiny Tim but for Decatur Celebration, an annual event about which I wrote a book (*Decatur Celebration: A History of the World's Fair of the Prairie* -- pretty sure you can get it on Amazon).

Tiny Tim played Celebration in 1993. It remains one of the most remarkable performances I've seen anywhere, let alone at Celebration. There are more people who found his show baffling, disconnected and disconcerting, all of which were features that made it great for me.

The idea of a large and tall man singing parts of songs while accompanying himself on a ukulele he'd carry in a brown paper bag? The image is as ridiculous as the idea of the singer having a three-octave vocal range and the knowledge and love of music to go from Rudy Vallee to AC/DC in consecutive songs.

Which he did.

At his Celebration performances, Tim was accompanied by a three-man band who had no idea what he was playing at any point. It wasn't their fault. It was Tim's style. A few months before he appeared in Decatur, I was told of a performance in another city. The leader of the evening's backup band asked for the show's set list, and Tim responded he had no idea what he would play until he was onstage.

At Celebration, he'd start a song by playing the verse and the chorus, and then change songs when he got partway through the second verse. The band lost its way regularly. The audience had the chance to replicate their experience when Tiny Tim encouraged them to sing along. Nobody really knew until he opened his mouth what Tim was going to sing.

It remains one of the most brilliant displays of stream-of-consciousness performance (while still being a show) that I've ever seen.

About every five minutes, he'd turn to the leader of the backup band, wave his hand and say, "Maestro, the key of 'A,' if you please," and the guys in the band would look at each other and shrug - they had no idea what song

Tim was going to play.

For that matter, neither did Tim. He never prepared a set list. At another location, when the leader of his locally hired backup band wanted to discuss a set list, Tim said, "Oh dear, no - I never know what I'm going to play until I go out on stage."

And tempo? Forget it. No one could ever tune into Tim's internal metronome. He'd start playing songs, then sing the same verse three times. He'd stop halfway through a chorus and start a new song, then he'd demand the audience sing along with a given song. (Most memorable: Making everyone sing along with the final line of "You're a Grand Old Flag.")

I'm glad I got to see that show. The only thing that would have made it better would have been if he'd done some kind of version of "You Make My Dreams."

||*| Breaking up with an album

(Feb. 6, 2015)

Sorry, *Trout Mask Replica.* I'm breaking up with you.

This isn't easy for me, please understand. You're special. You ask the people who love you for reasons why they do, and the first thing they talk about is how special you are. There's a club of people who love you, and they fill rooms and discuss their love and congratulate each other on how vast their love is and point out nuances and … adore the smell of their own farts.

Yeah, there, I said it. And I don't even mean it in a bad way. I have works with whom I have my own rooms and gangs. The big one, of course, is The Beatles. If you can't understand how great and influential they were and are, we cannot interact. You don't have to think The Beatles are the greatest thing ever, or even like them. But if you cannot even acknowledge their greatness and influence, I can't grasp the world in which you live.

That's snobbery. But that's just a fraction of mine. Here's a story that shows the depth, breadth and pettiness of my snobbery. (And you may enjoy it more, because I get my come-uppance at the end.)

104

About 15 years ago, I met a guy who was the creative force behind one of my favorite albums of the previous year. (It's at #226 on The Big List.) As we spoke, our love for a very specific type and era of music became clear. He topped my Beau Brummels original issues with his rare British Small Faces 45s. My *Smile* bootleg, he felt, was topped by his rare edition of The Zombies' *Odessey and Oracle.*

This was the foundation of The Great *Pet Sounds-Odessey and Oracle* War of WhateverYearThatWas. For at least 45 minutes, we each passionately broke down segments of our favorite of the two albums. (After, that is, I recovered from the shock of him declaring *Odessey and Oracle* a better album than *Pet Sounds*" That already, to me, bordered on heresy. Respecting his appreciation of music, and still more than a little awestruck to be talking to a musician whose work I adored, I gave him plenty of leeway.)

We broke our passions down to single notes, single vocal quivers, ingenious uses of silence. Each of us greeted the other's presentation with agreement. "Yes, you're absolutely right about that. Brilliant. BUT …"

I cannot ever make anyone understand how much I loved having this argument.

We didn't resolve the question between us, but I honestly felt we both agreed I'd put forth a better case. So when I told the story for years afterward, I would say I "won" the "argument," as though that mattered.

Fast forward a decade-plus. I'm sitting down and listing my favorite albums, a regular exercise I've always enjoyed, and I'm pondering expanding the list to dozens or even hundreds of favorites, because I've always kind of wanted to do that.

Without hesitation, *Odessey and Oracle* was in the top 20. Down into the 40s was *Pet Sounds.*

Now, I'm certain had I made my list 15 years ago, *Pet Sounds* would have been much higher. But what The Big List tells me in this case is I was in error, and it's been corrected in the last 15 years.

Thanks, Mike Jarvis.

See, that's the kind of passion I'm talking about it. I love it in anyone about anything. I can really get carried away alongside the enthusiasm of others. If you're passionate about a pyramid scheme, you could get me close to emptying my wallet. If you *really* wanted to drive to Vegas tonight, I'd probably be putting gas in the car somewhere in Missouri before I realized the degree of bad in the adventure to which I'd agreed.

But if you love comedy or movies or especially music with a passion and can communicate that, well, you're my favorite kind of person.

And while I don't mind loving the same music everyone else loves, I also enjoy finding my way around some weird music that catches my ear, and when I can find my way in to that kind of music, I've gained admission to a special, exclusive club. Those clubs don't look down on people sitting outside. In fact, if you're interested in coming in, they'll stumble over themselves trying to open doors for you to help you on your journey.

Don't make the mistake of agreeing to allow me to help you down a musical path. Express a slight interest in Frank Zappa, and you'll get a disc full of MP3s and a daily request for your impressions so I can feed you more of what you like. I'm a music pusher. I get paid in feedback from the person who receives.

I'm in some of those exclusive clubs, the stuff a select group "gets." Big Star, Small Faces, Lindsey Buckingham solo, Soft Boys/Robyn Hitchcock, The Jam, Zappa. (Some clubs are larger than others, and there's tons of cross-memberships.)

I always wanted to join the *Trout Mask Replica* club. It's by Captain Beefheart, it's produced by Zappa, and everything I read about it says it's something I need in my library, understanding it will help me understand other things and give depth to my music love.

Well, yeah, I want *that* to happen.

So for years and years, I've tried to understand *Trout Mask Replica*. I'd listen to it at least one day every year. I'd listen to it the way I normally listen to music (doing something to keep my hands busy while processing). I'd listen exclusively. I'd listen with a baseball game on TV, the sound muted. I'd listen while reading to essays about how great it was, and struggle to hear the things mentioned in what I was reading. I just never really quite caught on.

When I was an active member of the Elvis Costello internet mailing list (late 90s), my efforts at understanding *Trout Mask Replica*, then at about 10 years running, was viewed with admiration by some and derision by others. I particularly enjoyed e-mail off-list with a person wholly impressed, if a bit confused, by my ongoing effort with *Trout Mask Replica*. I introduced them to Material Issue and *International Pop Overthrow* (No. 158 on The Big List), so it was a win for everyone.

(See? Another person brought into another exclusive club.)

But *Trout Mask Replica* continues to elude me. About an hour ago, just looking through folders on my computer looking for something new to sample, I put on an album by Swedish prog-metal band Opeth.

How I got to Opeth was interesting in its own right. I was reading Prog Rock magazine's list of the top 150 prog albums, and a couple of names I didn't know kept popping up: Opeth, and Steven Wilson. I picked up a few of their albums and set them aside for the time when the mood struck me.

That happened today, and the album I listened to was *Blackwater Park,* an album Wilson produced for Opeth.

It's great. From the first minute, I wanted to hear more.

(Wait. Did he just sing something about "Dracula's balls"?)

I don't always advocate judging an album after first listen. Lots of things can be influencing an experience, positively or negatively. But this album gave me more joy in 120 seconds than *Trout Mask Replica* did in 120 listens.

I'm letting go of things. *Trout Mask Replica* is one.

I'm sorry. I gave it dozens of chances. I made my very best effort.

Ask anyone. It's not you. It's me.

"I always tell the girls, never take it seriously, if ya never take it seriously, ya never get hurt; ya never get hurt, ya always have fun; and if you ever get lonely, just go to the record store and visit your friends." -- Penny Lane (Kate Hudson) in *Almost Famous* (2000)

***

Here's the thing about anybody's list of favorite entertainment -- you're never going to agree with the person. You don't share their experience.

But I know Penny Lane's feeling about her musical friends. We all do. Even if you don't feel exactly like Penny Lane and her fellow Band Aids did. I didn't hang with the musicians I loved, not when I was in high school and not in 2000. You probably didn't, either. But that didn't matter. They were all friends.

I can't even look at the line without choking back tears, or even shedding some. And not about the same thing Penny Lane was talking about in that wonderful, wonderful film. So wonderful, in fact, that is justifies the careers of both Kate Hudson and Cameron Crowe.

In spite of how many boring, pretentious, one-act-too-long films Cameron Crowe puts out, he wrote and directed that beautiful movie, and crafted that beautiful line. And it was Kate Hudson who delivered that line and embodied Penny Lane with an irresistible charm and innocence. (In spite of, you know, all that sex. It was the early 70s, after all. Everybody was getting laid, except for the writers.)

The Motion Picture Academy doesn't like music movies much. Crowe got his Oscar. Hudson, in a horrible injustice, did not get hers. Let's face it, Eddie Murphy was a lock for the Oscar in *Dreamgirls* until he didn't get it. Still, hearing Hudson deliver that line in the theater immediately put me in the fetal position, eyes tearing.

I KNEW THAT FEELING.

I obviously didn't feel exactly like Penny Lane and her fellow Band Aids. I didn't hang out with the musicians I loved, not when I was in high school and not in 2000. But that didn't matter. They were all my friends.

I listened to the records repeatedly. I pored over the covers, looking for minutiae. (The "L.I.L.Y." and the insects on the cover of Paul and Linda McCartney's *Ram* album [No. 76 on The Big List] puzzled me for years. Then I either figured out or read that the insects were beetles having sex, and McCartney seemed a little more daring. And the "L.I.L.Y." stood for "Linda I love you," which made McCartney seem like more of a wimp. It was that kind of decade.)

These people who made this magic that was entering my ears became my friends. I memorized portions of Nicholas Schaffner's wonderful *The Beatles Forever*. I repeatedly read *The Rolling Stone Record Review Volume II*. (It took some time for me to find the first volume.) I memorized lines from that, and it definitely informed my own writing and attitudes about music.

I'd devour the monthly rock-and-roll *Creem* magazine, even the ones I didn't, couldn't, and in some cases never would understand. I'd devour the odd special publications I'd stumble across. *Rolling Stone* put out an 87-page book of some of their pieces about The Who. I focused on the interviews with Pete Townshend. He wrote the bulk of *Tommy* and *Who's Next,* was intelligent, thoughtful and well-spoken, and he became my spirit guide. Listening to the depressing *The Who By Numbers* (No. 77 on The Big List, right behind *Ram*) found Townshend and me in similar places, despite his success and Britishness and my teenage anger and confusion and my Middle Americanism. What did this tail-end baby boomer, a weak but kind of intelligent kid who was being raised conservative Christian in a corner of southern Minnesota, have in common with somebody whose youth was spent in bomb shelters and grew up playing around war rubble? Somehow, Townshend reached out and I heard him.

My mother would walk in on me listening to "How Many Friends" and scowling and wonder exactly what my problem was. My problem, simply put, was I was 16, confused, angry and horny. (My completely missing the sexuality in "Dreaming From the Waist" only shows how confused, angry and horny I was.)

***

"Some kid writes in to me and says, 'I've got all your records and I listen to your music all day long and I look at your pictures all the time and I write to you and all I get is a bleedin' autographed picture. You don't know how much time I spend thinkin' about you lot.' I write him back and say, 'You don't know how much time I spend looking at and thinking about teenagers.' "
- Pete Townshend, January 3rd, 1974, *Rolling Stone*

***

When I listen to *The Who By Numbers* now, I don't necessarily think it's a great album. But I love it. It's a part of who I am. It's vital. The music you love as a teen is the music you'll love most the rest of your life. Of my 40 favorite albums, only two came out after I was 25.

Those albums may not all be as great as I argue. But enough of them wrap around my ears like a perfect brain blanket. Not consciously, but almost certainly, I'm back in my basement room in Dodge Center, Minnesota, cupping my headphones tightly to my head to try to decode the time signature for Led Zeppelin's "Black Dog." Trying to understand what John Bonham was playing at the beginning of "Rock and Roll." I never accomplished that, but I still love listening to it. Like a lot of music I consider difficult to understand, it's still easy to listen to when the artists know what they're doing.

The 1970s have a negative image on many levels. One is criticism of the music. I passionately derided one critic of me by saying, "There was plenty of good music in the 1970s, and we listen to it all the time now. Your generation was just too lazy to look for the good stuff after radio stopped handing it to you."

That was a little too cruel. You could say that about music of any generation. I try to remind myself of that when I cringe at people confessing love for some of the more corporate MTV pop from the 1980s. I shouldn't cringe. As much as I dislike much of what MTV made popular, as frustrated as I got with acts I loved chasing that pop sheen the network

111

pushed, that's what shoved me toward Shriekback and Robyn Hitchcock and Cocteau Twins, to mention just three acts heavily represented in my top 100.

You always remember your first love, even after you're well past it. You can still taste the pain of that love dissolving. For me, the beauty is that my first love has never abandoned me, never let me down, has always been there for me. Some of these albums have given me a lifetime of pleasure. They have been in my world continually longer than anything, with the exception of my family and a handful of school friends.

Do I love *The Beatles* (a/k/a *The White Album*) more than my father, mother and sister?

Probably not.

But I don't think I'd feel comfortable answering that question under oath.

**

You inevitably haven't read, heard or seen everything on anybody's list of favorite art, especially if that list has any depth or heft. I've never come across someone's a list of 50 or 100 "best" or (my preferred term) or favorite albums and known all of them. If your list has *Sgt. Pepper's Lonely Hearts Club Band* in the top 20 or 30 you're like most respected professionals. They put it now lower than that. It's a barometer.

Sgt. Pepper is barely in my top 10 favorite Beatles albums. If that seems odd to you, we still might agree on music. But you'd have to examine the other material on my list to see where my musical tastes lie.

I don't expect my list to be what many would consider typical. It has no Michael Jackson, no U2, no Motown albums. It's light in R&B, rap, jazz and soul. It probably leans a little too much on the early 70s, I suspect because that was the most influential period, the period where I'd live with individual albums for weeks at a time. Once again, this emphasizes how music shapes our lives. For many of us, we're born to it. Get married to it. Die to it.

You won't agree with everything here. You might find some stuff to explore. Better yet, you might find some stuff to avoid.

(an asterisk denotes that an essay accompanies that album)
1. *The Beatles (The White Album)*, The Beatles (1968)
2. *World So Bright*, Adam Schmitt (1991)
* 3. *Blood on the Tracks*, Bob Dylan (1975)
4. *Tonight's the Night*, Neil Young (1975)
5. *Underwater Moonlight,* The Soft Boys (1980)
6. *Katy Lied,* Steely Dan (1975)
* 7. *Squeezing Out Sparks*, Graham Parker (1979)
* 8. *Get Happy!!*, Elvis Costello (1980)
9. *Joe's Garage (Acts I, II and III),* Frank Zappa (1979)
10. *The Records*, The Records (1979)
11. *Led Zeppelin IV* (1971)
12. *The Wall*, Pink Floyd (1979)
13. *The Dark Side of the Moon*, Pink Floyd (1973)
14. *Odessey and Oracle,* The Zombies (1968)
15. *Everybody Knows This Is Nowhere,* Neil Young (1969)
16. *Machine Head*, Deep Purple (1972)
17. *Every Picture Tells a Story*, Rod Stewart (1971)
* 18. *English Settlement,* XTC (1982)
19. *Animals*, Pink Floyd (1977)
20. *Marshall Crenshaw* (1982)

* 21. *Who's Next*, The Who (1971)
22. *Mistakes*, Gruppo Sportivo (1979)
* 23. *This Year's Model,* Elvis Costello (1978)
24. *Abbey Road*, The Beatles (1969)
25. *Fragile*, Yes (1971)
26. *Rocks*, Aerosmith (1976)
27. *Sound Affects*, The Jam (1980)
28. *You Are What You Is*, Frank Zappa (1981)
29. *A Night at the Opera,* Queen (1975)
30. *Psonic Psunspot*, XTC/Dukes of Stratosphear (1987)
* 31. *Energized*, Foghat (1974)
32. *Revolver*, The Beatles (1966)
* 33. *Billion Dollar Babies*, Alice Cooper (1973)
34. *Band on the Run,* Paul McCartney and Wings (1973)

35. *Ringo*, Ringo Starr (1973)

36. *Message from the Country*, The Move (1971)

37. *Jam Science*, Shriekback (1984)

38. *We're Only in it for the Money,* Frank Zappa/Mothers of Invention (1968)

39. *Venus and Mars*, Wings (1975)

40. *Oil and Gold,* Shriekback *(1985)*

41. *Bridge of Sighs*, Robin Trower (1974)

42. *Pet Sounds*, Beach Boys (1966)

43. Ro*ugh Mix*, Pete Townshend and Ronnie Lane (1977)

* 44. *SMiLE*, Brian Wilson (2004)/*Smile*, The Beach Boys (1966-1967, 2011)

* 45. *The Bis-Quits* (1993)

46. *Love Junk*, The Pursuit of Happiness (1988)

47. *whitechocolatespaceegg*, Liz Phair (1998)

* 48. *The Pilgrim*, Marty Stuart (1999)

* 49. *100 cc*, 10cc (1975)

50. *The Right to Be Italian*, Holly and the Italians (1981)

51. *After the Gold Rush*, Neil Young (1970)

52. *Aqualung*, Jethro Tull (1971)

53. *Hooverphonic Presents Jackie Cane*, Hooverphonic (2002)

54. *Pretty Little Lonely*, Michael Petak (1994)

55. *Rust Never Sleeps*, Neil Young (1979)

56. *Singles '96-'06*, Hooverphonic (2006)

* 57. *Goodbye Yellow Brick Road,* Elton John (1973)

58. *I Often Dream of Trains,* Robyn Hitchcock (1984)

* 59. *I'm With Stupid*, Aimee Mann (1995)

* 60. *Moondance*, Van Morrison (1970)

61. *Breakfast in America,* Supertramp (1979)

62. *Decade*, Neil Young (1977)

63. *Pump*, Aerosmith (1989)

64. *Cosmo's Factory*, Creedence Clearwater Revival (1970)

65. *Magical Mystery Tour*, The Beatles (1967)

66. *Treasure*, Cocteau Twins (1984)

67. *Peggy Suicide*, Julian Cope (1991)

68. *Physical Graffiti,* Led Zeppelin (1975)

69. *A New World Record*, Electric Light Orchestra (1976)
70. *Toys in the Attic*, Aerosmith (1975)
71. *Don't Shoot Me, I'm Only the Piano Player*, Elton John (1973)
72. *Zoot Allures*, Frank Zappa (1976)
73. *The List,* Rosanne Cash (2009)
74. *Dreamboat Annie*, Heart (1976)
* 75. *Ram*, Paul and Linda McCartney (1971)
76. *The Who By Numbers*, The Who (1975)
* 77. *Graceland*, Paul Simon (1986)
* 78. *Hotel California*, Eagles (1976)
* 79. *Legend*, Poco (1978)
80. *Big World*, Joe Jackson (1986)

81. *Stands for Decibels*, The dB's (1981)
* 82. *Dog Problems*, The Format (2006)
83. *Randy Newman's 'Faust'* (1995)
84. *Tommy*, The Who (1969)
* 85. *Pink Pearl,* Jill Sobule (2000)
86. *Sheik Yerbouti*, Frank Zappa (1979)
87. *Imperial Bedroom,* Elvis Costello (1982)
88. *Plastic Ono Band*, John Lennon (1970)
89. *Wish You Were Here*, Pink Floyd (1975)
90. *She*, Willie Wisely (1996)
* 91. *Empty Glass*, Pete Townshend (1980)
92. *Highway 61 Revisited*, Bob Dylan (1965)
93. *Killer*, Alice Cooper (1971)
94. *Them Or Us*, Frank Zappa (1984)
95. *Rumours*, Fleetwood Mac (1977)
96. *Aja*, Steely Dan (1977)
97. *Meaty Beaty Big and Bouncy*, The Who (1971)
* 98. *Hey Jude/The Beatles Again,* The Beatles (1970)
* 99. *Sandinista*, The Clash (1980)
100. *King of America,* Elvis Costello (1986)

* 101. *Rhythm Nation 1814,* Janet Jackson (1989)
102. *Arizona Bay*,"Bill Hicks (1993)
103. *Gaucho*, Steely Dan (1980)
104. *Some Girls*, The Rolling Stones (1978)

105. *Talking Book*, Stevie Wonder (1972)

106. *In Utero*, Nirvana (1993)

107. *Help!* The Beatles (1965)

108. *Blonde on Blonde*, Bob Dylan (1966)

109. *Houses of the Holy*, Led Zeppelin (1973)

* 110. *All Things Must Pass*, George Harrison (1970)

111. *Rubber Soul*, The Beatles (1965)

112. *Daryl Hall and John Oates* (silver album) (1975)

* 113. *Velvet Underground and Nico,* Velvet Underground (1967)

114. *Q: Are We Not Men? A: We Are Devo*, Devo (1978)

115. *Repercussion*, The dB's (1982)

116. *Argybargy*, Squeeze (1980)

117. *The Big Express*, XTC (1984)

118. *Born to Run*, Bruce Springsteen (1975)

119. *Mind Games*, John Lennon (1973)

120. *Can't Buy a Thrill*, Steely Dan (1972)

121. *Apostrophe ('),* Frank Zappa (1974)

* 122. *Introducing The Beatles,* The Beatles (1964)

123. *Nevermind*, Nirvana (1991)

124. *Southern Rock Opera*, Drive-By Truckers (2002)

125. *London 0 Hull 4*, The Housemartins (1986)

* 126. *Hot Rocks 1964-1971*, The Rolling Stones (1971)

* 127. *Never Mind the Bollocks, Here's the Sex Pistols*, Sex Pistols (1977)

* 128. *Raspberries* (1972)

* 129. *Sgt. Pepper's Lonely Hearts Club Band*, The Beatles (1967)

130. *Girlfriend*, Matthew Sweet (1990)

131. *Deja Vu*, Crosby, Stills, Nash and Young (1970)

132. *Live at the Portland Arms*, The Soft Boys (1983)

* 133. *Nilsson Schmilsson*, Nilsson (1971)

134. *Fleetwood Mac,* Fleetwood Mac (1975)

135. *The Rutles* (1978)

* 136. *Fegmania!*, Robyn Hitchcock (1985)

137. *The Best of The Guess Who*, The Guess Who (1971)

138. *Security*, Peter Gabriel (1982)

139. *The Six Wives of Henry VIII*, Rick Wakeman (1973)

* 140. *The World is a Ghetto*, WAR (1972)

141. *Odds & Sods*, The Who (1974)

142. *Stevie Wonder's Original Musiquarium I,* Stevie Wonder (1982)

143. *Volunteers*, Jefferson Airplane (1969)

144. *Good Old Boys*, Randy Newman (1974)

145. *Underdog Victorious,* Jill Sobule (2004)

146. *Close to the Edge*, Yes (1972)

147. *The Who Sell Out,* The Who (1967)

148. *The Stranger*, Billy Joel (1977)

149. *Trouble in Paradise.* Randy Newman (1983)

150. *Layla and Other Assorted Love Songs,* Derek and the Dominos (1970)

151. *Black Ribbons*, Shooter Jennings & Hierophant (2010)

152. *Innervisions*, Stevie Wonder (1973)

153. *Tea for the Tillerman*, Cat Stevens (1970)

154. *Skylarking*, XTC (1986)

* 155. *Brain Salad Surgery*, Emerson Lake and Palmer (1973)

156. *American Stars n Bars*, Neil Young (1977)

157. *International Pop Overthrow*, Material Issue (1991)

* 158. *Fables of the Reconstruction,* R.E.M. (1985)

* 159. *The Third Reich 'n Roll,* The Residents (1976)

* 160. *The Gold Experience*, Prince (1995)

161. *Whatever*, Aimee Mann (1993)

162. *Heaven Tonight,* Cheap Trick (1978)

* 163. *Bare Trees,* Fleetwood Mac (1972)

164. *A Whiter Shade of Pale*, Procol Harum (1967)

165. *Pronounced*, Lynyrd Skynyrd (1973)

166. *Black Sea,* XTC (1980)

167. *Harvest*, Neil Young (1972)

168. *Bookends*, Simon and Garfunkel (1968)

169. *Love Symbol Album*, Prince (1992)

170. *Imagine*, John Lennon (1971)

171. *Led Zeppelin II* (1969)

172. *Honky Chateau*, Elton John (1972)

173. *My Aim is True*, Elvis Costello (1977)

174. *Brothers in Arms*, Dire Straits (1985)

175. *Tusk*, Fleetwood Mac (1979)

176. *Sit Down and Listen to Hooverphonic,* Hooverphonic (2003)

177. *Still Crazy After All These Years*, Paul Simon (1975)

178. *Sladest*, Slade (1973)

179. *Quadrophenia*, The Who (1973)

180. *You Will Go to the Moon*, Moxy Fruvous (1997)

181. *The Thorns* (2003)

182. *Surrealistic Pillow*, Jefferson Airplane (1967)

183. *Sheer Heart Attack*, Queen (1974)

* 184. *White Light/White Heat*, Velvet Underground (1968)

185. *Greendale*, Neil Young (2003)

* 186. *Little Queen*, Heart (1977)

187. *Sign o the Times*, Prince (1987)

188. *Tapestry*, Carole King (1971)

* 189. *Burn*, Deep Purple (1974)

190. *New York*, Lou Reed (1989)

* 191. *Who Are You*, The Who (1978)

192. *The Rise and Fall of Ziggy Stardust*, David Bowie (1972)

193. *Book of Hours*, Green Pajamas (1987)

* 194. *We're An American Band*, Grand Funk (1973)

195. *Big Money Item*, Greenberry Woods (1995)

196. *Llamalamp*, The Oohs (2006)

* 197. *The Chicago Transit Authority* (1969)

198. *II*, Bachman-Turner Overdrive (1973)

199. *Music From Big Pink*, The Band (1968)

200. *Deluxe*, Better Than Ezra (1993)

201. *Diamonds and Pearls*, Prince (1991)

202. *Bridge over Troubled Water*, Simon and Garfunkel (1970)

203. *Greatest Hits*, Sly and the Family Stone (1970)

204. *Dusty in Memphis*, Dusty Springfield (1969)

* 205. *Jazz*, Queen (1978)

206. *Purple Rain*, Prince (1984)

207. *Fulfillingness' First Finale*, Stevie Wonder (1974)

208. *Like a Prayer*, Madonna (1989)

209. *Garbage* (1995)

210. *Drums and Wires*, XTC (1979)

211. *Songs in the Key of Life*, Stevie Wonder (1976)

212. *In City Dreams*, Robin Trower (1977)

213. *Jackie*, Jackie DeShannon, (1972)

214. *Even in the Quietest Moments...,* Supertramp (1977)

215. *Stand!* Sly and the Family Stone (1969)

216. *There Goes Rhymin' Simon*, Paul Simon (1973)

217. *Laurel Canyon*, Jackie DeShannon (1968)

218. *Dance to the Music*, Sly and the Family Stone (1968)

219. *Starting Over*, Raspberries (1974)

220. *True Blue,* Madonna (1986)

221. *State of Our Union,* Long Ryders (1985)

222. S*taying Out Late With Beat Rodeo*, Beat Rodeo (1984)

223. *Kiko*, Los Lobos (1992)

224. *Do You Believe In Magic*, Lovin' Spoonful (1965)

* 225. *The Beat and the Time,* Lackloves (2004)

226. *Exodus*, Bob Marley and the Wailers (1977)

227. *Pretenders* (1980)

* 228. *Jesus Christ Superstar* (1970)

* 229. *Chicago V* (1972)

230. *Werewolves and Lollipops*, Patton Oswalt (2007)

231. *Golden Bisquits*, Three Dog Night (1971)

232. *Legend*, Bob Marley and the Wailers (1984)

233. *American Highway Flower*, Dada (1994)

234. *Armed Forces,* Elvis Costello (1979)

235. *Willy and the Poor Boys,* Creedence Clearwater Revival (1969)

* 236. *Out of the Blue,* Electric Light Orchestra (1977)

237. *London Calling*, The Clash (1979)

238. *A Different Story*, Deadeye Dick (1994)

239. *Ray of Light,* Madonna (1998)

240. *Destroyer*, Kiss (1976)

* 241. *Sail Away*, Randy Newman (1972)

242. *Free-for-All*, Ted Nugent (1976)

243. *Songs for Drella*, Lou Reed and John Cale (1990)

244. *The River & the Thread*, Rosanne Cash (2014)

245. *Let It Be*, The Replacements (1984)

246. *Outlandos d'Amour*, The Police (1978)

247. *Looking On*, The Move (1970)

248. *Beggars Banquet,* The Rolling Stones (1968)

249. *God In Three Persons,* The Residents (1988)

250. *Parsley, Sage, Rosemary and Thyme*, Simon and Garfunkel (1966)

251. *West Side Story* (soundtrack) (1961)

252. *There's a Riot Goin' On*, Sly and the Family Stone (1971)

253. *Running with Scissors*, "Weird Al" Yankovic (1999)

254. *Live Rust,* Neil Young (1979)

* 255. *Something/Anything?* Todd Rundgren (1972)

256. *Sgt. Pepper's,* Big Daddy (1992)

* 257. *Dottie's Charms*, Jill Sobule (2014)

258. *Blast From Your Past,* Ringo Starr (1975)

259. *Greatest Hits,* Cat Stevens (1975)

260. *Xanadu* (1980)

261. *Styx II*, Styx (1973)

* 262. *The Completion Backward Principle*, The Tubes (1981)

263. *Stray Cats* (1981 UK only)

264. *Forever Your Girl,* Paula Abdul (1988)

265. *My Fair Lady* (Broadway cast) (1956)

* 266. *Sing it Again Rod*, Rod Stewart (1973)

267. *Stranger in Town*, Bob Seger (1978)

268. *Oklahoma!* (film soundtrack) (1955)

269. *Celebrate: The Three Dog Night Story, 1965-1975*, Three Dog Night (1993)

270. *Recorded Live*, Ten Years After (1973)

271. *Hotter than July*, Stevie Wonder (1980)

272. *Ogdens' Nut Gone Flake*, Small Faces (1968)

273. *Dare to Be Stupid*, "Weird Al" Yankovic (1985)

274. *Synchronicity*, The Police (1983)

275. *That Thing You Do!* (film soundtrack) (1996)

276. *Seduced by Money*, Thieves (1989)

277. *Lumpy Gravy*, Frank Zappa (1967)

278. *Portable Life*, Danielle Brisebois (1999)

279. *1962-1966,* The Beatles (1973)

280. *Gordon*, Barenaked Ladies (1992)

281. *Broadway the Hard Way*, Frank Zappa (1988)

282. *Are You Experienced*, Jimi Hendrix Experience (1967)

283. *Green River*, Creedence Clearwater Revival (1969)

284. *In Search of the Lost Chord*, Moody Blues (1968)

285. *Shaved Fish*, John Lennon (1975)

286. *Dog and Butterfly*, Heart (1978)

287. *Madman Across the Water*, Elton John (1971)

* 288. *At the Ryman*, Emmylou Harris (1992)

* 289. *Exile in Guyville*, Liz Phair (1993)

290. *Centerfield*, John Fogerty (1985)

291. *The Cars* (1978)

292. *Freedom*, Neil Young (1989)

293. *Go Insane*, Lindsey Buckingham (1984)

294. *Shazam*, The Move (1970)

* 295. *Taking Liberties*, Elvis Costello (1980)

* 296. *The Hoople*, Mott the Hoople (1974)

297. *Bargainville*, Moxy Fruvous (1993)

298. *shock/denial/anger/acceptance*, Rick Springfield (2004)

299. *A Hard Day's Night,* The Beatles (1964)

300. *East Side Story,* Squeeze (1981)

301. *The Presidents of the United States of America* (1994)

302. *The Future Is Medieval"/'Start the Revolution Without Me,* Kaiser Chiefs (2011)

303. *Waka/Jawaka,* Frank Zappa (1972)

304. *Buddy Holly Lives*, Buddy Holly (1978)

305. *Eye of the Zombie*, John Fogerty (1986)

306. *Out of the Cradle,* Lindsey Buckingham (1992)

* 307. *Double Fantasy,* John Lennon/Yoko Ono (1980)

308. *Toulouse Street*, The Doobie Brothers (1972)

309. *The Hollies' Greatest Hits* (1973)

* 310. *Flaming Pie*, Paul McCartney (1997)

311. *Tupelo Honey*, Van Morrison (1971)

312. *Pandemonium Shadow Show,* Nilsson (1967)

313. *I'm Everyone I've Ever Loved,* Martin Mull (1977)

314. *Simple Dreams*, Linda Ronstadt (1977)

315. *So Beautiful or So What*, Paul Simon (2011)

* 316. *Bad Girls*, Donna Summer (1979)

317. *Time and a Word*, Yes (1970)

318. *Long Misty Days*, Robin Trower (1976)

319. *Care*, Shriekback (1983)

320. *This is The Moody Blues*, The Moody Blues (1974)

321. *Paul Simon* (1972)

322. *Especially for You*, The Smithereens (1986)

323. *The Slider*, T. Rex (1972)

* 324. *A Retrospective*, Linda Ronstadt (1977)

325. *Weird Scenes From Inside the Goldmine*, The Doors (1972)

326. *Ten*, Pearl Jam (1991)

327. *History: America's Greatest Hits*, America (1975)

328. *Piano Man*, Billy Joel (1973)

329. *Changesonebowie*, David Bowie (1976)

330. *Control*, Janet Jackson (1986)

331. *Hot Rats*, Frank Zappa (1969)

332. *Alive!*, Kiss (1975)

333. *Frampton Comes Alive*, Peter Frampton (1976)

334. *The Great Twenty-Eight*, Chuck Berry (1982)

* 335. *No Quarter (Unledded)*, Jimmy Page and Robert Plant (1994)

336. *The Point*, Nilsson (1971)

337. *Sticky Fingers*, The Rolling Stones (1971)

338. *Faithful*, Todd Rundgren (1976)

* 339. *It'll End in Tears*, This Mortal Coil (1984)

* 340. *Back to the Egg*, Wings (1979)

341. *41 Original Hits from the Soundtrack of American Graffiti* (1973)

342. *#1 Record/Radio City*, Big Star (1972/74)

343. *Crowded House* (1986)

344. *The Original Soundtrack*, 10cc (1975)

345. *Ambrosia* (1975)

346. *Sunshine on Leith*, Proclaimers (1988)

347. *It's Only Rock 'n Roll*, The Rolling Stones (1974)

348. *Amanda Leigh*, Mandy Moore (2009)

349. *Tunnel of Love,* Bruce Springsteen (1987)

350. *Teaser and the Firecat*, Cat Stevens (1971)

* 351. *All the Best Cowboys Have Chinese Eyes,* Pete Townshend (1982)

352. *Retrospective*, Buffalo Springfield (1969)

* 353. *Poodle Hat*, "Weird Al" Yankovic (2003)

354. *Yours Truly, Angry Mob*, Kaiser Chiefs (2007)

355. *Queen Elvis*, Robyn Hitchcock (1989)

356. *Seven Separate Fools,* Three Dog Night (1972)

357. *Josie and the Pussycats* soundtrack (2001)

358. *L.A. Woman*, The Doors (1971)
359. *Countdown to Ecstasy*, Steely Dan (1973)
360. *The River*, Bruce Springsteen (1980)
361. *Around the World in a Day*, Prince (1985)
362. *The Magician's Birthday,* Uriah Heep (1972)
363. *The Game,* Queen (1980)
364. *Foghat*, Foghat (1972)
365. *Sentimental Hygiene*, Warren Zevon (1987)

No. 365. *Sentimental Hygiene*, Warren Zevon (1987) -- I never would have guessed how much I liked the first album he put out after a best-of package. Every story is every song is one I can easily picture. My favorites: "Sentimental Hygiene," "Reconsider Me"

No. 364. *Foghat,* Foghat (1972) -- Their slinky version of "I Just Want to Make Love to You" is the definitive one for me. Their originals almost match the astonishing cover versions. My favorites: "Maybelline," "I Just Want to Make Love to You"

No. 363. *The Game*, Queen (1980) – One of four Queen albums on this list. Their last gasp. Everyone makes an effort to overcome "Another One Bites the Dust," and they succeed well enough. My favorites: "Rock It (Prime Jive)," "Crazy Little Thing Called Love"

No. 362. *The Magician's Birthday,* Uriah Heep (1972) – Of course I realize the bombast is atrocious. The keyboard squeal on "Sweet Lorraine" sounds like banshees, or cats being strangled. At least this doesn't have "Easy Livin'" and its buzzsaw guitar. To Teen Tim, this was wondrous, especially when they put a kazoo and the song "Happy Birthday" in the middle of the 10-minute title cut. Favorite songs: "Sweet Lorraine," "The Magician's Birthday"

No. 361. *Around the World in a Day,* Prince (1985) – The last thing I expected as a follow-up to *Purple Rain* was this blissful psychedelia, which I enjoy more than almost anyone I know. Most people were looking for *Purple Rain II* instead of this bit out psychedelic wonder. This is one of five Prince albums on the list. Favorite songs: "Raspberry Beret," "Pop Life"

No. 360. *The River*, Bruce Springsteen (1980) – One of three Springsteen albums on the list. A classic example of "Oh, hey! This song is on this album!" Bloated, but in a productive enough way. At his most irritating, Springsteen is too wordy and the songs are a verse of two too long. But there's still enough fun here to consider this worthwhile. Favorite songs: "Crush on You," "Cadillac Ranch"

No. 359. *Countdown to Ecstasy,* Steely Dan (1973) – It felt like a step back to me when I first heard it. I just wasn't ready for it. It's remarkably dark for its time. The first of five Steely Dan albums on this list. Favorite songs: "Bodhisattva," "My Old School"

No. 358. *L.A. Woman*, The Doors (1971) – The charm I find here is what irritates others. I love how they're chasing their muse methodically and patiently (what else is the music on "Riders on the Storm"?) instead of violently shaking the listener. Instead of continually yelling over a busy band, like he did earlier in his career, Jim Morrison is singing over a different kind of Doors. He's even whispering to great effect on the album's last song. Favorite songs: As cliche as it is, "Riders on the Storm" and "L.A. Woman"

No. 357. *Josie and the Pussycats* soundtrack (2001) – Before actually watching and listening, I underestimated both the film (a clever and deep parody of teen culture) and the music. The music is solid power pop, by turns catchy and comic. Favorite songs: "Turn Around," "3 Small Words"

No. 356. *Seven Separate Fools*, Three Dog Night (1972) – Perhaps nostalgia clouds my brain, but this holds up to me as their best non-compilation album. The first side is near-perfect. The single "Black and White" is followed by a Randy Newman song (they've already had success with his work), then a floating keyboard piece leads into "Pieces of April," one of those quiet acoustic songs at which they excelled. "Going in Circles" is a vocal tour de force, and "Chained" is the same, except rockier. Favorite songs: "My Old Kentucky Home," "Going in Circles"

No. 355. *Queen Elvis*, Robyn Hitchcock (1989) – This almost marks the end of Hitchcock playing rockier songs with a band. For "One Long Pair of Eyes" to not be a songwriter's greatest effort means he's written a lot of great songs. Favorite songs: "One Long Pair of Eyes," "Freeze"

No. 354. *Yours Truly, Angry Mob,* Kaiser Chiefs (2007) – If an album could make this list based on one song, "Ruby" is a good enough tune. I don't think these guys have recorded a thing that I dislike. Favorite songs: "Ruby," "Everything is Average Nowadays"

***

No. 353. *Poodle Hat,* "Weird Al" Yankovic (2003) – One of three Yankovic albums on the list. What a diverse group he goes after: Eminem, Billy Joel, Zappa, Backstreet Boys, "angry white boy"s. Favorite songs: "Hardware Store," "Ode to a Superhero" (It's stunning to me as a Zappa fan that I do not list the Zappa style parody contained herein.)

I'm always amused to see assorted folks in the blogosphere giving love to "Weird Al" Yankovic and saying "it's OK to like him again."

See, I never stopped.

And I've never stopped taking grief for it. I've had dozens, if not hundreds, of people roll their eyes at me for being a Yankovic fan for -- well, for Yankovic's entire career, I guess. In the mid-1990s, I had him autograph a copy of his first commercial single, the TK Records release of "Another One Rides the Bus." His eyebrows went up when he saw it, and at least seemed somewhat appreciative that someone had been following him for so long.

How much do I like Yankovic? I don't think his song parodies are that great anymore. I liked "The Saga Begins," in which he retold the plot of *Star Wars Episode I: The Phantom Menace* to the tune of "American Pie," writing the song prior to the film's release, basing the lyrics off information he found on "Star Wars" rumor websites. And "Ode to a Superhero," the "Spider-Man"/"Piano Man" mash-up from *Poodle Hat,* was inspired.

But it's been the original songs and style parodies that have caught my ear. "Albuquerque" from 1999's *Running With Scissors,* was 12 hilarious and inspired minutes, and "Truck Drivin' Song" from that same album was an outrageous and entertaining cross-dressing tale.

Poodle Hat includes "Bob," a Dylan tribute whose lines consisted of palindromes ("Madam, I'm Adam," "Do geese see God" and my favorite, "Lisa Bonet ate no basil") and "Hardware Store," which features some amazing vocal gymnastics. When I interviewed him in the early 2000s, Yankovic was reluctant to talk about how much time it took him to record the vocals for the song, which was indicative of the guy's humble nature off-stage.

But for me, the true tour de force on *Poodle Hat* is "Genius in France," one of Yankovic's "style parodies," in which he playfully nudges an artist's musical style rather than a specific song. "Genius In France" parodies one of my favorite performers, Frank Zappa, in such a fantastic way that I don't know whether to laugh, cry, or just be stunned.

***

No. 352. "*Retrospective*, Buffalo Springfield (1969) – I might have known just the big hit except for this compilation, a vital part of any 1970s teen boy's collection. They're one of the least poppy acts that broke through as a pop act. They didn't do a dozen versions of "For What It's Worth." "Mr. Soul" and "Expecting to Fly" and "Broken Arrow" are all really adventurous works, especially at the time. Favorite songs: "Bluebird," "Rock and Roll Woman"

***

No. 351. *All the Best Cowboys Have Chinese Eye*s, Pete Townshend (1982) – The last time I was willing to follow him anywhere. This was truly a worthwhile adventure into adventurousness. Favorite songs: "Stop Hurting People," "Slit Skirts"

One prejudice or conceit that I've had to abandon is considering any version of a song "definitive." This is true especially since the beginning of broader video production and consumption.

The difference became painfully clear for me as a friend and I discussed Monty Python pieces. We both knew the works front and back. When we broke down the language and inflections, we slowly came to realize we had memorized different versions. Mine was based on the television broadcasts. I was a little younger than the demographic Python targeted, but I was still in the audience. I saw the *Holy Grail* and *Brian* films in the theater on first-

126

run. I had the records in my collection, but to me they were just intended as something to remind me of the TV series.

My friend memorized the audio recordings, reasoning that the recorded versions had at least as much legitimacy as the video versions. They did, after all, go to the trouble of re-recording the bits most of the time.

To me, this was heresy. The video was clearly canon. That's what established them. And if you knew details about how the records came to be – essentially recorded a Python's backyard shed – that gave even less legitimacy to making the recorded versions canon.

My friend didn't let up, though, insisting their version of Python was just as valid as mine.

How can I argue? I've got a whole thing of it going on myself. It's requiring a mind reset that's a struggle.

But my teen years were filled with a strange phenomenon that threw the idea of "definitive" into a muddle. The bizarre recorded music trait of the 1970s was songs edited down for radio airplay.

I know the 1970s didn't launch it. I suppose the first big one was "Light My Fire" with three minutes excised. I know I heard hideous edits of "Whole Lotta Love," although I'm not sure I ever saw a 45 rpm record of the song. That three-minute "Light My Fire," meanwhile – if anybody in my circle had a 45, that was the one they had.

"Locomotive Breath," Pink Floyd's "Money," "Carry On Wayward Son," "(Don't Fear) The Reaper," "Frankenstein," even "Kodachrome" – some of the versions of songs that became definitive to my ear were songs that had been edited. ("Kodachrome" had the word "crap" beeped out in the southeastern Minnesota market where I was listening. To quote my father, I shit you not.) I'd hear the original versions eventually, and appreciated them more. But I was always fascinated with the idea of scissoring a song to make it in some way more palatable.

Maybe that's why I have less of an issue with sampling and will regularly argue that people can use sampling as a base on which to build wholly unique new art. To me, the line between inspiration and theft is far more clear than it is for many others. I side with the secondary creators more than originators would prefer.

Sometimes, the originators don't give you a lot of help. There are multiple mixes of Frankie Goes to Hollywood's "Relax." Some are more palatable than others. I'm always going to prefer the video version, the version with the "live" performance and ultra-high powered flashlights that appeared to be floodlights. Others have walked away wholly unimpressed. To me, it will always be the definitive version.

The Killers' "Somebody Told Me" exists in close to a dozen versions. The ones I know best are the album version and a mix that features an extra keyboard, and the vocals seem a bit more lively. Interestingly, I enjoy both equally.

The Ting Tings' " That's Not My Name" is one of those songs that you know after hearing it once if you ever want to hear it again. I did and I do. I spent a lot of time with a lot of people introducing them to the tune. One of the versions i would use was a video of a live version from SXSW. In that version, they stretch out the start a bit, and the conclusion adds in a bunch of vocal histrionics by Katie White. For me, it's a pleasant addition to an already great song. But for a friend who first heard the live version, that was the one that "got the song right."

The thing is, even though I disagree, I could still hear exactly what my friend was saying.

Ultimately, the discussion turns on which version of the performance you consider " definitive." For me, that version has almost always been the recorded version. That's generally the first version I've come across. That's also the version over which the artist has the most control over the permanent pieces they know will be presented to a mass audience.

But then video comes in and messes stuff up, doesn't it? "Two Tribes" is a great Frankie Goes to Hollywood song, but you can get your hands on other horrific versions. So do I love the song or the soundtrack of a film? I readily confess images from the video stream in my head when I hear the song.

Pete Townshend, as he has been wont to do my entire life, adds to the problem.

"Slit Skirts" is the closing song on his *All The Best Cowboys Have Chinese Eyes* album. (In one review I read, it was politely described as "unfortunately titled.") Townshend also released a video album featuring some songs from the audio album. It also has a live version of "Slit Skirts" that's similar to the album version, but also features a harmonica part that elevates the song for me.

The video for "Face to Face" makes the version Townshend released on the *White City: A Novel* sound like a demo, and a poor demo at that. After seeing that video repeatedly, when I was first listening to the album and that song came up, I was crushed. It was a weak recording with little energy. In the video, with the appearance of Townshend's daughter Emma to do the middle "rap," the song almost exploded off the television. Meanwhile, Pete's performance of the bit on the album closes the coffin on the tune.

I know which versions I consider "definitive."

Townshend had as much control over all of those versions as any artist did. He doesn't seem to indicate what he considers definitive. I've done it for him.

Some artists' definitive versions cannot be captured. However beautiful the recorded version of Robyn Hitchcock's "Raymond Chandler Evening" turned out to be, it was never going to be the definitive version for me, because I heard what I consider to be the definitive version when I saw him perform it in concert, and no one else can hear that version of it. It was a combination of the moment, the mood in the air, and maybe sitting next to a good friend.

Of course, given how often Hitchcock changes words, phrases and lines with assorted live performances of certain songs, maybe he sees the recorded version as a marker among the way and the song as an ever-evolving piece.

That seems to be what Dylan does, anyway.

***

No. 350. *Teaser and the Firecat*, Cat Stevens (1971) – This is probably as much of a hippie-folkie compendium as there is on this list. I defy you to not be taken by the beauty of the songs. Favorite songs: "Morning Has Broken," "Peace Train"

No. 349. *Tunnel of Love*, Bruce Springsteen (1987) – This album proved he had quiet depth to go along with the arena bombast of *Born in the USA*. He also found an economy of words to make his lamentations punch you in the gut. Favorite songs: "Brilliant Disguise," "Tunnel of Love"

No. 348. *Amanda Leigh*, Mandy Moore (2009) – I followed her career because people I respected said she was more than a Disney pop queen. This was the point where she proved them right. Favorite songs: "Fern Dell," "Merrimack River"

No. 347. *It's Only Rock 'n Roll*, The Rolling Stones (1974) – I didn't know they were supposed to be over the hill. It felt like they'd just started. Favorite songs: "Ain't Too Proud to Beg," "If You Really Want to Be My Friend"

No. 346. *Sunshine on Leith*, Proclaimers (1988) – I found their hit single annoying. Its cloying tone and thick accents sound like, as I eventually learned, this album on speed. I ducked the album until swayed by a friend to uncover the beauty and brilliance in its concept of, quite simply, "home." A nice place to be. Favorite songs: "Sunshine on Leith," "I'm on My Way"

No. 345. *Ambrosia* (1975) – An unlikely cross of prog rock and sparkling AM pop. With lyrics for one song taken from Kurt Vonnegut's *Cat's Cradle*. Vonnegut's 1963 novel contained the lyrics of a song sung by characters in the book. Ambrosia set the lyrics to music, Vonnegut liked it and got a co-writer credit. I never tire of pointing that out, because it shows people I can read stuff besides lyric sheets. Favorite songs: "Nice, Nice, Very Nice," "Holdin' on to Yesterday"

No. 344. *The Original Soundtrack,* 10cc (1975) – Three-quarters of a brilliant album with an amazing first side. That breathtaking hit single "I'm Not in Love," the one with the orchestra of "ahh"s, is even more breathtaking here at its full six-minute length. It says something to me when "I'm Not in Love" is my fifth-favorite song on the album. Favorite songs: "Une Nuit a Paris (One Night in Paris)," "Blackmail"

No. 343. *Crowded House* (1986) – One of many 1980s pop bands whose debuts promised more potential than was eventually delivered. I've never forgiven The Bangles for not being what I thought they were, a Beatles-esque group that could modernize the sound and make a 1980s recreation of the British Invasion. The Bangles' efforts turned more toward a popular mainstream sound. Crowded House went the other direction, and not always in a good way. They never approached this again, which doesn't diminish its brilliance one iota. Favorite songs: "Something So Strong," "Now We're Getting Somewhere"

No. 342. *#1 Record,* Big Star (1972) – Responsible for much of the music I love that followed in its style wake. It's guitar pop with soaring harmonies, a template for exactly the kind of music I have adored for a half-century. In an alternate universe, Big Star is The Beatles. And so are a lot of performers I love -- The Lackloves, The Records, The Handcuffs, The Raspberries, Badfinger, Marshall Crenshaw, Cheap Trick, The Oohs, the *Girlfriend*-era Matthew Sweet. Favorite songs: "The Ballad of El Goodo," "Thirteen"

No. 341. *41 Original Hits from the Soundtrack of American Graffiti* (1973) – The manner by which a number of people my age without older siblings were introduced to pre-Beatles music. Fine flick, fun music. Favorite songs: "Come Go With Me," "Little Darlin'"

***

No. 340. *Back to the Egg,* Wings (1979) – By this time, Paul McCartney was regarded by almost anyone still interested in him as bloated and self-indulgent. That was difficult to argue against. I still like the production tricks, things that could only have come from inside the head of someone like McCartney. I take a lot of grief for liking this album. I'm good with that. Favorite songs: "Spin It On," "Arrow Through Me"

I've criticized Paul McCartney any number of times. When McCartney disappoints me the most is when it doesn't seem as though he's trying. He disappointed a number of people in 1979 with *Back to the Egg,* which many found dull.

I even had a friend who said, "If the rumors about his death had come around after *Back to the Egg,* I could have believed them."

But I always liked *Back to the Egg.* Paul McCartney's work in the 1970s was always shrouded in some kind of mystery, even at that point when Wings was one of the most popular bands in the world. From the bizarre covers of *Ram* and *Red Rose Speedway* (with its Braille message on the back) to all of the posters and stickers and other junk thrown into the *Venus and Mars* package (not to mention the weird cover), McCartney's albums seemed to arrive from another planet.

And here was an album where on the cover, the band members were literally looking down on Earth. The opening cut sounded like somebody tuning a radio. A spoken-word piece was featured on the second side. Two two-song "medleys," back-to-back on the B side. (Or, the "over easy" side. Sheesh.) And the "Rockestra," used by McCartney on two tracks, featured members of The Shadows (Hank Marvin), Pink Floyd (David Gilmour), The Who (Pete Townshend and Kenney Jones), Led Zeppelin (John Bonham and John Paul Jones), The Faces (Ronnie Lane) and Procol Harum (Gary Brooker).

Sure, it can be a little exhausting. Critic Robert Christgau was especially unimpressed, writing: "Sixteen titles on an untimed LP that must run forty minutes if not fifty - or seventy-five. When he's on, Paulie's abundant tunefulness passes for generosity. Here he's just hoping something will stick."

But a lot of it stuck with me, especially "Arrow Through Me," in which McCartney tarted up a sweet little pop song with a "horn" section playing in 7/4 time over a 4/4 time backing.

That 7/4-4/4 trick, and the beauty of the line "Come on, get up, get under way, bring your love" makes me forgive the what's-he-talking-about couplet of "You wouldn't have found a more down hero/If you'da started at nothing and counted to zero."

Huh?

A bootleg called *Egg Salad* features some early mixes and rough tracks of cuts from the album and from its era, and reminds me that whatever I think of McCartney now, there really was a time I thought he could do no wrong.

***

No. 339. *It'll End in Tears*, This Mortal Coil (1984) – I'm amused that comedian Patton Oswalt mentioning this in his act probably reached more people than those who'd previously heard it. At this time, I thought the 4AD label was infallible, and this set was just more proof. Favorite songs: "Holocaust," "Song to the Siren"

When I was in my early 20s, there were two record labels that consistently had my interest.

Rhino Records put out the goofiest stuff imaginable. *Rhino Royale* and *Circus Royale* collected offbeat comedy songs, as did their Dr. Demento releases. Wildman Fischer found a home on Rhino, as did Barnes and Barnes and Henny Youngman. By the time Rhino was re-releasing Beau Brummels albums, I was hooked enough to be on the company's mailing list, and I often thought anything on Rhino was worth purchasing.

The other was 4AD, which is apparently now described as a gathering of "goth-pop" performers. I didn't know what it was called in 1983, which was about the time I dived in, but I found it delightful, haunting, beautiful and hypnotic. The label boasted such diverse acts as Cocteau Twins (with an album yet to come on this list), Modern English ("I Melt With You") and M/A/R/R/S ("Pump Up the Volume"). So not everything was going to be to my liking. I still remember putting on an Xmal Deutschland album and thinking, "What the hell is this supposed to be? Music?" But it was always going to be interesting.

Only a handful of people in mu hometown were aware of 4AD records, but

I was the only person for whom the record store would set aside each 4AD release, knowing I would buy it. I subscribed to a mimeographed fanzine that went out in the mail at intermittent times in which the editor would include painstakingly transcribed interviews and news about 4AD acts culled from international press.

In late 1984, 4AD issued an album by a band of which I'd never heard, This Mortal Coil. The album was *It'll End in Tears*. This Mortal Coil was described as a 4AD "supergroup," a gathering of members of the label's bands recording cover versions under the This Mortal Coil name.

But I didn't know they were cover versions. I recognized some of the names eventually – Alex Chilton, Roy Harper, Tim Buckley, Colin Newman. I had Chilton and Newman albums at this point. And I'd heard the Tim Buckley song – "Song to the Siren" – when he performed it at the end of an episode of *The Monkee*s. I just didn't realize it.

The album was a revelation. I played it continually. I found the bleak mood comforting, the ethereal voices and production deep and intriguing.

Subsequent releases by the This Mortal Coil collective weren't as attractive for me. In part because *It'll End in Tears* prompted me to go out and dig into the source material, and as I got deeper into those original pieces, the copies were less interesting. Also, my tastes as the decade went on took me deeper into pop on one end, and Frank Zappa's experimentation on the other.

I always thought I was fairly alone in my passion for This Mortal Coil and *It'll End in Tears* in particular. I certainly never encountered anyone who enjoyed the stuff as much as I did. So imagine my surprise when listening to comedian Patton Oswalt's great *Werewolves and Lollipops* album, and he was in the midst of a fresh rant about the Kentucky Fried Chicken bowls.

Oswalt said, ""Is there a way that the bowl can play This Mortal Coil's I*t'll End In Tears* album while I'm eating at 2 in the morning in my darkened apartment, just kinda staring into the middle distance?" I was so excited. HE knew that album too. Although I found recordings where the song he wanted playing was Pink Floyd's "Great Gig in the Sky."

In late 2007, the collected works of This Mortal Coil – B-sides and special contributions elsewhere also included – were released in a four-CD box called *This Mortal Coil*. I excitedly dove in, eager to experience the material that was so important 25 or so years ago, this time with fresh and more educated ears.

And I found … a curiosity. Kind of like that experience of listening to someone else play their versions of songs from their record collection when you already have the originals.

The songs are still beautiful, the recordings are still moody and spooky and an appropriate soundtrack for a goth haunted house, or for eating a Kentucky Fried Chicken failure bowl. And I'm glad I have them – there may be a time when it comes in handy to point out to a modern teen that they and their peers did not create goth mood music.

But in general, when I need to hear these songs. I'm going to the originals. For which I thank This Mortal Coil.

***

No. 338. *Faithful*, Todd Rundgren (1976) – It was the side of covers (including a version of "Good Vibrations" that was a hit single) that drew me in, then the second side of originals kept me around. Favorite songs: "Love of the Common Man," "Boogies (Hamburger Hell)"

No. 337. *Sticky Fingers*, The Rolling Stones (1971) – A real zipper on the cover? Yeah. Crazy dark music inside? Even better. Art with an edge, the best kind. Favorite songs: "Brown Sugar," "Bitch"

No. 336. *The Point!* Nilsson (1971) – Watched the TV movie, loved the story, had to have the album. It's a nifty discrimination parable, delivered to me via animation in 1971. The only round-headed person in a village of people with points for heads, is banished from the village, goes on an adventure, and returns a hero. That's a crude outline, but if this is where my love of good concept albums was born, well, thank you Harry Nilsson. Favorite songs: "Everything's Got 'Em," "Me and My Arrow"

***

No. 335. *No Quarter (Unledded)*, Jimmy Page and Robert Plant (1994) – I only saw a connection to Led Zeppelin in some of the songs used. These were (largely) whole new takes on Zeppelin songs. Favorite songs: "Yallah," "Gallows Pole"

Robert Plant is Led Zeppelin's David Gilmour (or Roger Waters), he's Led Zeppelin's Paul McCartney (or John Lennon), he's Led Zeppelin's Don Henley (or Glenn Frey).

He's either the talent that stirred the group, the guy the rest of the band couldn't do without, or the guy whose obstinacy about the band and his work with them fires the passions and the anger of fans.

Fans want what they want, and in examples of these four performers (and dozens of others, make no mistake), the issues between the two leaders (Jimmy Page fills the role of Plant's opponent) are what prevent (or prevented) a harmonious coexistence, more quality music, and (in the case of Led Zeppelin) one (or, in the case of Eagles, multiple) reunion shows and tours.

Only in 2014, Plant was really spitting on a lot of people. He was wrong, and he's getting spanked by his peers, and they seem to have discovered what a number of Led Zeppelin fans have felt for a long time – Plant is more interested in paying lip service to some kind of artistic muse than he is invested in protecting Led Zeppelin's legacy.

He's mostly interested in the attention that once being a part of Led Zeppelin brings him. Consider the incendiary quotes from the 2014 Rolling Stone interview where Plant talks about a Led Zeppelin reunion tour yet again.

Among Plant's broadsides:

* "A tour (after Led Zeppelin's 2007 O2 reunion show, a concert for which the band rehearsed for a year) would have been an absolute menagerie of vested interests and the very essence of everything that's (expletive) about big-time stadium rock. ... I'm not part of a jukebox."

* Talking about bands (like Eagles. The Rolling Stones and presumably Steely Dan) who have reunited and been touring essentially on the nostalgia bandwagon: "I hope they're having a real riveting and wonderful late middle age. Somehow I don't think they are."

* "Do you know why the Eagles said they'd reunite when 'hell freezes over,' but they did it anyway and keep touring? It's not because they were paid a fortune. It's not about the money. It's because they're bored. I'm not bored." (Eagle Don Henley responded. The best quote? "I really wish [Led Zeppelin] would get back together because they were one of the greatest bands of all time. I think maybe Robert is worried about hitting those notes. He may not be able to unbutton his shirt any more.")

Plant has a caustic sense of humor, and sometimes I find it amusing. At a press conference for the 1994 Page-Plant tour, undertaken without John Paul Jones, Led Zeppelin's other surviving member, Plant was asked about Jones. "He's parking the car," Plant said. Jones was not, and remains not, amused.

Plant's attitude would be fine -- were he not the instigator of much of the Led Zeppelin talk. He was the reason for their reunions, he continued to perform songs he and Page wrote for the band in his solo shows, and worst of all, he continued to dangle the possibility of a reunion.

Rolling Stone essentially asked why he wouldn't rule out another reunion. "I don't think there's any reason for me to do that. Otherwise we've got nothing to be mystic about … Everything will develop as it develops. All doors are open. All phone lines are open. I don't hear from anybody. Talk is cheap … But I just think everything has to be new. Then you can incorporate history."

All right then. To me, the telling word in that quote is "mystic." It often struck me that Robert Plant was torn between demanding the respect he deserves as one of rock's great front men, and being embarrassed by the extremes of his youth with the band. (Did he listen or think about his interjections on live versions of "Stairway to Heaven" - "the forests will echo with laughter … DOES ANYBODY REMEMBER LAUGHTER?"

and "there's still time to change the road you're on ... I HOPE SO" and, starting a later verse, "WAIT A MINUTE! WAIT A MINUTE!" - and cringe a little bit, and wish to avoid reliving those youthful moments? Maybe, and who could blame him?)

Perhaps Plant was so concerned about protecting his legendary frontman status that he didn't want to reveal what he might have seen as shortcomings during a lengthy reunion. He probably well remembered the 1970s tours, where a younger band who should have been in prime condition was as likely to not be clicking on all four cylinders as it was to be solid and splendid. Just listen to some of the live tapes.) Maybe he and Jones were irreconcilable. Maybe he just didn't want to sing the songs any more.

Plant backed away from a tour idea after the reunion show, turning his back on what experts predicted could be rock's first billion-dollar tour. That frustrated me as a fan, but many of Plant's backers were able to convince me that Plant following his artistic muse was what was best for everyone. He went on to a Grammy-winning collaboration with Alison Krauss.

But Plant continued to trot out something Zeppelin related – often discussing a reunion – every time he had something of his own to sell. It reminded me of McCartney dusting off a "new" Beatles story, or hinting at some kind of potential upcoming Beatles release, every time he had a new album to promote.

Was it the right of both Plant and McCartney to trade on their legacies for promotional purposes now? Certainly. Is it my right as a fan of both, and particularly their original bands, that I got frustrated with the up-and-down, back-and-forth nature of their attitudes?

You bet. That's what this was all about.

***

No. 334. *The Great Twenty-Eight*, Chuck Berry (1982) – As I was building my appreciation for rock's pioneers, this issue of Chess sides (his original label) was a priceless replacement of my copies of his later Mercury re-recordings. These sounded right. Favorite songs: "No Particular Place to

No. 333. *Frampton Comes Alive*! Peter Frampton (1976) – It's too easy to forget how perfect this album was for its time. A blend of AM radio hits with FM classic rock workouts. It chased me into his back catalog, which was better than I expected. Sure, he picked the best/most popular songs from those studio albums, but he could have flipped out a half-dozen songs and the live/best of would have been no worse. Favorite songs: "Doobie Wah," "Lines on My Face"

No. 332. *Alive!*, Kiss (1975) – Like *Frampton Comes Alive!*, this was a greatest-hits by a band that had no real hits yet. Whatever they did to embed themselves in my skull started with this crazy breath of fresh air. Favorite songs: "Strutter," "Rock and Roll All Nite"

***

No. 331. *Hot Rats*, Frank Zappa (1969) – It was well after Zappa's 1993 death that I found this, which helped me better grasp modern jazz in general. Favorite songs: "Peaches En Regalia," "The Gumbo Variations"

(March 2005)

We often get out of art what we take in and are willing to put into it. And even if we come to different conclusions about ambiguous points, we're not "wrong." And, in fact, we can come to different conclusions and disagree about art altogether.

That happened to me while reading Barry Miles' biography of Frank Zappa. (Miles has also written biographies of Jack Kerouac, William Burroughs and Paul McCartney.)

I had just finished reading a section about Zappa's song "We're Turning Again."

In Miles' view (and, to be fair, in the view of some Zappa fans and sidemen), "We're Turning Again" is a tasteless song that mocks many of Zappa's friends and contemporaries from the 1960s, including Jimi Hendrix (who played with Zappa's Mothers of Invention during one show), Janis Joplin (with whom Zappa had an affair), Keith Moon (who appeared in Zappa's film "200 Motels") and Jim Morrison and Mama Cass (both of whom, early in their careers, discussed Zappa producing their bands' records).

The lyrics are uncompromising in their contempt of the 1960s hippie lifestyle and attitudes, essentially mocking those who insist on living in the past by mythologizing its "martyrs." In the song, hippies are depicted as people who feel like they could have made everything all right had they only been present to cheer up Joplin and Moon as they careened toward drug-induced deaths, or tend to Morrison and Hendrix in their stupors, or prevent Cass from choking.

(Zappa often reworked his songs in concert before recording and releasing them, and the original versions of the song were much crueler, although in those versions, Zappa was not singing about an outside group - he included himself as a member, using "we" instead of "I.")

At least I always heard it as mocking an audience that turned drug burnouts into martyrs.

Some of Zappa's musicians hinted at dissatisfaction with the song, and Miles blatantly feels it mocks the deaths of the five icons mentioned. Miles calls it one of Zappa's worst songs.

Miles and I disagree on the interpretation of the song, but even accepting Miles' analysis, I don't think the song is tasteless or mocking of the deaths. It's merely using the deaths to show a way *not* to live. It's mocking self-destruction, if anything.

Everything's open to interpretation. But I rarely feel as off-base as I felt reading that segment of Miles' book.

***

No. 330. *Control*, Janet Jackson (1986) – It was shocking because she wasn't a little girl any more. It got repeat plays because she met the production team of Jimmy Jam and Terry Lewis and they wrote some great

140

stuff. Favorite songs: "Nasty," "What Have You Done for Me Lately"

No. 329. *Changesonebowie*, David Bowie (1976) – A great starter set for me before I got into Bowie's albums proper. It was much easier for me to get in via the poppier of his music. Favorite songs: "Young Americans," "Golden Years"

No. 328. *Piano Man*, Billy Joel (1973) – Fascinating how the formula here was a template for Joel's best work: Epic opener ("Travelin' Prayer"), hit single ("Piano Man"), lengthy workout piece (both "The Ballad of Billy the Kid" and "Captain Jack"). *The Stranger* had "Movin' Out (Anthony's Song)," two huge singles ("Only the Good Die Young" and "Just the Way You Are," which I don't care whether I ever hear again) and a tour de force workout in "Scenes From an Italian Restaurant." And with *The Nylon Curtain,* he opens with the epic "Allentown," has the big single "Pressure" and the workouts "Scandanavian Skies" and the unsurpassed "Goodnight Saigon." Favorite songs: "Piano Man," "The Ballad of Billy the Kid"

No. 327. *History: America's Greatest Hits*, America (1975) – I can't underestimate the quality and importance of greatest hits albums from my high school years. America was an acoustic-tinged soft pop group who had a couple of hits on each album, albums that were expensive to a kid in junior high. When the best-of albums came along, it showed they had 40 minutes' worth of fantastic music, and they were way more than "A Horse With Name." "Muskrat Love," meanwhile, remains inexcusable. Favorite songs: "Ventura Highway," "Daisy Jane"

No. 326. *Ten*, Pearl Jam (1991) – With each of their subsequent releases, I've come to realize how solid this album is, and how much it's the only thing by them that I need. Though I don't doubt their sincerity and I know millions of people disagree, I found each subsequent album a watered-down version of this both lyrically and musically. These guys and U2 just never connected with me. Favorite songs: "Jeremy," "Even Flow"

No. 325. *Weird Scenes Inside the Goldmine*, The Doors (1972) – I'm disinclined to reveal how much of my teens was spent listening to "When the Music's Over." And "Five to One" was and is, frankly, terrifying. A teenager in a midwest small town was inclined to hide under the bed when

Jim Morrison sang "No one here gets out alive" and "They got the guns but we got the numbers." Favorite songs: "Five to One," "When the Music's Over"

***

No. 324. *A Retrospective*, Linda Ronstadt (1977) – Exactly the compilation I needed from Ronstadt at the time, it gathered up all I needed from her Capitol albums. It made me regret buying *Silk Purse* solely for "Long Long Time," which is a classic breakup song and, according to a contemporary list in *Rolling Stone* magazine, the perfect antidote to the Sex Pistols, and vice versa. Favorite songs: "You're No Good," "Silver Threads and Golden Needles"

When John Lennon was murdered, an older colleague told me he was beginning to understand that the most difficult part about growing older was seeing the demise of your icons - whether by actual physical death, or by their inability to continue doing what they did.

We were both sports writers, so the decay of Willie Mays' talents was on our mind.

Both that co-worker and I have seen too many our icons fall in the 33 years since Lennon's murder. But for some reason, I was truly struck with sadness that Linda Ronstadt has reported her singing career concluded because of Parkinson's disease.

(Just to get this out of the way, while Ronstadt is quoted in the story as saying, "No one can sing with Parkinson's disease. No matter how hard you try," there are therapy singing groups for individuals with the disease.)

Ronstadt has been a lot of different things in her career - down-home farm girl (and isn't *Silk Purse* one of the craziest album covers ever?), rock-n-roller (she was the concert highlight in the film *F.M.*), romance paperback cover, teen queen, chanteuse and whatever the hell she thought she was when she posed for Annie Liebovitz and *Rolling Stone* in 1978 wearing nylons and a red negligee.

A lot of Ronstadt's work fell well outside my ears. I loved the country-rock

142

thing she started with, and I liked the early Peter Asher albums a lot. In spite of myself, and in spite of the painfully shiny polish producer Asher put on *Living in the USA*, I enjoyed that too. When she appeared to laser target the mainstream into the early 1980s, I lost interest, and it went away altogether when she went to lounge and cabaret songs with *What's New*.

But even before that, Ronstadt had established herself as a great cover singer. Whether it was her or Asher or Andrew Gold (or any combination), Ronstadt's covers of previous hits are often perfect. Among her covers that at least match the quality of the originals are "That'll Be the Day," "It's So Easy," "You're No Good," "Silver Threads and Golden Needles," "Will You Love Me Tomorrow," "When Will I Be Loved," "The Tracks of My Tears," "Someone to Lay Down Beside Me," "Blue Bayou," "Back in the U.S.A.," "Ooh Baby Baby," "Just One Look," "Hurt So Bad," "Get Closer" and "I Knew You When."

Those all, by the way, were released in a 10-year period.

And it leaves out the greatest piece of all.

If the only thing Linda Ronstadt had recorded in her life was 1975's "Heat Wave," she would be justifiably remembered.

"It's the singer and not the song that makes the music move along." —
'Join Together,' the Who, 1970

Well, maybe, and maybe not.

One of rock music's eternal mysteries for me is how songs become 'standards.' I don't think too many have been written in the 21st century, but that's OK. Pondering the standards that do exist causes me to get caught in that horrible whirlpool vortex, the one you get into when you try to ponder the size of the universe, of George Lucas' wallet, or why in the hell people bought John Tesh albums.

The two strongest examples of standards in post-1960 popular music are "Blowin in the Wind" and "You Are the Sunshine of My Life."

I don't remember the first time I heard "Blowin in the Wind." It was

143

probably the same way much of the world heard it, by Peter Paul and Mary. Although it could just have easily been any of the number of teenage girls who astonished the 5-year-old me in 1964 by reacting to the folk music boom by actually picking up acoustic guitars and PLAYING THEM IN PUBLIC! Singing and everything.

To this day, I find myself enjoying folk music, often in spite of myself (hello, Jewel). Some of the pieces of the folk music lexicon frustrate me. The lyrics can be predictable. The tone can be wildly optimistic or incredibly sociopathic as the singers share their wonder or their anger with the world, "The Man" or someone who dun them wrong. But I still adore the form if it's done with sincerity. I wonder how much listening to those musicians when I was 5 years old has to do with my appreciation.

One of the first albums I purchased was Bob Dylan's *The Freewheelin' Bob Dylan*. It was the early 70s, I was 12 or 13, and I could have picked any one of Dylan's earlier albums out of the $2.99 bin at a Woolworths in Austin, Minnesota, but I grabbed *Freewheelin'* because it had a lot of songs on it, and I recognized the title "Blowin' in the Wind."

As I listened to all the songs, I started wondering if Dylan was just making up the lyrics as he went along. (I made a similar mistake years later when I'd listen to Frank Zappa's jazz-based pieces and think the band was making everything up as they went along, and just happening to end at the same time.) In both cases, it slowly dawned on me that some thought was going into this — somebody was actually *writing* this stuff.

It's impossible for me to grasp the concept that a man as young as Dylan was writing such timeless lyrics as you find in "Blowin' in the Wind." Astonishing.

The first time I heard "You Are the Sunshine of My Life," I knew Stevie Wonder had found another pop chestnut to cover. After all, this was the guy who pulled old songs out of somewhere and revamped them for a current audience, right? And there was no way anyone writing music at the time could have come up with a bridge as wonderful as you find in that song ("You must have known that I was lonely/Because you came to my rescue …"). Right?

144

But Stevie wrote that song.

Again, a classic. A song anyone can sing, and (within reason) sound good singing. A song so timeless that even though you know someone *wrote* it, maybe the chances are good that the writer was actually channeling it, divinely inspired by whatever divinely inspires songwriters.

Key to both songs is the following point: If you're somewhat able to stay in key, you can sing both of them, and any clown passing by can recognize that it's a great song. (If you're singing the Dylan song, you may not even have to stay in key.) The better the singer, the better the song sounds, but both songs transcend the performer.

So it's the SONG, not the singer.

Whenever I'm with you ...

One of the greatest rock and roll songs ever written is "Heat Wave." Martha & the Vandellas had a hit with the original in 1963, The Who covered it a couple of years later, and in my book, Linda Ronstadt's 1975 version is the definitive one. In fact, all of these versions are so enjoyable, I couldn't imagine the song done poorly.

Until, that is, I listened to a version recorded by a band known as The Half Dozen, found on the otherwise excellent *The Big Hits of Mid-America: The Soma Records Story 1963-1967.* But the glass is half-full: This version does so many things wrong, it points out everything *right* about the others.

Instead of a nice syncopated Motown-style beat with a solid feeling of where the bass is, their version opens sounding tinny and devolves into what sounds like a cocktail party band's first clumsy attempt at playing what the 1964 kids wanted to hear. If you want to know the sound of a song being choked of its soul, listen to this one. And wonder whether drummer is deliberately trying to make listening to this song hurt.

Martha & the Vandellas brought the song to listeners' ears, and remains the one many hear in their heads when the song is mentioned. To me, it's great, but just a baseline for what was to come.

When Electric Light Orchestra's "Roll Over Beethoven" was a hit in 1972, *American Bandstand* played a 'megamix' (long before we knew that word) of the song through the decades — Chuck Berry, the Beatles, and ELO. A friend listening said he found the Beatles' version the weakest.

Many years later, as The Lovely Mrs. Cain and myself waiting patiently to observe a mediocre film at the Rock and Roll Hall of Fame, I found my eyes wandering to the 12- or 15-minute montage playing on the video bank across the way. It covered a basic history of music. Apparently, however, not basic enough. When Aretha Franklin appeared on the screens, one observant fellow in line with us pointed out to those with him, "That must be Janis Joplin."

Each time the video loop showed The Beatles, The Who, The Hollies or The Kinks in their resplendent early- and mid-60s glory, I thought, "You know, if I had to limit myself to one time period for music, this is the one I'd pick." Short and clever pop songs, ringing guitars, a steady beat, harmonies, and especially the occasional clever lyric -- all things I love dearly.

And The Lovely Mrs. Cain has often pointed out how I tend to like earlier, "rougher" versions of bands, before they sand off the rough edges and turn into another cookie cutter outfit. Mrs. Cain's theory is I can hear things in the music that aren't there, like potential and glockenspiels.

Now back to "Heat Wave"

Which is one explanation of how I can find The Who's pale copy of "Heat Wave" enjoyable. I'm hard-pressed to think of a Who song prior to the *Who Are You* album that doesn't excite me. (For crying out loud, I'm usually the one pointing out the songs from *Quadrophenia* and the B-sides from the post-*Tommy* morass to anyone willing to listen.) So maybe this is irrational, but I get a tremendous kick out of hearing four guys who clearly *love* Motown music do their best to mimic it. Maybe better than any of their British peers, but still kinda weak. Lovable, but weak.

And in spite of all that, I *prefer* the Who's version to Martha & the Vandellas'. No apology offered, and none needed. If the most well-known version of a song is your favorite, great. It's also great if you, for example, prefer Bob Dylan's version of "All Along the Watchtower" to Jimi Hendrix's wild reimagining of Dylan's song. We'd disagree, but obviously neither of us is wrong.

Which brings us to Linda Ronstadt's version of "Heat Wave." Or, better put, Linda Ronstadt's and Andrew Gold's. Gold arranged and played all the instruments, and does the lion's share of the backing vocals. And it's his subtle shadings instrumentally that drive the song forward. Ronstadt's version is a song that starts at a crescendo, *then* builds. Gold slyly hides a piano and a string arrangement, and has backing vocals so simultaneously impromptu and tight that I defy you to do anything but tap your foot (or drive 15 miles an hour over the speed limit) when it comes on.

Thread in a perfect guitar solo, one so perfect that I can't imagine the song any other way. And Ronstadt's near-hoarse and infectious "yeah-yeah, yeah-yeah" on the outchorus, and you've got a slice of pop heaven, and the best thing Linda Ronstadt ever recorded. And I've said and will continue to say a lot of nasty things about Linda Ronstadt. I'm just a bad, bad boy. But she's recorded a lot of inspired music as well.

Nothing more inspired than "Heat Wave."

So maybe it *is* the singer …

***

No. 323. *The Slider*, T. Rex (1972) – It wasn't until well after T. Rex frontman Marc Bolan's death that I knew anything other than "Bang a Gong (Get It On)." I blame both my own and Middle America's general reluctance to embrace glam rock. This is a solid one. Favorite songs: "Metal Guru," "Telegram Sam"

No. 322. *Especially for You*, The Smithereens (1986) – A ton of bands came into my life around this time, bringing high expectations that couldn't be fulfilled, even though none of us knew it at the time. This just sounds like a tough and rockin' band. Favorite songs: "Blood and Roses,"

No. 321. *Paul Simon* (1972) – The first time I heard this, I thought the split with Art Garfunkel was going to benefit all of us. The cover photo is a tight facial shot of Simon wearing a hooded parka. It took me a long time to figure that out, and the cover remains, for reasons I can't explain, one of the strangest things I've seen. Favorite songs: "Mother and Child Reunion," "Me and Julio Down by the Schoolyard"

No. 320. *This is The Moody Blues,* The Moody Blues (1974) – A perfect introduction for what the band's albums proper were like. This best-of sampled from their first seven albums. It took the band's signature concept pieces like spoken poems and song suites fully intact in spirit if not in style. By the time I started digging into their catalog up to this album, I was both prepared and pleased. Favorite songs: "Ride My See-Saw," "The Story in Your Eyes"

No. 319. *Care*, Shriekback (1983) – The description I read in a magazine (*Penthouse*, of all places) was intriguing, hinting at something slinky and hypnotic and mysterious. The music was intoxicatingly different. They were far ahead of their time. By the time people were talking to me about "club dance music" in the late 1990s, I would think, "I've heard Shriekback do this already." Favorite songs: "Lined Up," "My Spine (is the Bassline)"

No. 318. *Long Misty Days*, Robin Trower (1976) – More of a transition album from his early "classic" period than I realized at the time. I played it a ton. I didn't like it as much as *Bridge of Sighs* (higher on this list), but I liked it more than *For Earth Below*, my first Trower album. Favorite songs: "Same Rain Falls," "Messin the Blues"

No. 317. *Time and a Word,* Yes (1970) – I still love playing "No Opportunity Needed, No Experience Necessary" and watching the listener's disbelief when the orchestra (and then the guitar) launches into "The Big Country." Their bloated double-LP set *Tales of Topographic Oceans,* with its four dense side-long pieces, was still three years away. This had a pile of different covers. Favorite songs: "Time and a Word," "No Opportunity Needed, No Experience Necessary"

***

No. 316. *Bad Girls*, Donna Summer (1979) – I had to catch up to this one. At the time, I'd lumped it in with much of the disco that I disliked. There's depth here. She'd already revolutionized music with "I Feel Love," and then came this buffet of beautiful vocals. I should have been paying closer attention. Favorite songs: "Dim All the Lights," "Bad Girls"

Donna Summer was voted into the Rock and Roll Hall of Fame posthumously. Just like Dusty Springfield and Frank Zappa. Nicely done, Rock Hall.

A long time ago, I said I thought Madonna should have in her house a statue of Donna Summer, and she should genuflect before it every day and thank the "Queen of Disco" (I guess that's what we're calling her) for giving Madonna a career.

I've long argued Summer's accomplishments as a recording artist lift her above genre and make her worthy of induction to the Rock and Roll Hall of Fame. She was nominated four times before her induction, so I had plenty of time to hone my arguments in defense of her.

Much of disco music really bothered me as the form worked its way into the mainstream in the late 1970s. What I hated was the automation. Disco records listed "BPM" – beats per minute. A great thing for dancers. An awful thing for musicians. In my world, music wasn't meant to be played to a metronome. If the music moved you to pick up the pace or slow it down just a bit, then that was the beauty of playing with other real live players. (One of my favorite 1970s singles, Johnny Rivers' "Blue Suede Shoes," was made better because the band picked up the pace as the song went, and it was almost out of control by the end. Exciting.)

I hated those artificial drum beats, even if they were played by real people.

But then I started reading stories about how Donna Summer was different, and I had to admit hearing some of those songs on the radio was like a curtain parting. You take disco versions of classic R&B songs ("Knock On Wood," "Never Can Say Goodbye") and follow them up with Donna Summer hits, and Summer was clearly in another universe.

Producer Georgio Moroder certainly had his hand in as well. But it was

Summer songs like her version of "Could It Be Magic" and especially the brilliant "I Feel Love" (probably still my favorite song of hers) that made me realize there was some substance there.

I jumped on board. And for a time, I was known in and around my circle of friends as the guy who owned Summer's double-LP *Bad Girls* (which featured another great great great song, "Dim All the Lights") but didn't own *Saturday Night Fever*.

Summer swiftly moved into the role of MTV star, and I suppose "She Works Hard For the Money" is her best-known song.

But when I think about Summer and argue about her importance as an artist, I point to those earlier songs. I know artificial beats are far more common in pop and rock now than they were in the 1970s. (I remember being crestfallen upon learning that the percussion on The Bangles' "Walk Like an Egyptian" was automated, but also figuring maybe that explained why I liked that song less than some of their other stuff.) And I also know that if true soul and passion is present in the recording, it can cover any of what my ear hears as mechanical flaws in that artificial sound. Or even that indeed someone who can work well with the tools can use that annoying inhuman perfection to enhance the song.

That's the thing I learned from Donna Summer's music. It wasn't a manufactured sound that could be purchased out of the box. It was something that helped form the frame and bed for some of the most memorable music in history.

And for those who argue Summer belongs not in the Rock Hall but in the Disco Hall, she was a founding inductee to the Dance Music Hall of Fame in 2004. The Bee Gees are in both. No reason Donna Summer can't be in both. Like Frank Zappa, Dusty Springfield, Miles Davis (Miles Davis is rock and roll and Donna Summer is not?), Don Kirshner, George Harrison and others, Summer fits one thing Hall voters like – she's dead, they didn't recognize her while she was alive, and now's a chance to play makeup.

Truth to tell, though, I don't need Summer in the Hall of Fame to legitimize what her music meant to me. In wrecking some of my preconceptions about what music was and was not, Summer helped set the table for my later acceptance of electronic music and avant garde music, and helped me accept things outside my scope as legitimate as sometimes exciting.

Donna Summer helped set the stage for me appreciating avant garde composer John Cage, who composed a song consisting of silence and wrote a piece in which an assortment of radios are tuned to different frequencies at specific times. If those aren't rock and roll, then nothing is.

***

No. 315. *So Beautiful or So What*, Paul Simon (2011) – I was disappointed by his output for 20 years, then stunned when this album grabbed me and wouldn't let go. There's enough of his old singer-songwriter style so it's still him. But the style experiments like the Broadway show his work with Eno masked inferior songs. This has the content, and enough experimentation to keep it interesting. Favorite songs: "Getting Ready for Christmas Day," "Rewrite"

No. 314. *Simple Dreams*, Linda Ronstadt (1977) – That rarest of commodities, an artist at their peak, straddling almost every style imaginable. She makes Buddy Holly and Warren Zevon her own, and does FM and AM pop-rock along with country. Favorite songs: "It's So Easy," "Poor Poor Pitiful Me"

No. 313. *I'm Everyone I've Ever Loved*, Martin Mull (1977) – He played plenty of songs from this album when he did the *Fernwood 2Night* TV show. He was at his peak here, especially with the filthy song that is only filthy in the listener's imagination. Favorite songs: "The Humming Song," "They Never Met"

No. 312. *Pandemonium Shadow Show*, Nilsson (1967) – Catching up with Harry Nilsson's output was as baffling as his early stuff was varied. This was great. He got fantastic a few years later. "You Can't Do That" is one of my five favorite Beatles covers. Favorite songs: "You Can't Do That," "Cuddly Toy"

No. 311. *Tupelo Honey*, Van Morrison (1971) – The artist himself claims to dislike this album, regarding it as leftovers. Even if so, it's from his strongest period as a writer. Favorite songs: "Wild Night," "Tupelo Honey"

***

No. 310. *Flaming Pie*, Paul McCartney (1997) – McCartney can go years between good albums, and I will keep listening, because he has things like this in him. It was 15 years since he'd done anything I listened to continually. I will listen to "Beautiful Night" any time it is on. Favorite songs: "Beautiful Night," "The Song We Were Singing"

In the 1970s, *Creem* magazine was my *MAD* magazine. *Creem* contained work by people as passionate about music as I was, and had the bonus of being really funny. The letters to the editor section was matched at the time only by *National Lampoon*'s letters to the editor, and both may have been equally fictional.

(A favorite from the time: "If voodoo works, [Journey singer] Steve Perry is in intense pain right now.")

When Blondie emerged, some people seemed to be confused about the group and Debbie Harry, often referring to the singer as "Blondie," infuriating fans who would exclaim "Blondie is a group!" It never seemed that complex to me. But I certainly understood the confusion. I showed a girl I was dating a picture of Led Zeppelin guitar player Jimmy Page, and she said, "Oh, so that's what Led Zeppelin looks like."

A *Creem* letter to the editor in the midst of the Debbie Harry debate asked the logical question: "If Blondie is a group, does that mean Debby Harry is a person?"

Such is the frame for the discussion about Paul McCartney's solo career - a frame of confusion. For me (and I'd dare say for many of us alive when The Beatles were a group and Paul McCartney was a person), everything after *Let It Be* is a solo effort from McCartney. I mean, I love his Wings bandmate Denny Laine. Laine sang one of my favorite songs, "Go Now," when he was with the original Moody Blues.

But I didn't scramble to buy *Band on the Run* because it had a Denny Laine song on it.

152

(I also file all Tom Petty albums in my collection under "P." When smart-alecks say, "What about The Heartbreakers?" I demand they name one Heartbreaker, and when they can't, I explain *that's* why he's under "P." I also suspect that trick wouldn't work so well now -- maybe after four decades, more fans have learned The Heartbreakers.)

Discussing *Time's* suggestion that McCartney's *Chaos and Creation in the Backyard* (2005) was his best solo effort, one friend admitted to not being aware of much of McCartney's solo canon. I listed the albums *Band on the Run, Venus and Mars* and *Wings Over America.* My friend, a little irritated, indicated knowledge of McCartney's *band* work - Wings was a group and McCartney's work with them was different than a solo album.

That left me a little taken aback. I'd never looked at it that way.

***

Sometimes, all it takes is someone with a clear head and a sure sense of what's right to straighten you out on some silly thoughts.

I hoped against hope for a reunion of The Beatles in the 1970s. My reasoning: If you took the best three songs off each solo album they released in the first five years after they split up (John Lennon's last album of original material in the decade came out in late 1974), you'd have a handful of really great records.

(Ones that people like me created by making our own Beatle album mix tapes. Hey, obsessiveness can be its own reward sometimes.)

In 1978, Mark Shipper wrote a faux history of The Beatles, *Paperback Writer.* (The full title was: *Paperback Writer: The Life and Times of the Beatles, the Spurious Chronicle of Their Rise to Stardom, Their Triumphs and Disasters, Plus the Amazing Story of Their Ultimate Reunion.*)

In the hilarious book, Shipper had The Beatles title their first album *We're Gonna Change the Face of Pop Music Forever.* John Lennon and Paul McCartney write a song called "Pneumonia Ceilings" with Bob Dylan and then lose the lyrics. When Lennon claims The Beatles are bigger than Jesus, he actually means they were taller. A collaboration between Lennon,

153

Yoko Ono and Sonny and Cher results in the Plastic Bono Band.

And ultimately, The Beatles reunite in 1979, and put out a terrible album.

Amid all the comedy, Shipper made a great point. It was silly to wait for a reunion. However good it turned out to be, it would never be as great as the reunion in my head (or on my mix tapes).

***

No. 309. *The Hollies' Greatest Hits* (1973) – Another greatest hits album from the 1970s with an absolutely awful cover. But a great way to link up the Graham Nash, Allan Clarke and Terry Sylvester years. And, blessedly, it left off "Jennifer Eccles," a piece of pop piffel that couldn't be much more annoying. Favorite songs: "Long Cool Woman in a Black Dress," "Long Dark Road"

No. 308. *"Toulouse Street,"* The Doobie Brothers (1972) – The prototype of an AM-FM crossover from the era. And they were eclectic enough to cover Seals and Crofts, Sonny Boy Williamson and The Byrds, and write "Listen to the Music," one of the great guitar songs of all time. Favorite songs: "Listen to the Music," "Jesus is Just Alright"

***

No. 307. *Double Fantasy*, John Lennon/Yoko Ono (1980) – He'd gone more than six years (even more of an eternity in the 1970s) with no new studio recordings. This could have been Lennon breaking wind for 30 minutes, and I'd have loved it. It was better than that, and Yoko's songs were solid too. Favorite songs: "(Just Like) Starting Over," "Hard Times Are Over"

I've truly enjoyed listening to the "stripped down" version of John Lennon and Yoko Ono's *Double Fantasy*.

When the album originally came out in 1980, I enjoyed it for three weeks. Then the man was murdered, and it forever tainted *Double Fantasy* for me. Instead of a beginning, it became an epitaph.

When Yoko Ono announced the release of the *Stripped Down* version of the album on close-to-the-30th-anniversary of its original release, I cynically thought, "Well, at least she's giving us something somewhat new instead of repackaging the same half-dozen albums in a new way." (Although she did that, too.) And I was interested, only because I have enough bootleg recordings of Lennon in the studio to suspect anything "new" would at least be interesting once.

I wasn't sure it was something I'd be willing to return to multiple times. But I have.

The loose Lennon found on these recordings is the man at his charming best. (And he didn't always have the charm on during these sessions. I have a bootleg of Lennon from the *Double Fantasy* sessions berating a session guitarist who keeps playing The Beatles' "She's a Woman" during every break.)

And Lennon's sense of humor is present, along with many references to his past, as a Beatle and otherwise. The first thing you hear is Lennon's voice saying, "This one's for Gene and Eddie and Elvis ... and Buddy," referencing 1950s singers Vincent, Cochran, Presley and Holly - a pretty good sign of where Lennon's mind was at the time, and of what was to come in the album.

The spoken part at the end of "Oh Yoko" is dramatically different. We don't hear Lennon asking Ono to not sell a cow and to hang around and talk, but we hear what one imagines would be one side of an end-of-the-day talk between the couple. It's pretty funny, too.

While Lennon sings "Along Came Jones" at the close of "I'm Losing You" (fairly disarming), Beatles references also dot the release. On the "Clean Up Time" outro, Lennon sings, "It's Christmas time, it's that time of year again," a throwback to The Beatles' Christmas fan club recordings.

And most surprisingly, at the start of "Woman," he repeats a mantra he used to keep The Beatles' spirits up in the early days: "Where are we going, fellas?" (The band would respond, "To the top, Johnny!" "What top?" he'd ask. And they'd yell, "To the toppermost of the poppermost, Johnny!")

Elsewhere, production and mix decisions lead to a different listening experience, significantly on "Watching the Wheels," where the piano comes through, and on Ono's "Yes I'm Your Angel," where Lennon's whistles are more prominent than on the original mix.

And maybe that's what makes *Double Fantasy Stripped Down* a listening treat for me, and why it doesn't feel like I'm revisiting Lennon's grave. I've never heard these songs this way before. They're very much alive.

***

No. 306. *Out of the Cradle*, Lindsey Buckingham (1992) – For a stretch, Lindsey Buckingham was infallible to me. This is the first of five albums on this list for him and his version of Fleetwood Mac. His having unique tunings for every song on the album is fantastic. Favorite songs: "Soul Drifter," "Don't Look Down"

No. 305. *Eye of the Zombie,* John Fogerty (1986) – I probably overrate this album since I saw him on this tour. It just seemed he was settling in on a recording routine, and then it was 11 years until another album. Great cover, though. Favorite songs: "Change in the Weather," "Soda Pop"

No. 304. *Buddy Holly Lives*, Buddy Holly (1978) – Vital. This was a horrible-looking package I picked up in the aftermath of the film *The Buddy Holly Story.* The content rises well above the appearance. Favorite songs: "Rave On," "Maybe Baby"

No. 303. *Waka/Jawaka*, Frank Zappa (1972) – Zappa's crazier jazz-based stuff took me longer to get into and appreciate. But "Big Swifty" always fascinated me from first listen, probably because he repeats a pretty simple refrain throughout.. Favorite songs: "Big Swifty," "Your Mouth"

No. 302. *The Future Is Medieval"/'Start the Revolution Without Me,* Kaiser Chiefs (2011) – Released as the former in the UK in 2011 (and my album of the year that year), a few songs were swapped out as it was released in the US a year later as the latter. They are my favorite 21st century band, and this is my favorite album by them. Favorite songs: "Little Shocks," "Starts With Nothing"

No. 301. *The Presidents of the United States of America* (1994) – An antidote to some of the grumpy grunge music of its time, I was taken by their willingness to be completely happy idiots. Favorite songs: "Kitty," "Peaches"

No. 300. *East Side Story*, Squeeze (1981) – By this point, you could fully believe their aspirations to Lennon and McCartney. More serious than their previous album (yet to come on this list), it was their last to have that rare combination of fun and gravitas. Favorite songs: "Tempted," "Messed Around"

No. 299. *A Hard Day's Night,* The Beatles (1964) – And we welcome my favorite group to The Big List, the first of 11 entries. The original British album, not the American film soundtrack. I love the power pop genre, which is particular about what it allows to call power pop. I call this album The Grandfather of Power Pop. Some people won't talk to me as a result. Favorite songs: "Can't Buy Me Love," "I Should Have Known Better"

No. 298. *shock/denial/anger/acceptance*, Rick Springfield (2004) – My public appreciation of this album led to some of the most severe internet backlash I've received, although that was before the internet was ruining people's lives daily. This is the whole package, a cross-section of his crooner-rocker-pop singer skills that never fails to impress even the most skeptical. Favorite songs: "I'll Make You Happy," "Alien Virus"

No. 297. *Bargainville*, Moxy Fruvous (1993) – What a fantastic statement. Complex arrangements on some songs, minimal on others. Intelligent lyrics, and four guys who could sing. A 20th century pop music style sampler. And addictively clever. Favorite songs: "King of Spain," "My Baby Loves a Bunch of Authors"

***

No. 296. *The Hoople*, Mott the Hoople (1974) – I thought this would be the album that broke them through huge. That's how it felt to me. It didn't work out like that. However much you appreciate Ian Hunter, you don't appreciate him enough. Favorite songs: "Born Late '58," "Roll Away the Stone"

I loved Mott the Hoople. Loved them. And they were one of those rare bands - The Jam is another that comes immediately to mind - that dissolved at or near their peak. (I know a band called Mott continued to release albums after Ian Hunter parted ways with them. I choose to ignore them, and you would be wise to do the same thing.)

And I didn't just dig *All the Young Dudes*. In fact, by the time they put out *Mott* in 1973, I was convinced they were one of the great bands of the age. (I thought that with all of the conviction and expertise one can have as a 14-year-old small-town Midwestern kid.)

There weren't a lot of us. In fact, the song I consider their greatest accomplishment is "All the Way From Memphis." Hey, it was good enough for Martin Scorsese to use as the title credits song for *Alice Doesn't Live Here Anymore*.

It's one of those songs that lives up to the promise of that opening piano riff. It starts at 100 mph, and only gets faster when the band kicks in.

But it never charted here.

Mott the Hoople didn't get the revival many of its 1970s peers enjoyed. They were certainly more successful in their homeland of Great Britain than over here.

There are any number of bands I like that I don't expect others to even remember. Mott the Hoople may be the most successful band on that list. They had four top 100 albums in the 1970s. They aren't exactly obscure, but I don't know many people familiar with them.

***

No. 295. *Taking Liberties*, Elvis Costello (1980) – This was his second 20-song album of the year. (The first occupies spot No. 8 on this list.) These outtakes and B-sides were largely new to me. Is it any wonder I considered him the most important artist in the world at this point? Favorite songs: "Getting Mighty Crowded," "Crawling to the U.S.A."

No. 294. *Shazam*, The Move (1970) – Heavier than what they were to become as they turned to quality pop. But it should have been perfect for

FM radio at the time. There's an eight-minute song about being institutionalized, for crying out loud. Favorite songs: "Hello Susie," "Cherry Blossom Clinic Revisited"

No. 293. *Go Insane,* Lindsey Buckingham (1984) – One of the greatest headphone albums on this list. He was able to indulge himself more than he ever had. In many ways, he's most interesting alone than with Fleetwood Mac. Favorite songs: "Go Insane," "Bang the Drum"

No. 292. *Freedom*, Neil Young (1989) – I had given up on him. How much did I adore the guy? This is the first of 10 albums by him on this list, and only one of those 10 was released after this. As comebacks go, this rivals John Fogerty and *Centerfield.* Favorite songs: "Rockin' in the Free World," "Wrecking Ball"

No. 291. *The Cars* (1978) – Is this what New Wave was supposed to sound like? Was this Devo with a huge dollop of pop sugar? All I knew at the time was when you heard The Cars on the radio, you knew it was different than everything else. Favorite songs: "You're All I've Got Tonight," "Bye Bye Love"

No. 290. *Centerfield*, John Fogerty (1985) – The biggest rock and roll comeback since Elvis. Fogerty has been a lot of things before and since, but this was probably the moment I loved him most dearly. Favorite songs: "The Old Man Down the Road," "Centerfield"

***

No. 289. *Exile in Guyville*, Liz Phair (1993) – The claim that this was an answer record to *Exile on Main Street* may be one of rock's great marketing efforts. It still amazes me how much Phair's career puts people on both sides of thrilled and annoyed. I'm there fully, on both sides. Favorite songs: "Flower," "Never Said"

You can argue Madonna is a polarizing figure, but it seems if you're looking from the start of the 21st century, Liz Phair has been the center of more intense discussions by people who care about the artistic and social functions of music more than any other female.

Not surprisingly, issues surrounding both Madonna and Phair focus at least sometimes and at least in part on their sexuality. Both are more pursuers/predators (at least in persona) than passive/victims, and it's probably not a stretch to think their behavior intimidates and influences some people involved in the discussion.

Seriously, do the sexual conquests of well-known male horndogs like Adam Duritz of Counting Crows or John Mayer ever enter discussions of *their* music?

So Phair marked the 15th anniversary of the release of her breakthrough first album, *Exile in Guyville.* The album was re-released, and she played the entire package in concerts. (Something she didn't do when it was released, thanks to well-publicized stage fright she's since overcome.)

The re-release was greeted by fond memories and of assertions that *Exile in Guyville* is her best album and that it's the most overrated indie album ever.

Others are entitled to their opinion, but no one, not even Phair herself, is going to convince me that *Whitechocolatespaceegg*, Phair's 1998-released third album, is not only the best thing she's ever done but also one of the five greatest albums of the 1990s.

I enjoy both *Exile* and Phair's second album, *Whip-Smart.* Both made my top 10 lists the years they came out.

I'm no non-stop Phair apologist, though. Her *Somebody's Miracle* album (2005) bluntly bored me. I couldn't believe it was the same artist I'd once called the best songwriter of the 1990s. And after being one of the oldest people in the audience at a sparsely attended Foellinger Hall show in 2003, Phair became one of those acts I'm glad I saw once, but have no interest in seeing again.

All that said, though, I remain baffled at the sexual politics played out in print and in discussion in Liz Phair's name.

Are we really that afraid of a woman who seems to be tough?

***

No. 288. *At the Ryman*, Emmylou Harris (1992) – Almost every Emmylou Harris show is worthwhile. This one was historic as well. I love the lack of overdubs. Favorite songs: "Walls of Time," "Get Up John"

It meant something, I think, when Emmylou Harris was leading a band with a guy playing honky-tonk-style piano, another guy on a dobro, another playing standup bass and yet another playing a slide electric guitar solo - all in the same song - and I found myself thinking, "How is it that she came to be considered a country singer?"

Sure, Harris crossed genres like a stone skipping across waters. But for decades, Harris has been a presence on the country charts.

I'm not sure I'd define Harris as country. I never have been sure about that. She considers herself country, and she learned a lot of its history from mentor Gram Parsons, about whom she still speaks. (She mentioned Parsons - who died in 1973 - twice during a concert I attended in 2012.) But Harris also did 40s swing (she had a hit with "Mr. Sandman" in 1981), Beatles ("Here There and Everywhere," 1976) and Chuck Berry ("You Never Can Tell," 1977). They all hit the country charts. They all should have crossed over. They all did, in my mind.

If Harris came along today, we'd call her Americana. That's what we call her spiritual children like Gillian Welch (whose "Orphan Girl" Harris recorded on 1995's *Recking Ball*, and it remained on Harris' setlists) and Alison Krauss. (Krass, Harris and Welch sang "Didn't Leave Nobody But the Baby" - the muses' song - together on the soundtrack for *O Brother, Where Art Thou?*)

But Harris is best described is as an original. She follows her own path, whatever she determines it to be. And she's talented enough to drag her audience along with her. Her *All-Music Guide* biography says it well: "With the exception of only Neil Young ... no other mainstream star established a similarly large body of work as consistently iconoclastic, eclectic, or daring."

We paid the extra price for the premium seats and a post-show meet-and-greet. I took along my vinyl copy of 1985's *The Ballad of Sally Rose* (long a favorite), hoping to get it signed. It's a concept album (she called it a "country opera") loosely based on her experiences with Gram Parsons. In the past, she called it a "huge commercial disaster" (although it was far from an artistic disaster). and when she saw me clutching my copy Friday night, she snatched it away, looked up at me and said, "You have one of about seven copies of this that sold."

***

No. 287. *Madman Across the Water,* Elton John (1971) – The only Elton John album like this. The songs are longer, and critics would argue the arrangements are bloated. If they are, they're bloated in the best possible way. Favorite songs: "Levon," "Tiny Dancer"

No. 286. *Dog and Butterfly,* Heart (1978) – I see this as their actual third album, after *Dreamboat Annie* and *Little Queen.* Not many acts start out of the box that strong. Heart did. Favorite songs: "Straight On," "Mistral Wind"

No. 285. *Shaved Fish,* John Lennon (1975) – A greatest hits album we needed, as it collected up some of his early 1970s non-album singles. I still can't forgive whoever is responsible for truncating "Give Peace a Chance." Favorite songs: "Happy Xmas (War Is Over)," "Instant Karma! (We All Shine On)"

No. 284. *In Search of the Lost Chord,* Moody Blues (1968) – What surprised me as I caught up with Moody Blues albums as an adult was the consistency and excellence of the first seven albums. This is my favorite now, and that could change in five years. Favorite songs: "Ride My See-Saw," "Legend of a Mind"

No. 283. *Green River,* Creedence Clearwater Revival (1969) – The toughest thing about any Creedence album is narrowing your 'favorite' songs down to two or three. And this is the first of three of their albums on this list. Favorite songs: "Green River," "The Night Time is the Right Time"

No. 282. *Are You Experienced,* Jimi Hendrix Experience (1967) – It's an album that seems so obvious now that it's almost overwhelming to consider how innovative and important it was in its time. Favorite songs: "Manic

Depression," "Fire"

No. 281. *Broadway the Hard Way*, Frank Zappa (1988) – Featuring Zappa's new songs from his 1988 tour, focusing on politics and social issues. He's blunt. And in retrospect, largely correct. This band was amazing. Favorite songs: "Any Kind of Pain," "Stolen Moments/Murder By Numbers"

No. 280. *Gordon*, Barenaked Ladies (1992) – However much more popular their later work was, I always preferred this one. It struck out of the blue, with each song its own fantastic little symphony. They earned the right to write "Brian Wilson." Favorite songs: "Hello City," "Grade 9"

No. 279. *1962-1966*, The Beatles (1973) – "I'd have just bought the Blue one *(1967-1970)*," my best friend said at the time. I didn't have the words to describe how much I loved The Beatles' early pop songs. They are the foundation of everything I love about music. Favorite songs: "She Loves You," "Can't Buy Me Love"

No. 278. *Portable Life*, Danielle Brisebois (1999) – Maybe the rarest album on the list. Promo copies were printed, but the album was never officially released. What was I supposed to do, erase it from my head? Especially with as good as this is? Favorite songs: "I've Had It," "Stop It Hurts You're Killing Me Don't Stop"

No. 277. *Lumpy Gravy*, Frank Zappa (1967) – There are enough versions of this for me to not remember which one is "official" and which ones have been released or bootlegged. Zappa called this and the surrounding group of albums of one piece. It all sounds good to me. Favorite songs: "Duodenum," "Take Your Clothes Off"

No. 276. *Seduced by Money*, Thieves (1989) – It had too much of each of its elements (pop, rock, country, honky tonk) to gain popular attraction. It was alternative country or Americana before either really existed. Favorite songs: "Everything But My Heart," "When I Wake With Someone New"

No. 275. *That Thing You Do!* (1996) – Just when I thought this kind of music (pure power pop) would never return to the mainstream again, it did with this. As with before, it didn't spark the genre explosion I'd hoped for.

But it left behind a great movie and soundtrack. Favorite songs: "Dance With Me Tonight," "That Thing You Do!"

No. 274 *Synchronicity*, The Police (1983) – Even at their peak, they were innovative and fantastic. Too bad the bass player was so difficult to get along with. Favorite songs: "Synchronicity II," "Murder by Numbers"

No. 273. *Dare to Be Stupid*, "Weird Al" Yankovic (1985) – This was where Yankovic set his bar, where the originals and the style parodies matched or bettered his mocking of previous chart hits. This showed he had some longevity. Favorite songs: "This Is the Life," "One More Minute"

No. 272. *Ogdens' Nut Gone Flake*, Small Faces (1968) – The novelty of the side two "concept" peters out after a few listens. But Steve Marriott knew his way around a tune, and if their catalog had been handled better, they might be a more legendary band. Favorite songs: "Lazy Sunday," "Afterglow of Your Love"

No. 271. *Hotter than July*, Stevie Wonder (1980) – His last home run (although he put out two more solid albums in the next 15 years). Go, now: listen to "Master Blaster" for about an hour. It'll be the best part of your day. My other favorite from the album is my nominee for Wonder's most amazing under-appreciated song. Favorite songs: "Master Blaster (Jammin')," "I Ain't Gonna Stand For It"

No. 270. *Recorded Live*, Ten Years After (1973) – I loved them because an older friend did, and that appreciation never died. They, to me, were the greatest of England's second-level blues bands. Great guitar work, and some of the most mush-mouthed vocals in rock history. Favorite songs: "You Give Me Loving," "I'm Going Home"

No. 269. *Celebrate: The Three Dog Night Story, 1965-1975*, Three Dog Night (1993) – What made this exciting was they used the more vibrant original 45 mixes in enough cases so the slightly more attuned listeners were able to think, "Yeah, that's what that was supposed to sound like." Their later (post-"Shambala") hits were much better than their chart positions indicated. Favorite songs: "Eli's Coming," "Pieces of April"

No. 268. *Oklahoma!* (film soundtrack) (1955) – This dominated the listening experiences of my childhood, before I was allowed to operate the record player. "Out of My Dreams" is one of the most beautiful songs written for musicals in the 20th century. Favorite songs: "The Farmer and the Cowman," "Out of My Dreams"

No. 267. *Stranger in Town*, Bob Seger (1978) – Seger solidified his position by duplicating the *Night Moves* album effort and doing it with better songs. "Old Time Rock and Roll" got the attention of a few people. Favorite songs: "Hollywood Nights," "Still the Same"

***

No. 266. *Sing it Again Rod,* Rod Stewart (1973) – A vital greatest hits package for me, a nascent Stewart fan as a teen. In spite of annoying cross-fading (to better fit in 51 minutes of music). It included (out of order) the second side of the "Every Picture Tells a Story" album, which will show up at No. 17. Also, the album was die-cut into a bizarre drink glass shape, making it pretty much impossible for me to stick the sleeve back in without destroying cardboard. Favorite songs: "Twistin' the Night Away," "(I Know) I'm Losing You"

I've never been ashamed to admit when I've misheard song lyrics. Sometimes, it shows how my mind works. (Overthink things? Me? Never.) And sometimes, it just gives people a reason to chuckle at me. You can be the judge on this one.

I was recently looking at the lyrics to Sam Cooke's "Twistin' the Night Away." Cooke sings "He's movin' with the chicken slacks."

Now, the first time I learned of the song was Rod Stewart's version with Faces. At 13, I had no idea what "chicken slacks" were. I assumed they were pants so tight they gave the appearance of longer legs - the guy looked like a chicken.

Imagine my shock to discover how much I'd complicated this. As apparently everyone who's ever heard the song realizes, Cooke is singing "chick in slacks." Now I could cite any number of reasons for mishearing it, most specifically the anachronism of the word "chick" dropped into a twist song. But it's probably easier to not even try, and just own my mistake and join everyone's laughter at it.

And unlike previous times, I won't even argue that my version is better.

***

No. 265. *My Fair Lady* (Broadway cast) (1956) – This is the one on which I grew up, thanks to my parents' enthusiasm for musicals. When asked my favorite musical, I always say, "For the 'traditional' and 'classic' musicals, it's *Oklahoma!* or *My Fair Lady*, whichever one I've seen most recently."Favorite songs: "I'm an Ordinary Man," "Just You Wait"

No. 264. *Forever Your Girl,* Paula Abdul (1988) – Before she was an insane reality TV judge and star, she sang infectious dance pop and made cool videos. I can still listen to this album without skipping a song. Favorite songs: "Straight Up," "Cold Hearted"

No. 263. *Stray Cats,* Stray Cats (1981) – My peer group was listening to this UK-only release 16 months before the US *Built For Speed,* which was a best-of the two UK albums they'd released. As such, "Rock This Town" was not the revelation to me that it was to those who heard that song first. Favorite songs: "Runaway Boys," "Fishnet Stockings"

***

No. 262. *The Completion Backward Principle*, The Tubes (1981) – Is it OK for bad boys to clean up and have a hit if they're doing it to pay bills? If the songs are this good, it's indeed OK. Favorite songs: "Talk to Ya Later," "Let's Make Some Noise"

Sometimes some of us are too clever for our own good, assigning to some works different purposes and reasons than they originally aspired to.

When interviewing Tubes lead singer Fee Waybill in 2007, I posited my theory about what was behind the band's 1981 album *The Completion Backward Principle.*

I acknowledged that my theory was a mishmash of interviews I'd read with Waybill, my knowledge of the band's raucous early career (which included

166

inspired but bank-breaking live shows, costly because of their extensive staging), listening to the album and making a few assumptions. With his permission, I ran through it.

"After six years of recording for A&M Records, The Tubes are up to their eyeballs in debt and no closer to having a hit record than they were when they started. They part ways with A&M and go to Capitol Records with the most crass of plans: They're going to create a hit record and give the world what it appears to want. This doesn't bother their fans, because the fans want the band to stay together, and if it takes an obvious AM- and FM-ready hits package to do it, that's what they'll do.

"In fact, The Tubes are so serious about becoming a hit-making band that they'll bring in producer David Foster (known at the time for his middle-of-the-road work with Kenny Rogers, Boz Scaggs, Alice Cooper and Earth Wind and Fire) and songwriter and guitar player Steve Lukather (a member of Toto and a studio player for, among others, Olivia Newton-John, Elton John and Hall and Oates). They'll dress up in suits as businessmen on the album and on the videos promoting the album. This will let the fans in on the joke a little more, and maybe give those fans a chance to forgive the band for its appearance in the film *Xanadu*."

"That's an interesting theory," Waybill said after taking a few moments to digest it. "I haven't heard that one before.

"But it's not quite accurate."

Ah, well.

The truth of the story, Waybill said, is less about life as performance art and more about people who loved to play music doing their best to continue to be able to do it for a living.

"We did leave A&M owing them millions," Waybill acknowledged. "They could never collect that, except through record sales. We never received any record royalties. The first four tours we did, we came home in the red. We didn't make any money."

The group went to Capitol Records and received a quick, harsh lesson in the realities of the business as it was 27 years previous.

"They said to us, 'A&M signed you because they thought you were cool.' Which was true. (Label co-owner) Jerry Moss loved us."

But, the Capitol folks pointed out, "They never intended to sell you." Which Waybill found accurate. "They made a half-hearted attempt to sell us on the first two albums," he said of A&M, "and we did the live album (1978's *What Do You Want From Live*) and they tried to push 'White Punks' again (as a single), but that was too controversial."

The result was an ultimatum.

"So before Capitol signed us," Waybill said, "they made it clear we had one shot to get a hit. So we knew that. 'One shot, and you're done. You've got a cult audience that will not support you to the point that you'll have a career.' "

The decision, the group felt, was easy.

"We made a conscious effort to be more commercial," Waybill said. "We had hardcore fans who said, 'Oh, you sold out.' What they didn't understand was we had to, or we wouldn't have had a career. We wanted to reach a lot of people."

Foster was one of the keys.

"We went through a lot of producers before we met David Foster," Waybill said. "Before we met him, we'd come up with great ideas that didn't pay off. We'd have great songs, but something would be missing. David had just gotten done producing 'Boogie Wonderland' for Earth Wind and Fire, and he's a genius.

"He made us work like we'd never worked before, but he'd find the things in the songs to make them work."

The story would be pointless and sad if there wasn't success tied to it. The resulting album, *The Completion Backward Principle,* was the band's first top 40 album, and it set the stage for the follow-up, *Outside Inside,* reaching the top 20. "Talk to Ya Later," the first single from *The Completion Backward Principle,* was a top 10 song. The lead single from *Outside Inside,* "She's a Beauty," got to No. 1.

That wink toward the original fans seemed to work, too. At least for some of them.

"We made a decision to reach out, to go for mass appeal," Waybill said, "but we also wanted to take the piss out of it. We slicked our hair back and put on the gray suits (for the photos and videos with *The Completion Backward Principle*) and parodied ourselves and groups like Journey, those groups who obviously went for the corporate thing and tried to be as commercial as possible."

Rounding off the package were audio clips slotted into the album. The clips were from *Your Hidden Success Mechanism,* a self-help book for salesmen by Stanley Patterson.

"Even though we did make a conscious decision," Waybill said, "we couldn't go all the way with it. We had to parody ourselves, try to make a joke out of it. But we loved those songs."

No joke.

***

No. 261. *Styx II,* Styx (1973) – The early 1970s was a perfect time to blend obvious pop with prog, and Styx was on the cutting edge. And they had a sense of humor. In one song, a man's tryst leads to him about to become a father and contracting an STD at the same time. Ahh, the 70s. Favorite songs: "You Need Love," "You Better Ask"

No. 260. *Xanadu* (1980) – I have defended and will continue defending this album through all mocking. It has its soulless disco elements, certainly. But both Olivia Newton-John and Electric Light Orchestra made sure the pop elements were top-notch, and they do a good job hiding the dreck. Favorite songs:"Don't Walk Away," "Magic"

No. 259. *Greatest Hits*, Cat Stevens (1975) – It was difficult to reconcile this album with the Cat Stevens I was learning about. The songs here come largely from three albums, and mainly being exposed to him through his singles, it would be years before I realized the quality of his discography. Favorite songs: "Sitting," "Oh Very Young"

No. 258. *Blast From Your Past,* Ringo Starr (1975) – Like John Lennon's *Shaved Fish,* this has value in what it collects. "It Don't Come Easy" makes its first appearance on an album, as does "Back Off Boogaloo." Favorite songs: "You're Sixteen," "It Don't Come Easy"

***

No. 257. *Dottie's Charms,* Jill Sobule (2014) – Sobule crafts her brilliant lyrics. Here, she conceived a concept album, and approached others to write the lyrics. Breathtaking, and entertaining. Favorite songs: "Flight," "Wedding Ring"

I love it when artists take risks. It's even better when the risks are huge and the outcome is spectacular.

Jill Sobule, a long-time favorite (you may remember her as the original "I Kissed a Girl" girl), swung for the fences, connected, and delivered a round-tripper. She took three crazy chances with her album *Dottie's Charms*.

1. CONTENT

Sobule had a charm bracelet of unknown origin. She decided to create a concept album based on the charms on the bracelet. A concept album. In 2014.

(Hey, I *love* concept albums. Some of my favorite albums are concept albums, and I always admire the effort even when I'm disappointed or embarrassed by the outcome. But concept albums are so ... so ... 1975.)

2. LYRICS

Sobule is a keen observer of the human condition, clever and empathetic, able to take a stranger's concerns and make them ours. (She's probably the closest we have now to early-1970s, in-his-prime Randy Newman.) Her songs about an exercise addict, Mary Kay LeTourneau, Joey Heatherton and a underage prostitute in Tel Aviv (yes, that's right) - and those are just examples - have made me deeply care about the subjects.

For the lyrics on this album, however, Sobule handed over lyric duties. After sending letters to some of her favorite writers, she sent those agreeable a charm and asked them to write a lyric about the piece.

She took one of her strengths, and turned the responsibilities over. The most surprising thing, though, is what happened next.

3. PRODUCTION AND MUSIC

Sobule hooked up with Mike Viola as producer. This is close to a dream team for me. Viola has recorded his share of fantastic music under both his name and as Candy Butchers, and his production on Mandy Moore's *Amanda Leigh* helped make that my favorite album of 2009. (Sobule's *Pink Pearl* was my favorite in 2000.)

Then she dabbled in styles in which she's never previously recorded, but sound perfectly natural. She manages to stylehop while always remaining Jill Sobule, to which I credit her voice. She is a believable (and yet utterly unbelievable, if you take my meaning) vocal actress. (And that's a compliment.)

"Flight" has crazy rhythmic production (handclaps and a prominent bass), a talk-singing vocal, and sounds flying from out of nowhere, and it's unlike anything she's ever done. It's also the first song from *Dottie's Charms* that I play for people. (Oh, and it has a tear-'em-up guitar solo I find as natural and iconic as her "I Kissed a Girl" solo.)

The breathy vocal on "Statue of Liberty" rounds out a haunting recording whose melody Randy Newman (there he is again) would have been proud to write. "Women of Industry" is a union rallying call that Billy Bragg could have written. (Again, meant as a compliment.)

"O Canada" feels like it could be laid over the base of "On Broadway" and fit perfectly. Even with a sitar solo. But the peak is "Wedding Ring."

A solemn song, Sobule set out musically to mimic early Elton John. She succeeds wildly. "Wedding Ring" could have fit on *Tumbleweed Connection* or *Madman Across the Water*, with a slide steel guitar and an incredible orchestral arrangement.

To top that off, the string break sounds like it could take the place (or be added) of the guitar solo in The Beatles' "Let it Be."

We rarely reward our greatest artists, and with the music market fractured, many of us never even get a chance to hear our greatest artists. I'm glad I've had the chance to follow Sobule's career. She's a pioneer - she crowd-funded an album via contributions from her fan base two years before Kickstarter came into existence. And more than 20 years into that career, she's sill coming up with fresh ideas and taking chances.

In the place where I'm at, we call that kind of stuff "genius."

***

No. 256. *Sgt. Pepper's,* Big Daddy (1992) – Big Daddy rearranged popular 80s songs 50s style. Then they took on The Beatles, in the styles of bebop poets, Little Richard, Johnny Mathis, The Coasters and more. When I first heard the Buddy Holly-styled "A Day in the Life," I burst into tears at the end. Favorite songs: "Being for the Benefit of Mr. Kite," "A Day in the Life"

***

No. 256. *Something/Anything?* Todd Rundgren (1972) – I've always said if he'd continued in this direction, he would have rivaled Elton John as the king of '70s pop. In spite of what Rundgren fans may think, I've never said anything in his career was a mistake. Favorite songs: "Hello It's Me," "Couldn't I Just Tell You"

Todd Rundgren is not in the Rock and Roll Hall of Fame, and should be.

Look, as far as the power pop music lover in me is concerned, Rundgren earned his Hall credentials with his 1972 opus *Something/Anything?* and his production work with XTC (*Skylarking*), Badfinger (*Straight Up*) and The Pursuit of Happiness (*Love Junk*). All fantastic and well worth your time.

The biggest problem with Rundgren's career? He's too talented.

Something/Anything? had three singles, and could have had six or eight. It's just that good.

Rundgren could have kept mining the "I Saw the Light"/"Hello It's Me" style of songwriting, and potentially been an American rival to Elton John on the pop charts for the rest of the 1970s.

But he decided to go in other directions. Thus, he created an odd fan base - some loved his pop music, some loved the progressive rock direction he took, and a select few loved it all. (And if you get around any of those people -- I know a couple of them -- you'll learn quickly that they love a lot of different kinds of music, and they're extremely passionate about all of it.)

Rundgren instead chose to follow his muse wherever it led him: Prog rock, jazz fusion and psychedelia with Utopia (with whom he also recorded some New Wave and an album full of Beatles send-ups); spirituality; one-man recreations of 1966 classics; TV and film composer; a capella; bossa nova; and Internet visionary.

I've seen Rundgren twice in the midst of all of this. Once was on Utopia's *Deface the Music* tour, promoting the previously mentioned Beatles send-up album. It was a great show.

But even better was one of Rundgren's solo shows a couple of years later, where he played guitar, piano, a wall of keyboards, and loaded backing tracks created by himself and Utopia members into a computer that sat onstage. (That was really curious to see, especially in the 1980s.)

The show was in a small theater, in front of a crowd consisting mostly of

Rundgren maniacs (like my brother-in-law, with whom I attended both shows). The most fascinating and frightening moment came as Rundgren, with a guitar strapped on and playing with pre-recorded bass and drums tracks, played "One World." As the final chorus rolled around, the audience as one began clapping and singing along, un-cued.

That's the kind of devotion Rundgren inspires. And the kind of talent he has.

***

No. 254. *Live Rust,* Neil Young (1979) – The conclusion of the decade he truly owned. Of his 10 albums on this list, seven were released in the 1970s. I saw this tour. I miss the "Road-eyes" (a version of Jawas from *Star Wars*) dancing during "Cinnamon Girl." Favorite songs: "Hey Hey, My My (Into the Black)," "Sugar Mountain"

No. 253. *Running with Scissors,* "Weird Al" Yankovic (1999) – He wrote the *Star Wars/*"American Pie" parody before seeing the film. Incredible. And it ends with 11 1/2 minutes of brilliant obnoxiousness in "Albuquerque." Favorite songs: "Albuquerque," "The Saga Begins"

No. 252. *There's a Riot Goin' On,* Sly and the Family Stone (1971) – The necessity of listening to Sly's albums as one piece has become more clear to me over the years. The mood of this is hopefully bleak or bleakly hopeful. It's inspiring. Favorite songs: "Family Affair," "(You Caught Me) Smilin' "

No. 251. *West Side Story* (soundtrack) (1961) – One of the first albums "everybody" owned. The largest seller of the decade. The populace isn't always right. This time they were. Favorite songs: "Jet Song," "America"

No. 250. *Parsley, Sage, Rosemary and Thyme,* Simon and Garfunkel (1966) – They got better than this. But they were already style-hopping and perfecting the forms at which they were best, especially the acoustic folk song. Favorite songs: "Homeward Bound," "A Simple Desultory Philippic (or How I Was Robert McNamara'd into Submission)"

No. 249. *God In Three Persons,* The Residents (1988) – A chilling piece. I don't go back to it often, but when I do, I find it overwhelming. I don't even hear it as tracks, so I'm not listing any favorite songs.

No. 248. *Beggars Banquet,* The Rolling Stones (1968) – The Summer of Love dissolved into this. Good music on both sides. We listeners won. I always considered this the most legitimate and honest of the Stones' styles. Favorite songs: "Sympathy for the Devil," "Doctor Doctor"

No. 247. *Looking On,* The Move (1970) – I didn't find them until 10 years later. By that time, I was plenty prepared for anything weird and out of the ordinary. That they did it so melodically was a bonus. Favorite songs: "Brontosaurus," "What?"

No. 246. *Outlandos d'Amour*, The Police (1978) – By this time, a lot of punk/New Wave seemed to be incorporating reggae rhythms, but these guys mixed in enough pop to make it palatable for those weary of reggae. And we'd never heard a song like "Roxanne." Favorite songs: "Next to You," "Roxanne"

No. 245. *Let It Be,* The Replacements (1984) – The point at which they started to do things just to annoy people coincided with better songs. Even the KISS cover song makes me smile. Favorite songs: "I Will Dare," "Androgynous"

No. 244. *The River & the Thread,* Rosanne Cash (2014) – It's a loose concept album, and contains some of her most solid originals. She does Americana like she invented it. Favorite songs: "A Feather's Not a Bird," "Modern Blue"

No. 243. *Songs for Drella,* Lou Reed and John Cale (1990) – We should all be allowed an elegy this beautiful. The stripped-down sound makes us concentrate on beautiful songs. Too bad these two had such trouble getting along. One of those albums that must be consumed as a whole. Favorite songs: "Work," "I Believe"

No. 242. *Free-for-All,* Ted Nugent (1976) – Nugent's most consistent album, one I can listen to without wanting to skip a track. It's out of control in the best possible way. Favorite songs: "Free-for-All," "I Love You So I Told You a Lie"

No. 241. *Sail Away,* Randy Newman (1972) – Discovering the beauty in this album set me up to love Newman for the rest of my life. It sounded like it might have come out of the 1920s, until you started concentrating on the words. Favorite songs: "Simon Smith and His Amazing Dancing Bear," "God's Song (That's Why I Love Mankind)"

(2012)

With Randy Newman making the cut for nominees for the Rock and Roll Hall of Fame, it's been interesting to observe the reaction.

No one seems to really want to rip Randy Newman, or ask whether what he does is really rock and roll, or criticize his output. It would almost be like blasting the artistic accomplishments of Walt Disney. Newman, thanks to his film scoring work, has become almost a favorite uncle.

After all, this is the guy who wrote "You've Got a Friend in Me," practically a Disney/Pixar theme. He wrote the Oscar-winning "If I Didn't Have You." And he wrote the song that rips my guts out every time I watch *Toy Story 2,* "When She Loved Me." (It's sung in the film by Sarah McLachlan. It's sadder than all of her ASPCA commercials combined, if you can imagine that.) That's the song for which Newman should have won an Oscar.

If I had a vote for the Hall of Fame, Newman would be in. (Even though he's publicly dissed it. So did the Sex Pistols. They belong in, and they are.) Since his first album in 1968, Newman has put out a dozen albums with dozens of fantastic songs, and really only one clunker of an album. (*Born Again* has a couple of great songs, but seems half-finished.)

Why the meager output? Lots of film work, some commercials, a musical – the man has almost continually been working in some form, except for a break to deal with Epstein-Barr disease. He came back with a vengeance a few years into the 21st century, making his public performances almost as common now as they were 30 years ago.

And I know it's easy to dismiss Newman because of his children's films work – even though I'll argue for a long time that those Pixar films are not strictly kid flicks.

The list includes what I consider one of Newman's most phenomenal songs – "Dixie Flyer." After years of what felt like similar arrangements of songs, songs that stood out primarily because of Newman's fantastic way with lyrics, here was a song that matched the sophistication of his words with some truly fantastic music.

There's also a handful of selections from his *Good Old Boys* album, which shines a light on northern-vs.-southern prejudice in a thoughtful way. It's not overstating to point out that listening to this album as a teen was one of the things that helped me realize there are multiple sides to every story. If you decide to pursue it, make sure you get the double-CD re-issue, which includes a disc called *Johnny Cutler's Birthday,* a collection of demos Newman proposed for a new album.

(If you're old enough to have seen the legendary prime time *Saturday Night Live* from Mardi Gras 1977, you've heard three songs from the *Good Old Boys* album.)

And failing that, go grab *Sail Away,* which often makes "500 best albums" lists. It features "Lonely at the Top," a song Newman once said he wrote for Frank Sinatra, and also offered to Barbara Streisand. (Its closing verse: "Listen all you fools out there, go on and love me, I don't care. Oh, it's lonely at the top.")

John Lennon also said he thought Sinatra would have done a great version of his "Nobody Loves You (When You're Down and Out)." ("Nobody loves you when you're old and grey/Nobody needs you when you're upside down/Everybody's hollerin' 'bout their own birthday/Everybody loves you when you're six foot in the ground")

Oh, Old Blue Eyes, what might have been …

***

No. 240. *Destroyer*, Kiss (1976) – It started with what sounded like a radio report about a death, briefly gave us a piece of the live "Rock and Roll All

Nite," and an actual song doesn't start until 90 seconds in. It was so lovably pretentious, and was one more notch in the belt of fantastic bombastic producer Bob Ezrin. I start listening even now, and want to hear it all. Favorite songs: "Detroit Rock City," "Shout It Out Loud"

No. 239. *Ray of Light,* Madonna (1998) – She'd been around almost two decades, and still was leading the way, this time bringing electronica to the mainstream. That it sounds tamer now shows what a breakthrough it was and how deep it went. With this, she earned Rock and Roll Hall of Fame induction. Favorite songs: "Ray of Light," "Skin"

No. 238. *A Different Story,* Deadeye Dick (1994) – If you ignore the *Dumb and Dumber* song (although I do like it), the album may be more palatable. This was a fantastic flash they were doomed to be incapable of matching. The lyrics are clever and solid. Favorite songs: "Like a Shadow," "Perfect Family"

No. 237. *London Calling,* The Clash (1979) – The first Clash album I heard, although I knew the band's name. "Train in Vain" set the hook, and the rest of the album drilled it in. Every man I went to college with loved "Death or Glory." Favorite songs: "Brand New Cadillac," "Train in Vain"

***

No. 236. *Out of the Blue,* Electric Light Orchestra (1977) – They were atop the pop pile at the time, and delivered a double album that was better than it had any right to be. The first side is practically perfect. Favorite songs: "Turn To Stone," "Mr. Blue Sky"

"I don't think I've ever heard any ELO."

My younger friend's admission left me both incredulous and irritated.

Electric Light Orchestra (ELO) is one of the most successful singles chart acts in history. As recently as 2004, they were in Billboard's top 100 of all time, ahead of such contemporaries as Fleetwood Mac, Aerosmith, Styx and ABBA, as well as such all-timers as Chuck Berry, Simon and Garfunkel and Creedence Clearwater Revival.

They never had a number one song. In fact, they had just seven top 10 hits. But their work was always around enough for people to be aware of it, to the point that they held Billboard's record for most top 40 hits without a No. 1.

A 2001 album, "Zoom," was greeted with indifference, although I put it seventh on my top 10 list that year, writing:

"A good release that had no place to go. What's the market for a revived band that last charted 15 years ago? Next to nonexistent, unfortunately. Writer Jeff Lynne hasn't lost his feel for catchy melodies, he's just lost a receptive audience. Too bad."

Somewhere along the line, though, some people remembered Electric Light Orchestra. In 2004, both Volkswagen and the trailer for the film *Eternal Sunshine of the Spotless Mind* used "Mr. Blue Sky" as background music. (One of my more amusing experiences was seeing both spots in one sitting before a feature film.) Monster.com used "Do Ya" in its commercials.

In 2006, a band called L.E.O. (get it? get it?) released an album called *Alpacas Orgling* that might as well have been a new Electric Light Orchestra recording. Lush music, multi-layered and effects-laden vocals, memorable choruses -- L.E.O. had ELO down to an irresistible science. I had it eighth on my year-end list, and called it "the greatest album Electric Light Orchestra ever made (except for *A New World Record*)."

***

No. 235. *Willy and the Poor Boys,* Creedence Clearwater Revival (1969) – There are three Creedence Clearwater Revival albums on this list. They were released in a period of less than 12 months. John Fogerty's consistency and passion remain remarkable. Favorite songs: "Down On the Corner," "Up Around the Bend"

No. 234. *Armed Forces,* Elvis Costello (1979) – He abandoned the breakneck punky garage sound for an Abba-ish pop sheen. The lyrics were more British, and turned even more so later. This is the album I recommend to pop lovers as an introduction to Costello. Favorite songs: "Accidents Will Happen," "Oliver's Army"

179

No. 233. *American Highway Flower,* Dada (1994) – The ease and depth with which the three band members layered the sound hypnotizes me to this day. The guitar work may be simple. It sounds complex. Great variety in song subjects too. Favorite songs: "All I Am," "Feel Me Don't You"

No. 232. *Legend,* Bob Marley and the Wailers (1984) – I didn't appreciate Marley in his prime as much as I do now. When I began to be able to differentiate the songs, I felt sorry for myself. Wish I'd realized his talent when he was alive. Favorite songs: "Is This Love," "Jamming"

No. 231. *Golden Bisquits,* Three Dog Night (1971) – That title remains a painful pun. But the album was a must for young teens (like me) who were tight of cash. That explains the presence of almost every compilation album on this list: I was buying singles and waiting for greatest hits packages. Favorite songs: "Mama Told Me (Not to Come)," "Eli's Coming"

No. 230. *Werewolves and Lollipops,* Patton Oswalt (2007) – The first of two comedy albums on the list. Their very attitudes make Oswalt and Bill Hicks the ultimate rock and rollers. At the peak of his breakthrough period. This is boiled down from a fantastic two-hour set where he displays his love of pop culture and contempt for a pre-packaged world. And it's a howler. Favorite pieces: "America Has Spoken," "At Midnight I Will Kill George Lucas with a Shovel"

***

No. 229. *Chicago V* (1972) – My first lesson in jazz rock. What made it most palatable, though, was "Saturday in the Park," one of my favorite songs ever. I cannot give the song enough accolades. It might be enough to put the album in this position by itself. But there's a whole lot more. Favorite songs: "Saturday in the Park," "Dialogue (Part II)"

(2006)

One interesting thing about growing older is the opportunity to see artistic icons swing through, reborn, again and again.

John Travolta, Frank Sinatra, Johnny Cash, Farrah Fawcett, Robert Downey, Aerosmith, Demi Moore, Elton John, Rob Lowe, Pee Wee

Herman, Sally Field, Burt Reynolds – they've all had some degree of comebacks in my lifetime. (Some welcome, some not so much so.)

Some art finds its way back around in curious fashion. Home video on DVD has made it possible for us to own full series runs of television shows in relatively compact form, giving many the opportunity (for good or ill) to revisit an old favorite show. The music business has mastered the art of selling us the same material over and over, via best-ofs, box sets, and re-mastered re-releases with bonus extra tracks! (Some of this behavior makes the companies putting out DVDs actually look restrained.)

But sucker that I am, if something's attractive, I snap it up, which is why I have six vinyl editions and four compact disc editions of Elvis Costello's *Get Happy!!* album.

So when Rhino Records reissued *Chicago V* with bonus tracks, it almost immediately found its way into my collection.

Chicago V was one of the first albums I bought with my own funds. (The Beatles' "red" and "blue" albums – *1962-1966* and *1967-1970* – being the very first.) More than anything else, I vividly remember the price sticker, a red-and-white one from Musicland (which eventually became Sam Goody's), and the $3.99 sale price.

The band Chicago has had its own series of runs falling in and out of favor since their first album came out in 1969, but when *Chicago V* came out in summer 1972, they were at the top of their game. The first single released from the album remains my favorite Chicago song – "Saturday in the Park." (And it still has one of the best openings of any pop song.)

But for me, at age 13, the key song on the release was "Dialogue (Parts I and II)."

Man, those guys loved their Roman numerals, didn't they?

"Part I" is a conversation between two people, Terry Kath (as the older person, challenging the college student with a series of questions) and Peter Cetera (as the head-in-the-sand youngster).

Honestly, the song feels as though it could have been written yesterday.

181

Kath wonders whether the student is tired of war, tired of seeing starvation, tired of repression. The short-sighted student really doesn't understand what he's being asked.

The key lines are Kath singing "Will you try to change things, use the power that you have, the power of a million new ideas?" and Cetera responding, "What is this power you speak of and the need for things to change? I always thought that everything was fine."

"Part II" is a simple singalong, consisting of just four lines. We can, Chicago tells us, "make it happen," "make it better," "save the children" and, most important, "change the world now."

The idea of this pounded into my head, listening to the song over and over. We really *could* make it happen, make it better, save the children, change the world now.

John Lennon's "Imagine" had been out the year before, and I fell in love with Lennon's idea that you had to picture something becoming a reality before it could actually be a reality. The idealism carried over into my public life, going door-to-door in my little southeastern Minnesota hometown and passing out literature for the individual I was supporting for president.

George McGovern.

Almost 35 years down the line, it's painfully obvious we didn't change the world. Kath couldn't even make it to the 1980s. John Lennon was murdered as 1980 drew to a close.

It's hard for me to determine what's more crushing – the fact that we didn't change the world, or that I was naive enough in 1972 to believe we could.

So I suppose I could be excused for the lump in my throat as I listened to "Dialogue Parts I & II" recently, especially when it got to the part about making it better and saving the children.

The Lovely Mrs. Cain likes to point out that by sponsoring children through charitable organizations, we're saving a few children, one by one. But I remind her that wasn't exactly what I had in mind when I was 13.

But thanks to the re-issue, the music is still there, and maybe it will inspire some 2006 13-year-old who can really make it better, change the world now, in a big way.

***

No. 228. *Jesus Christ Superstar* (1970) – Divisive in its time and always eye-opening. Popular music that was discussed (not simply condemned) from pulpits. And some rocking stuff to boot. Never mind that it unleashed Andrew Lloyd Webber on us. And how cool was is that Jesus was the same guy who sang "Smoke on the Water"? Favorite songs: "Heaven on Their Minds," "Superstar"

Jesus Christ Superstar wasn't the first rock opera. That honor goes to The Pretty Things' 1969 album *S.F. Sorrow,* although The Who likes to make the claim with 1969's *Tommy.* And *Jesus Christ Superstar* creators Andrew Lloyd Webber and Tim Rice conceived, wrote and performed portions of *Joseph and the Amazing Technicolor Dreamcoat* the year before the original *Jesus Christ Superstar* recording was released.

But it was *Jesus Christ Superstar* that caused all the troubles.

(If you're a *Joseph* fan, that's fine, but in terms of controversy, *Joseph* is Justin Bieber and *Jesus Christ Superstar* is Christina Aguilera flubbing the national anthem before the Super Bowl.)

In the months after the album's 1970 release, *Jesus Christ Superstar* couldn't escape the attention of anyone who was awake. Religious figures argued its significance and its place in society. (And sometimes critiqued the music as well. One Catholic newspaper observed in 1971 that "the music often sounds like howls from Hell!")

Released in January 1971, the single of "Superstar" by Murray Head (Judas in the original recording) made it to the top 15. A month later, Helen Reddy's version of "I Don't Know How To Love Him" – her first hit single – also reached the top 15. The recording of the same song by Yvonne Elliman from the original album released as a single in April 1971 made the top 30.

The album spent close to two years on the charts, including three weeks at No. 1 in 1971. Other No. 1 albums that year included George Harrison's *All Things Must Pass,* Janis Joplin's *Pearl, Four Way Street* (Crosby, Stills, Nash and Young), John Lennon's *Imagine, Sticky Fingers* by The Rolling Stones and Carole King's *Tapestry.*

Jesus was running in pretty elite pop culture territory at the time.

But if you were a youngster just trying to enjoy the album and maybe delve a little bit from it, you were assailed from all sides. Since the music was about a religious figure, it couldn't be "cool," one side would argue. Another would insist the music was fantastic. Some said it was distorted, twisting a two-millennia-old story to fit 1970s mores. Some called it preachy.

(Someone standing in a pulpit and accusing a piece of art of being "preachy"? Let's just say the irony didn't escape a tweener in southeastern Minnesota.)

Lost in the controversy over the content and interpretation of *Jesus Christ Superstar* is how important it turned out to be in the musical education of thousands, if not millions, of young listeners at the time of its release and since.

Let's face it: Attracting the interest of a youngster is difficult for opera. It's often sung in a different language, the excellent singers are doing things difficult for the average listener to imagine or replicate, and the stories are sometimes over the heads of the listeners.

But a Bible story? Sung in English by rock singers, led by the lead vocalist for Deep Purple? Now *that* was something youngsters could grasp.

Like *Tommy* a year earlier, *Jesus Christ Superstar* used a number of standard opera motifs, readjusted slightly for rock audiences. Changes in tempo and mood: check. A tragic central figure punished just for being who he is: check. (Tommy may be the most Christlike fictional character created in the history of music. Even moreso than Roger Waters' Pink.) Repeated motifs and callbacks in lyrics, music and tone: check.

The writers may have been young punks with little respect for their elders, but they also clearly had studied the masters of their art.

Jesus Christ Superstar upped the ante with unlikely time signatures as well. While many pop songs are written in 3/4 or 4/4 time, "Heaven on Their Minds" - the first song in "Jesus Christ Superstar" - includes a section in 7/4. "Everything's Alright" is in 5/4.

Decades of listening have continued to allow new treats to be unveiled. When seeing a 1995 touring production starring *Jesus Christ Superstar* film star Ted Neely, the priests at the conclusion of "This Jesus Must Die" emphasized the similarity between the music in the title line and the singing of the name "Figaro" from *The Barber of Seville* was hilarious.

(Yes, that was me laughing on the right side of the balcony. Sorry about that.)

Jesus Christ Superstar was such a fixture in the life of me and many contemporaries that it's strange now to be around people who don't know the work.

This isn't intended as a discussion about how tough we had it listening to *Jesus Christ Superstar* in the early 1970s, or a condemnation of those who don't know the opera or its history. It's more an expression of surprise that something once so controversial seems to have slowly glided into the mainstream.

We never would have guessed.

***

No. 227. *Pretenders*, The Pretenders (1980) – Chrissie Hynde was the first "rock chick" who earned my attention strictly for the music. What a tough band. And no matter what she did in its wake, I remained interested. Favorite songs: "Precious," "Tattooed Love Boys"

No. 226. *Exodus*, Bob Marley and the Wailers (1977) – I had to backtrack for this one. My peers were listening to it while I was finding punk and

New Wave imports. Glad I caught up. Favorite songs: "Three Little Birds," "One Love/People Get Ready"

***

No. 225. *The Beat and the Time,* The Lackloves (2004) – A miracle out of Milwaukee. A power pop band that adapted any number of my favorite styles from the mid-1960s, and did them close to the originals, but still with a twist. I've always described Lackloves as The Beatles had John Lennon decided to take over everything. Favorite songs: "The Radio's Mine," "Nowhere Near Here"

(April 2005)

(As I say elsewhere and often, Mike Jarvis was right. The Zombies' album is the better effort.)

As The Grip Weeds wound down their set Beat Kitchen (I know, I know - Who? Where?), there were about 25 people in the audience. But they were all passionate about what they were hearing.

Earlier that evening, The Lackloves played a set. Their album, *The Beat and the Time,* was No. 2 on my top 20 list the previous year. After the set, I grabbed the band's lead singer and songwriter as he walked by my table, and we began discussing music, both The Lackloves' and others'.

Before long, we were discussing the merits of The Zombies *Odessey & Oracle* and The Beach Boys' *Pet Sounds* (The Zombies have better songs, we agreed, but we agreed to disagree on which was the better album, since I think *Pet Sounds* is one of the greatest heartache pieces of art ever developed), whether he should buy Rick Springfield's latest album (he should), and what defined true rock and roll stage behavior (throwing a bass guitar at a stage light and shattering it may be bad form and may irritate the club's owners, but it *is* rock and roll).

One of the reasons arena shows started to turn me off was the distance from performers. (As much as I'd love to discuss "Cinnamon Girl" and Jimmy Reed with Neil Young, I never will.) At International Pop Overthrow, they carry their equipment past you on the way to the stage. (One of my favorite

International Pop Overthrow memories is sitting at a table with Springfield's The Oohs and listening to Brian Curtis supply the missing harmony line into my left ear as the band onstage played The Monkees' "Pleasant Valley Sunday.")

(2007)

International Pop Overthrow is an annual event in Chicago. (And elsewhere, but the only ones I've been fortunate enough to attend have been in Chicago. Although the year they started in Chicago - 2002 - I had been considering flying to Los Angeles to the place where the event was originally based. The Chicago shows saved me the time and expense of a trip.)

IPO (which is what we "aging hipsters" call the event) is a festival featuring power pop music. (Think The Raspberries' "Go All the Way," Katrina and The Waves' "Walking On Sunshine," Fountains of Wayne's "Stacy's Mom" or even The Beatles' "A Hard Day's Night.")

(Hey! Thanks to *Guardians of the Galaxy,* The Raspberries and "Go All the Way" are suddenly relevant again!)

The two-week festival features close to 150 different acts, each playing 35- to 40-minute sets. One writer called it speed-dating for music fans, and that description is as accurate as it is humorous.

One 2007 show featured two of my favorite acts -- The Lackloves, whose *The Beat and the Time* was No. 2 on my 2004 albums list, and The Handcuffs, whose *Model for a Revolution* was No. 3 in 2006.

The Handcuffs, whom I love, played their debut gig at an IPO show. I blogged about it, and in the comments, singer Chloe F. Orwell, wrote: "The show you saw was our first show. I swear, we're better now." I didn't think she needed the qualification. They put on a good show. I dug it, and so did the audience.

I'd never been real close to the stage for them before, usually because my seat is more comfortable. The first time I'd seen Orwell sing, she was doing so for a band called Big Hello. Orwell and phenomenal drummer Brad Elvis evolved from that effort to The Handcuffs.

187

After seeing that Big Hello show, I wrote that while the band was setting up, I rolled my eyes in frustration and irritation as "somebody's kid sister" wrestled with setting up keyboards. Minutes later, that kid sister stepped in front of the monitors and started belting a song, pinning my ears to somewhere in the back of the room.

A few years later, due to a couple of unexpected happenings, I wound up 10 feet from the stage, and got the full force of The Handcuffs' hammer. Man, were they powerful. It was impossible to take my eyes off Chloe, except to see Brad Elvis play drums.

A few months before that, I stood inches from former Missing Persons and Frank Zappa drummer Terry Bozzio at a soundcheck, trying to figure out how he does what he does. (I couldn't, by the way.) The power from Bozzio's bass drums literally blew my hair back. At that IPO show, Brad Elvis was doing the same thing. (Or maybe it was Chloe's vocals blowing my hair back.) They went seamlessly from one song into the next, and would have been a mind-blower, except I knew how good they were.

At every good show I attend, there's at least one song that jumps out unexpectedly. Via either its placement in the set or the mood of the place or the performance, the song is elevated in my estimation just because of that one performance. (Which may be the best argument in favor of live shows I can some up with.)

In The Handcuffs' show, it was "All Shine On." I think it may have suffered by being between two rocking songs I like even more on their album. But placed about two-thirds of the way through the set, it was a startling departure, and by the time Chloe was singing the a capella piece at the end, I was almost in tears.

But you want to know the weirdest thing? As great as that set was, it wasn't even the best set I saw that night. That's because the Milwaukee-based Lackloves came out and played an unbelievable set.

The Lackloves are a driving force of power pop with guitar-based tunes, tight harmonies and an ability to, my buddy Jeff Markland loved to say, "bring the rawk."

They put on one of the greatest IPO sets I've seen. They'd changed lineups since the previous time, losing a bass player and a guitar player. But they added a bass player who was really busy (and I mean that in a good way). They were playing songs from their upcoming new album, and what it sounded like to me was The Beatles in 1966 if John had said to Paul and Ringo, "OK, you're my backup band now, and Paul, you can sing harmonies once in a while."

A sound which, of course, is right in my wheelhouse.

Then after they played a couple of new songs, they said, "We're going to do some covers." I kind of grimaced a bit, because I like a band in an IPO setting to maybe do one or two covers. To say two songs into the set that you're going to do "some covers" is not a good sign.

And then they played The Zombies' "Tell Her No." Without the important keyboard. As a three-piece. And it was great. I was stunned.

Then they played The Turtles' "Elenore," which has a horn section, which they did not. And they pulled that one off, too.

But what stunned me the most was their encore.

Now understand, bands don't get encores at IPO. It's a tight schedule. This was just the third one I'd seen. And I'd never heard of the first band getting one. But The Lackloves did.

And they did a rock and roll version of "Across the Universe" that was breathtaking. During breaks, guitar player Mike Jarvis dropped in riffs from other Beatles songs, like "I Feel Fine" and "Ticket to Ride" and "Can't Buy Me Love."

It was great.

The best thing about all of it was the performance prompted me to go back to *The Beat and the Time* when I got home. It was every bit as good as I remembered. And the thrilling thing was there was a chance the best is still to come.

A little while after I wrote that, I wrote this about that album that was to come:

Mike Jarvis would likely be just as happy if popular music had stopped evolving in 1966.

Of course, had that been the case, Jarvis' band The Lackloves would be riding high on the charts and his name might be as well-known as John Lennon. (With whom Jarvis shares some nice vocal traits. In fact, I've described The Lackloves in their current form as ""The Beatles in 1966 if John had said to Paul and Ringo, 'OK, you're my backup band now, and Paul, you can sing harmonies once in a while.' ")

As it is, fans of The Lackloves - and I'm one - need to be satisfied with the wonderful music that seems to flow effortlessly from the pen of Jarvis.

The Lackloves are a Milwaukee-based trio whose new album, *Cathedral Square Park* (named after a Milwaukee location), is a lock to land a spot on my list of 2008's best albums.

I'd love to be able to describe this music as: Light entertainment that you'll enjoy if you like 1960s guitar- and vocal-based pop, but it won't change your life. The problem is, I can't look at it that way, because this trio - to a small degree, admittedly, but it's true nevertheless - has, in fact, changed my life.

It goes back to a moment in 2005 when, after The Lackloves played a set at International Pop Overthrow, I happened to see Jarvis passing by and mentioned how much I liked his band.

One thing led to another, and before I knew it, Jarvis and I were sharing adult beverages and arguing about whether The Beach Boys' *Pet Sounds* or The Zombies' *Oddessy and Oracle* was the better album, discussing how we came to discover The Move, and bemoaning how horribly The Small Faces had been treated by American record companies.

It was a geek moment to beat all geek moments.

I wouldn't presume to call Jarvis or his bandmates "friends." We've seen each other two or three times, tops. But I admit to a fondness for these guys as musicians and as people.

That said, it all wouldn't matter if *Cathedral Square Park* were a mediocre album. But the fact is, it's a great album. In a year of a lot of great albums, The Lackloves rise above the pack to my ears with a nice little retro package featuring tributes to The Beatles, the Byrds, The Beach Boys and even Buddy Holly.

It's all done with an unassuming charm, without a hint of irony, and with the most important thing of all - songs.

***

No. 224. *Do You Believe In Magic,* Lovin' Spoonful (1965) – This is their debut. They were right at the top of the pops artistically with this one as well. Major leaguers. Favorite songs: "Do You Believe in Magic," "Did You Ever Have to Make Up Your Mind?"

No. 223. *Kiko*, Los Lobos (1992) – I'm not proud to admit that I considered them just this side of a novelty act before this album. It surprised me more than it should have. It remains classic. Favorite songs: "That Train Don't Stop Here," "Kiko and the Lavender Moon"

No. 222. *Staying Out Late With Beat Rodeo,* Beat Rodeo (1984) – I can allow detractors their complaints: It's lightweight, musically and lyrically; its country lands to much on the side of pop; and it's forgettable. I can see how all of those points would be true for someone else. Not for me. Favorite songs: "Just Friends," "Falling Out of Love"

No. 221. *State of Our Union,* Long Ryders (1985) – "Looking for Lewis and Clark" is one of the greatest album openers ever. The best, most-sincere compliment I can give them is I always found them to be authentic. Favorite songs: "Looking for Lewis and Clark," "State of My Union"

No. 220. *True Blue*, Madonna (1986) – The album that convinced me she was more than a pop tart. There's some seriously diverse styles here. And she co-wrote and co-produced everything. Favorite songs: "True Blue," "La Isla Bonita"

No. 219. *Starting Over,* Raspberries (1974) – They seemed at the time to me to simply be a good singles band. But like Creedence Clearwater Revival, the hits were the cream of a fantastic crop. Favorite songs: "Overnight Sensation (Hit Record)," "Play On"

No. 218. *Dance to the Music,* Sly and the Family Stone (1968) – I probably should flip this with *There's a Riot Going On* (No. 253) when I revise the list. It's one of the most influential soul records of its time. Favorite songs: "Dance to the Music," "Higher"

No. 217. *Laurel Canyon,* Jackie DeShannon (1968) – It might as well be the soundtrack to pre-Charles Manson California. It's a vital snapshot of a place in time. Favorite songs: "Laurel Canyon," "The Weight"

No. 216. *There Goes Rhymin' Simon,* Paul Simon (1973) – This was back when Paul Simon and Stevie Wonder went back and forth winning best album Grammys. This was was varied and solid. Who could have guessed he was just getting started? Favorite songs: "Loves Me Like a Rock," "Kodachrome"

No. 215. *Stand!,* Sly and the Family Stone (1969) – Every song on this album is great. One could argue the title cut is Sly's greatest song. I'd disagree ("If You Want Me To Stay"), but I could help you make your case as well. Favorite songs: "I Want to Take You Higher," "Stand!"

No. 214. *Even in the Quietest Moments...,* Supertramp (1977) – Building toward their ultimate achievement. "Give a Little Bit" is unique, and their most distinctive radio tune. Favorite songs: "Give a Little Bit," "From Now On"

No. 213. *Jackie,* Jackie DeShannon (1972) – This album comes across like she's living in her own world, and blessing us with some music from it. Why has Van Morrison never recorded "Vanilla 'Olay"? Favorite songs: "Vanilla 'Olay," "Only Love Can Break Your Heart"

No. 212. *In City Dreams*, Robin Trower (1977) – The drift toward funk (Rustee Allen joined the band on bass straight from The Family Stone) didn't bother me, because the guitar work was so soulful. He lost me after this one, though. Favorite songs: "Somebody Calling," "Farther On Up the Road"

No. 211. *Songs in the Key of Life,* Stevie Wonder (1976) – It wasn't unexpected that he put out a great album. Look at the roll he was on at the time. But it was audacious that he put out two albums plus a four-cut EP. Not for nothing is it both Elton John's and George Michaels' favorite album. Favorite songs: "I Wish," "As"

No. 210. *Drums and Wires*, XTC (1979) – This was an odd step toward the mainstream based on what they'd done previously. But Colin Moulding sure wrote some sweet palatable songs for this one. Favorite songs: "Ten Feet Tall," "Real by Reel"

No. 209. *Garbage* (1995) – I'm not sure I laughed as hard at anything in 1995 as when I first heard Shirley Manson sing "Pour some misery down on me." It's like the perfect song for nihilism. And you can tap your foot to it. Favorite songs: "Only Happy When It Rains," "Queer"

No. 208. *Like a Prayer,* Madonna (1989) – This was the one. This put her ahead of Michael Jackson and Bruce Springsteen for most artistically significant act of the 1980s. She was doing what she wanted, without apology, and love it or hate it, she demanded attention. I loved it. Favorite songs: "Like a Prayer," "Cherish"

No. 207. *Fulfillingness' First Finale,* Stevie Wonder (1974) – This album is just plain funky. How can you resist "Boogie On Reggae Woman"? It represents the tough side of Wonder for me. Favorite songs: "You Haven't Done Nothin'," "Boogie On Reggae Woman"

No. 206. *Purple Rain*, Prince (1984) – Not his best. That was yet to come. But definitely the one that made you pay attention. I could do without ever again hearing "When Doves Cry," and when you play "Let's Go Crazy," be sure it's the full 7 1/2-minute version. Favorite songs: "I Would Die 4 U," "Let's Go Crazy"

***

No. 205. *Jazz*, Queen (1978) – Even a college roommate regularly waking me from a deep sleep by blasting "Mustapha" couldn't stop me from loving this album. Favorite songs: "Bicycle Race," "Don't Stop Me Now" (2015)

I've long loved Queen's "Don't Stop Me Now." I love it to the point that I was briefly upset to find the TV show *Super Fun Night* had used it as a theme song. The song deserved better.

A friend passed along to me a cartoon creation where inked figures of singer Freddie Mercury acted out the song.

My friend didn't know the song. She just thought it was cool because it was Freddie Mercury. "I like Freddie, and I know you LOVE Freddie, so I had to send it." And she was delighted to listen to the song.

As she listened, I thought, "Yeah, I DO love Freddie. It never occurred to me before, but I do."

There are four Queen albums on The Big List, including this first one. Here's where they rank:

29. *A Night at the Opera* (1975)
183. *Sheer Heart Attack* (1974)
205. *Jazz* (1978)
363. *The Game* (1980)

And there are songs on all the other albums around this period that I love dearly: "Keep Yourself Alive," "Somebody to Love," "Tie Your Mother Down," "Spread Your Wings," "Need Your Loving Tonight," "Sail Away Sweet Sister," "Crazy Little Thing Called Love."

Just keep "Another One Bites the Dust" away from me.

I was a teenager in the closeted 1970s when Freddie Mercury became a public figure. His sexuality never troubled me. Thinking about whether performers were gay was something I didn't spend much time on. I knew if I admitted to liking lightweight pop acts, my own sexuality would be questioned. But I also knew that would happen if I wore purple socks on

Thursday. (Yeah, that was a thing at my school.)

How did I battle it? I didn't admit to liking some Partridge Family songs, and kept my passion for the Raspberries pretty close to my vest. But I also made a point to wear purple on as many Thursdays as possible.

As much as they wanted us to, I don't think many boys my age made Queen rock royalty. I remember being stunned at one point when a close friend started trashing "Keep Yourself Alive," which was my favorite Queen song for a long time, and if not for how much I adore "Killer Queen," it might still be. (I would never have realized what Moet & Chandon was without it. Although that's not the only reason it's probably my favorite Queen song. But then again, there's " '39" …)

If we were talking "heavy" bands, Led Zeppelin and Pink Floyd were the huge acts in my teen years. Deep Purple and KISS made their runs, early and late in the 70s. Aerosmith was a band we could actually see in concert.

But Queen didn't fit as "heavy." Too many ballads, too many sweet songs, and what the hell was "Bohemian Rhapsody," anyway? And then things got far less interesting. I was confused by *Hot Space,* and annoyed enough with *The Works* that I gave up on them. Which made their Live Aid appearance far more interesting. Were people really still big fans of Queen? Apparently so.

(And everybody who heard fascism and Nazism in the footstomps of "We Will Rock You" flipped out as soon as they saw thousands of people with their arms over their heads, clapping in rhythm.)

But yeah, I think I did and do love Freddie. I think Freddie is why I loved especially Mika's first album, and his first song. (I'd share "Grace Kelly" with friends who dug Queen, and their reaction was mixed. I was just amazed by the voice, and appreciative of Mika name-checking Mercury.)

I'd like to think Mercury would smile at that.

As my friend listened to "Don't Stop Me Now," she suddenly said, "This is where 'Wicked' got the idea for its songs." I laughed. That may or may not have been true. But I also couldn't help but think of Mika's "Popular Song," which lifted directly (and credited properly) from "Popular" from "Wicked."

Freddie Mercury's been dead for 24 years. I am now 11 years older than Mercury when he died. But he still rules his area of pop culture.

***

No. 204. *Dusty in Memphis*, Dusty Springfield (1969) – One of the greatest soul albums ever, and easily her best. Even at that, I probably have this a shade too high. Favorite songs: "Son of a Preacher Man," "Just One Smile"

No. 203. *Greatest Hits*, Sly and the Family Stone (1970) – Shows exactly how perfect they were for three years. The hits just kept on comin'. Favorite songs: "Hot Fun in the Summertime," "Everybody Is a Star"

No. 202. *Bridge over Troubled Water,* Simon and Garfunkel (1970) – Deservedly one of the best-selling albums ever. And it's not even my favorite by them. Favorite songs: "Cecilia," "The Boxer"

No. 201. *Diamonds and Pearls*, Prince (1991) – From a time when he could do no wrong in my book. His early 1990s were an amazing creative resurgence. Favorite songs: "Diamonds and Pearls," "Gett Off"

No. 200. *Deluxe,* Better Than Ezra (1993) – They were unjustly grouped with grunge-wannabes. There are many more styles on display here. Favorite songs: "In the Blood," "Coyote"

No. 199. *Music From Big Pink*, The Band (1968) – It still seems to have come from another planet out of nowhere. Every time I listen to it, I think, "No wonder The Beatles loved these guys." Favorite songs: "I Shall Be Released," "The Weight," "This Wheel's On Fire"

No. 198. *II*, Bachman-Turner Overdrive (1973) – They were one of those 1970s bands who had radio hits, but the albums were equally important. This was their peak for albums, but there were still plenty of hits coming. Favorite songs: "Let It Ride," "Give It Time," "Takin' Care of Business"

***

No. 197. *The Chicago Transit Authority* (1969) – This version of the band would not have recognized the band they became. Which is neither praise nor criticism. Favorite songs: "Beginnings," "Questions 67 and 68," "Does Anybody Really Know What Time It Is?"

(This was written in 2011. Their Rock n Roll Hall of Fame dispute -- Peter Cetera refused to appear -- and the blistering later-period-band-sanctioned documentary *Now More Than Ever* made it pretty clear little had changed.)

It's always sad and a little troubling when rock bands divide into camps. Those attending Chicago's shows will get a clear look at that.

Chicago has been around for years, releasing its first album in 1969. Four of the seven founding members have been constant since — Robert Lamm, James Pankow, Lee Loughnane and Walter Parazaider. Drummer Danny Seraphine was dismissed by the group in 1990 in a contentious debate. Guitar player Terry Kath died tragically from a self-inflicted gunshot wound during some drunken play in 1978. And singer and bass player Peter Cetera — whose voice is closely identified with the band even to this day — left contentiously in 1985.

Cetera is gone, but his songs are not. Looking over current Chicago concert set lists, about half of the songs performed will have Cetera's prints all over them, as a singer, a songwriter or both.

That's fine. Plenty of groups tour with a good part of the creative force behind that band not present. But it's the amount of Cetera material — and the things the founding members of the band snipe back and forth at one another — that's troubling.

Cetera's voice was present from the beginning with Chicago (or Chicago Transit Authority, the name under which the band released its first album). He sang "25 or 6 to 4" and "Questions 67 and 68" on that tremendous, sprawling double-album debut. He shared the lead vocal on two of the band's greatest early-period singles, "Dialogue" and "Saturday in the Park." (All of those songs were written by Robert Lamm. This is important, considering what happened later.) He sang "Just You N Me," "(I've Been) Searchin' So Long," "Call on Me" and "Old Days." He co-wrote and sang "Feelin Stronger Every Day" and wrote and sang "Wishing You Were Here."

And that's kind of where the trouble begins. A number of huge subsequent Chicago hits were sung by Cetera. "Baby, What a Big Surprise," "Hard to Say I'm Sorry," "Hard Habit to Break," "You're the Inspiration" and the big one: "If You Leave Me Now."

"If You Leave Me Now" may be the most well-known Chicago song to a new generation, thanks to its use on "South Park" and in commercials. But it was a last-minute addition to the album. Some members of the band were dissatisfied with the softer, ballad-heavy direction. In an interview in the *Classic Rock AOR* magazine, Lamm said, "Some of us resented ("If You Leave Me Now") because it wasn't cool."

Producer David Foster took the template provided by the success of the song and ran it into the ground. He used Cetera's smooth, radio-friendly voice as his lead soldier, and Chicago became the ballads band.

Gone were the extended jazzy instrumental segments. Gone was much of the classical music-based sophistication. And gone was the guitar of Terry Kath, which made a song like "(I've Been) Searchin' So Long" more a rocker with its gorgeous solo on the outro.

But Kath left by his own hand. He accidentally killed himself in 1978, playing with a gun he didn't believe was loaded. His death and Cetera's influence were practically concurrent events. Lamm said, "Terry would have opposed the balladic direction that we were sucked into. He'd put a stop to that, or he'd have left the band."

Cetera, who has rarely spoken about his time in Chicago since his 1985 departure for an initially wildly successful solo career, takes his share of shots at his former bandmates in that same *Classic Rock AOR* magazine. Cetera says he stepped up his role because of other members' drug and alcohol abuse. Loughnane responds, "… when it comes to derogatory comments about his association with Chicago, may we suggest that (Cetera) have a Coke and a smile and shut the (expletive) up."

Yeah. Ugly.

And that would be that, except Chicago still seems pleased to cash the checks off Cetera's back. They hate those ballads, but people going to those shows will hear them all, especially the later-period hits written and sung by Cetera: "Baby, What a Big Surprise," "Hard to Say I'm Sorry," "You're the Inspiration." And especially "If You Leave Me Now."

The song is the focus of a promotion of Chicago's website. Fans can bid on a package that includes a meet and greet, two "premium" tickets, backstage passes and the opportunity sing "If You Leave Me Now" on-stage with the band. The auction prices begin at $500. The resulting funds go to the American Cancer Society.

So it's a good thing the song is there. The band can at least be more magnanimous with it than they're willing to be with one another.

***

No. 196. *Llamalamp*, The Oohs (2006) – I'm continually amazed that this was recorded within an hour's drive of my house. One of the greatest power pop albums ever. Favorite songs: "Pretty," "Get It Straight," "That's What She Said"

No. 195. *Big Money Item*, Greenberry Woods (1995) – I love this even more as I listen again and realize it's not only great music, but amazing style parodies as well. Favorite songs: "Back Seat Driver," "Baby You Can't Get It Back," "Nice Girl"

***

No. 194. *We're An American Band*, Grand Funk (1973) – By this time, I was ignoring the grief I'd get for liking them, and just digging how much I was liking each album more than the previous one. That original copies were pressed in gold vinyl was fantastic. Favorite songs: "We're an American Band," "The Railroad," "Loneliest Rider"

(2003)

Grand Funk Railroad is touring without Mark Farner.

It's a sad story, another of those surreal moments that somehow crushes a piece of idealism one didn't even know still existed. More than many of their peers, Grand Funk often had a 'Three Musketeers'-like aura, and imagining two carrying on without a third - especially without Farner - was

199

an unlikely as Creedence Clearwater Revival going on without its songwriter and lead singer, John Fogerty.

But guess what? Creedence Clearwater Revisited tours even now, two members of the original band with a sound-alike standing in for Fogerty.

And the fashion in which the break continues to be handled is disconcerting. Grand Funk's official Web site has no mention of Farner, and its shows are disappointing fans around the country who see five people on stage, but none of them is the guy who sang ""Closer to Home.""

Farner, who lost a court case trying to prevent use of the Grank Funk Railroad name, seems disappointed but resigned to the chicanery of his former bandmates. (Although trotting out a cliche like ""You give a thief enough rope and he'll hang himself"" certainly means Farner is stinging a little more than he's willing to let on.)

But Farner is resolute with his pride that his shows are exactly what they're described as being - the guy who wrote most of the songs singing them. He laughs when he points out three men replaced him in the touring Grand Funk (including a former Kiss guitar player and, as Farner gleefully quoted a Florida newspaper review, "a guy who replaced a guy who replaced a guy who replaced the original singer for .38 Special").

Grand Funk without Mark Farner? That's just not right.

***

No. 193. *Book of Hours,* Green Pajamas (1987) – A few years later, when Seattle became a national musical hotbed, I was convinced someone would find these guys. They're practically baroque, and practically perfect. Favorite songs: "Ain't So Bad," "Paula," "Men in Your Life"

No. 192. *The Rise and Fall of Ziggy Stardust,* David Bowie (1972) – You don't need to understand the concept at all when "Suffragette City" grabs you by the ears and pulls you in. Favorite songs: "Hang On to Yourself," "Ziggy Stardust," "Suffragette City"

No. 191. *Who Are You,* The Who (1978) – I listened to a lot of this through tears, mourning Keith Moon. Pete Townshend's personal battles are well on display, but didn't affect his adventurousness. Favorite songs: "New Song," "Had Enough," "Who Are You"

(2015)

The tap dance that Who fans to in attempts to justify their beliefs that what's left of the band is an ongoing vital concern, as important as it's ever been?

Laughable. And it continues to be.

Nevertheless, I'm reluctant to give any kind of take on the band's plans for a 2015 tour. It's just not worth it to endure the wrath of a fan who wasn't alive the last time Pete Townshend or Roger Daltrey - the two surviving members of the group - last put out any music that mattered. The fans who still are able to differentiate between a "farewell" tour and a "one last time" tour and a *Quadrophenia* tour and a "new mediocre album" tour and ... Those fans' wrath is a loud, steadfast and angry thing.

But it doesn't matter that it's been approaching four decades since there's been a Who album anyone should be encouraged to hear. Which isn't a criticism. The Rolling Stones, Eagles, The Beach Boys - they pack stadiums and arenas playing their vintage hits. If there are fans who want that, good for them. Here's your opportunity.

But in discussing the realities of the tour, Daltrey sounds a lot like Rolling Stones guitar player Keith Richards, who essentially has said the band is doing its job by playing songs the paying fans want to hear.

You won't find a dozen fans who love The Who more than I do, especially if you stop after Keith Moon's 1978 death. But I'm not interested in seeing the band ever again. I saw them with Kenney Jones as their drummer, and I was somewhat disappointed. I know it would be even more so now. For me, the beauty of what Pete Townshend does as a writer and performer is the breathtaking nature of taking chances. A formal rock concert setting these days is no place to take chances. There are lighting cues and curfews and the next week of shows to worry about. Everything has to be planned tightly. The show starts at 7:05, and you're on your way home to the babysitter by 10.

Keith Moon would never have stood for the kind of regimented scheduled required today. Keith Richards never used to.

"... most people that want to come to a show want to hear what they grew up with," Daltrey told *Rolling Stone.* "We will always sell more tickets if we play the hits. ... It's easy for fans to stick their heads in the sand and not understand the economics of touring. ... There might be 40,000 total people in America who want to hear 'Slip Kid.' That won't be enough to put us on the road."

And that is both what will convince thousands to part with their cash to see The Who, and what will keep me at home. It seems to me everybody will be a lot happier this way.

(Predictably enough, when this was published, the angry Who fans descended like starving buzzards. One decided I was not a true fan because I originally wrote Keith Moon died in 1977. That was lazy, but memorization of dates is not a measure of fandom. More laughably, I was castigated because true fans call the *Who Are You* album *WAY.* I responded I had never seen that acronym before, and if somebody thought that won them the Biggest Fan title, congratulations. The guy still never disclosed his age to me. Although there was a suspiciously familiar contemptuous tone. I thought it might have been 16-year-old me time traveling and being a smartass.)

***

No. 190. *New York,* Lou Reed (1989) – I've long suspected this album means so much to me because it was the first one that sunk in after a huge life event. Reed was real, and for the first time, I felt like I was living a real with him. Favorite songs: "There Is No Time," "Busload of Faith," "Dirty Blvd."

***

No. 189. *Burn*, Deep Purple (1974) – Even with a new singer and bass player, the juggernaut continued with what ended up being one of their greatest records. At this time, I was convinced Ritchie Blackmore was infallible. Favorite songs: "Burn," "You Fool No One," "Lay Down, Stay Down"

"We're as valid as anything by Beethoven."

Deep Purple keyboard player and founding member Jon Lord said that in the 1970s. Lord retired from Deep Purple in 2002.

Lord was the centerpiece of Deep Purple classic rock classics like "Highway Star" and "Lazy," and was responsible for probably my favorite rock keyboard solo, in the song "Smooth Dancer." I'm still not sure what I like about it, but it makes me want to get up and dance around the office.

Lord was unique among rock keyboard players by running a Hammond organ through a Marshall stack of amplifiers. It gave him a distinct sound, and allowed him to compete with guitar player Richie Blackmore. (There was a time when Deep Purple was in the Guiness Book of World Records as the world's loudest band. No, that title wasn't just a "This Is Spinal Tap" joke. It actually happened.)

Lord said the difference between him and many keyboard players was he did not approach the Hammond like a piano, but like an organ, and that helped form his distinct sound. I don't know enough about keyboard playing to speak to that. I do know I saw Deep Purple a couple of times, and even at the time of the "Mark II reunion" – the 1984 reunion of the "classic" (i.e. *Machine Head*) Purple lineup – Lord would literally rock his Hammond standard when soloing. I always wondered how the heck he kept it under control enough to not have it crash to the ground.

Lord was plenty diverse in his work. He was behind the Deep Purple *Concerto for Group and Orchestra* album recorded in 1969 with The Royal Philharmonic, and he continued to work in the "classical" field in recent years, along with other styles and artists.

But for me, Lord was and always will be the thing that made Deep Purple different from its 1970s metal peers like Led Zeppelin and Black Sabbath.

He had style, and class, and a sound and technique all his own.

***

No. 188. *Tapestry*, Carole King (1971) – I've finally settled on love in my love-hate relationship with this album. King wrote great songs. It wasn't her fault our parents loved them too (back when that was a much bigger deal than it is now). Favorite songs: "I Feel the Earth Move," "So Far Away," "It's Too Late"

No. 187. *Sign o the Times,* Prince (1987) – After everything he'd done in the previous five years, he decides to throw out another double album? That was top-to-bottom solid? Amazing. I was at a club where "The Cross" was played, pre-release. The crowd listened in silence for five minutes, then exploded in applause. For a record. Favorite songs: "U Got the Look," "Starfish and Coffee," "I Could Never Take the Place of Your Man"

***

No. 186. *Little Queen,* Heart (1977) – This was the first time I was in on the ground floor of a band, and they started great and stayed great. Because it just had the one hit single ("Barracuda"), this one seemed a little more exotic. The renaissance fair cover photo helped too. Favorite songs: "Love Alive," "Kick it Out," "Say Hello"

A box set of a band's recordings should, assuming you're a fan, easily remind you of why you're a fan.

But in that rare, special instance - like for me with *Strange Euphoria,* a three-CD 51-cut collection issued by Heart - I'm reminded of what I don't like about the band as well.

To explain this, I've got to go back in time and discuss how Heart was perceived in the late 1970s. Because it's going to sound ridiculous.

There was a time when a number of us music fans considered Heart to be the logical heir to Led Zeppelin.

It feels comical just to type it now, but it's true. Just as there was a time when choices for pop supremacy came down to Dave Clark Five or The

204

Beatles. Yeah, it's silly now, but there was a time when it was a legitimate question.

In 1978, you could make the case that Heart was ahead of Led Zeppelin at its own game. Now, this requires ignoring the release of the album *Magazine*, essentially a collection of demos, rough mixes and live stuff that the group didn't want out. It was released by the spiteful independent label that released Heart's first album, the great *Dreamboat Annie*. ("This is like a greatest hits album all by itself, isn't it?" my young brother-in-law said when he first heard the album all the way through, and he was pretty much correct.)

Heart followed *Dreamboat Annie* with *Little Queen*, perfecting the template of the first album with their most solid collection of songs, from the sizzling single "Barracuda" to the beautiful "Say Hello" to the classic rocker "Kick It Out" (which songwriter/singer Ann Wilson was reluctant to put on the album, she revealed). And they followed that up with *Dog and Butterfly,* which felt majestic. It had the "Straight On" single, the concert pleaser "Cook With Fire," and the second side was bookmarked by the title cut and the powerful "Mistral Wind," which I've recently read referred to as the band's "Stairway to Heaven," which really isn't far from the mark.

And it was at this time - the end of 1979 - that I saw the band in concert. When they encored with Led Zeppelin's "Rock and Roll," while we might have laughed at some bands trying it, we accepted it from Heart. It was like the torch was being passed, or at least was being carried at a time when we weren't sure what the heck Led Zeppelin was going to do next.

But in retrospect, the cracks were apparent. The opening act, Player, played exactly 45 minutes. After a break of exactly 30 minutes, Heart played for exactly 90. And we all went home. It may have been coincidence. It may also have been a case of extreme clock-watching. And when I later heard that Heart had disintegrated as a unit to the point where members were put on salary and fined for not being on time and other disruptive behavior, I know what I thought was probably going on that night in 1979.

Bebe Le Strange, the next Heart album, was just weird. It didn't have the combination of acoustic and electric charm as its predecessors. The band seemed to be carving a new direction, and it wasn't one those of us who viewed them as a female Led Zeppelin wanted to follow. They became an afterthought.

Until the MTV explosion, and Nancy Wilson's bustiers. Now, we all loved the bustiers, but the music had deteriorated to the point where we'd watch the video with the sound off. The screechy arena rock of "Never" and especially "Alone" made the Zeppelin-type Welsh-folk of "Dream of the Archer" feel like another world away.

And I'd check in with Heart every once in a while despite it all. As their box set shows, they still could write a great song. The version of "Never" here is a live, semi-unplugged version with Led Zeppelin's John Paul Jones on mandolin. And it's tasty.

In 2004, the Wilson sisters put out an album called *Jupiters Darling,* which would have appealed to fans of their late 70s style. But too much time had passed, and independent recording companies being what they are, the label folded owing the band thousands of dollars.

Strange Euphoria does a superb job in a role I never expected - at the same time, it reminds me what I loved about this band and the potential I saw in what they were doing, and the tremendous disappointment I felt when they had their second wave of success playing what I thought were inferior songs in style and substance, for an audience that never would have appreciated what the band was when it started.

***

No. 185. *Greendale*, Neil Young (2003) – At the time, few people, especially Neil Young fans, had much interest in a concept album about ecology. And to many, these songs all sounded the same. If true, that was still fine by me. And the lyrics were what mattered most. Favorite songs: "Double E," "Grandpa's Interview," "Sun Green"

***

No. 184. *White Light/White Heat,* Velvet Underground (1968) – Loud, fast and experimental, and maybe even sometimes unlistenable for some. Scary

206

audio experiments. And instantly memorable. Favorite songs: "The Gift," "White Light/White Heat," "Sister Ray"

I knew The Velvet Underground before I knew *of* The Velvet Underground.

Which is not to say I knew of The Velvet Underground before I heard The Velvet Underground. Although that's also true.

I have no idea why it came back into my head, but I found myself thinking of the song "The Gift" on the first Velvet Underground album. To call it a "song" is a bit of a misnomer. It's a spoken-word piece with music. The band recorded one of its jams, and member John Cale read a story composed in college by fellow band member Lou Reed.

The version presented above is a disservice to the listener. The original is a true two-channel stereo production. The music comes from one channel, and the story comes out of the other speaker.

I don't remember when I first heard the song, but I know it was after 1988, because I bought my copy of *White Light/White Heat* at a store in Illinois. Of course, I'd heard plenty *about* the Velvets by then, and to my surprise, I was aware of a couple of their songs ("Femme Fatale" and "Venus In Furs," from their first album, both of which I presumably heard in films).

(*White Light/White Heat* is not an easy listen, particularly when you don't know what you're getting into. Much of the album is a guitar-bass-viola-primitive drum drone, keeping in the spirit of composer Reed's assertion that "One chord is great, two chords are OK, and three chords are jazz." By the early 90s, I was a big fan of the album and the band, because I'd found my way in. Visiting my college roommate at his house, I talked him into removing their first album from his "trade" pile by playing "Femme Fatale" and "Venus In Furs" and talking him through them.)

When "The Gift" came on, I concentrated on the story, and thought, "Wait a minute - I know this." It turned out I'd read the story told in the song in either my high school freshman or sophomore literature class. (I remember realizing earlier - but again, after the fact - the same book contained a chapter from Kurt Vonnegut's *Cat's Cradle.* I vividly remember reading the chapter when I read the full Vonnegut book and thinking "I know this ...")

However you want to slice it (no pun intended, for those who already know the story of "The Gift"), that was a pretty hip literature book to be throwing at young teens in the 1970s. And try as I might - and normally I'm pretty good at this - I couldn't find any trace of the book's title or other contents anywhere on the Web.

***

No. 183. *Sheer Heart Attack,* Queen (1974) – The album that put them on notice for me. At their best, they regularly style-hopped the way they do here. Favorite songs: "Brighton Rock," "Killer Queen," "Now I'm Here"

No. 182. *Surrealistic Pillow*, Jefferson Airplane (1967) – I confess my early prejudices against hippie folk music had me coming to this late. To my shame and regret. They were really distinct talents. Favorite songs: "Somebody to Love," "Today," "White Rabbit"

No. 181. *The Thorns* (2003) – A brief (unfortunately, their sole album) return to the lyrical harmonies and laid-back sounds of California, early 1970s. Gorgeous. Favorite songs: "No Blue Sky," "Runaway Feeling," "Blue"

No. 180. *You Will Go to the Moon,* Moxy Fruvous (1997) – The first thing I heard by them was a distorted banjo mangling the riff to "Last Train to Clarksville." Four years later, I'd seen them perform live in excess of two dozen times. Favorite songs: "Your New Boyfriend," "Kick in the Ass," "Michigan Militia"

No. 179. *Quadrophenia,* The Who (1973) – I didn't know I was supposed to be disappointed in this. It was dense and English, but I felt like if you knew anything about the band (and I did), this wasn't that difficult to grasp. Favorite songs: "The Real Me," "Love Reign O'er Me," "5:15"

No. 178. *Sladest*, Slade (1973) – If this were the first Slade album you heard, you couldn't be blamed for buying into the hype they earned as England's biggest band at the time. Their later MTV renaissance was embarrassing to those bragging up this version of their music.

Favorite songs: "Gudbuy T'Jane," "Skweeze Me Pleeze Me," "Get Down and Get With It"

No. 177. *Still Crazy After All These Years,* Paul Simon (1975) – He was riding one of music's hottest artistic streaks. The three songs I list as favorites are unmistakably Simon, and also impossibly distinct. Favorite songs: "Still Crazy After All These Years," "50 Ways to Leave Your Lover," "Gone at Last"

No. 176. *Sit Down and Listen to Hooverphonic,* Hooverphonic (2003) – A trip-hop band demonstrates its songs are "real" by performing them with an orchestra. It works, bringing out unheard beauty in the songs, and pointing out the quality of the writing. Favorite songs: "One," "Vinegar and Salt," "The Last Thing I Need is You"

No. 175. *Tusk,* Fleetwood Mac (1979) – The whole is definitely greater than the sum of its parts. The sound of a band that can do anything it wants, and a lead guitar player taking it to the extreme. Both of those sentences are intended as compliments. Favorite songs: "Sara," "Tusk," "Not That Funny"

No. 174. *Brothers in Arms,* Dire Straits (1985) – A huge step forward for them, although ardent fans could be forgiven for being upset at some mainstream concessions. One of MTV's most improbable success stories. Favorite songs: "So Far Away," "Money for Nothing," "Brothers in Arms"

No. 173. *My Aim is True,* Elvis Costello (1977) – As a matter of fact, he *was* angry, which was a huge part of the appeal to me. As much as I loved this album, I never dreamed he'd make four more in the next 10 years that I'd rank ahead of this. Favorite songs: "I'm Not Angry," "Watching the Detectives," "Mystery Dance"

No. 172. *Honky Chateau,* Elton John (1972) – The peak of his pre-pop dominance. William Shatner aside, "Rocket Man" is still a brilliant song. He moved closer to mainstream success after this, leaving a whole group of fanatics who swear this is his last good album before selling out. Favorite songs: "Hercules," "Susie (Dramas)," "Rocket Man"

No. 171. *Led Zeppelin II* (1969) – Even if you don't like this album, you've heard it dozens of times. Recorded all over the world and sounding like it, this is the template for their style-hopping and their proficiency. Favorite songs: "The Lemon Song," "Whole Lotta Love," "Ramble On"

No. 170. *Imagine*, John Lennon (1971) – It says a lot that songs like the title track and the hilariously angry "How Do You Sleep?" don't even make my top three favorite songs on the record. Favorite songs: "Gimme Some Truth," "It's So Hard," "Oh! Yoko"

No. 169. *Love Symbol Album*, Prince (1992) – Another of his albums that works better as a whole than in its pieces. "Sexy MF" makes me laugh as well as want to dance. Favorite songs: "My Name is Prince," "Sexy MF," "Damn U"

No. 168. *Bookends*, Simon and Garfunkel (1968) – A concept album, more subtle than most and more mature for its time. Favorite songs: "America," "A Hazy Shade of Winter," "Mrs. Robinson"

No. 167. *Harvest*, Neil Young (1972) – If this was the sugar newcomers needed to swallow what was to come from Young, that was fine. The hints of everything about his future find their seeds here. Favorite songs: "Alabama," "The Needle and the Damage Done," "Words (Between the Lines of Age)"

No. 166. "Black Sea," XTC (1980) – That cover sure wasn't a New Wave group. But the contents were. It proved earlier albums weren't a fluke, and what followed was even more amazing. Favorite songs: "Respectable Street," "Generals and Majors," "Love at First Sight"

No. 165. *Pronounced*, Lynyrd Skynyrd (1973) – It seems pretty obvious to call this the pinnacle of Southern rock. Not everyone thinks so. Not everyone laughs as much as I do during "Gimme Three Steps," either. Favorite songs: "Tuesday's Gone," "Gimme Three Steps," "Free Bird"

No. 164. *A Whiter Shade of Pale*, Procol Harum (1967) – "Repent Walpurgis" is a sadly underrecognized instrumental classic. For some reason, it's wildly important to me to point out my album cover was burgundy and gray and called *A Whiter Shade of Pale*, not the black and

210

white cover just called *Procol Harum.* Favorite songs: "A Whiter Shade of Pale," "Conquistador," "Repent Walpurgis"

***

No. 163. *Bare Trees*, Fleetwood Mac (1972) – One of my first "FM" albums. I wasn't hearing any of these songs on any stations I listened to. Still, these were good. What else was missing in my life? I was on my way to finding out. Favorite songs: "Homeward Bound," "Bare Trees," "Child of Mine"

Fleetwood Mac could have been a completely different band when they made their breakthrough to the mainstream.

In this alternate universe, if we've heard of Lindsey Buckingham or Stevie Nicks at all, it's for entirely different reasons.

The 1972 Fleetwood Mac release *Bare Trees* seemed to set them up for a huge mid-1970s breakthrough. They would have at least been some version of Foghat or Blue Oyster Cult or even Aerosmith, a tough little band that rocked its way through package tours especially of the Midwest and rode to extended success with the assistance of hip FM radio stations, and maybe once in a while got some play on an adventurous AM station.

The Fleetwood Mac that made *Bare Trees* had two guitar-playing songwriters, the rocking blues aficionado Danny Kirwan and the complex melodicist Bob Welch. And both were at the height of their game.

If you need further proof, this is the original source of Welch's 1977 hit single "Sentimental Lady." His re-working of it later was merely a shade more polished. It was a great track, but wasn't the standout track on "Bare Trees."

The standout tracks were written and sung by Kirwan. Each side kicks off with a great rocking blues-based piece sung and written by Kirwan, "Child of Mine" and the title track. He also contributed the beautiful instrumental "Sunny Side of Heaven," which caps off the album's powerful first side.

Christine McVie is known to those who came to Fleetwood Mac through their Buckingham-Nicks breakthrough as the woman who wrote the love songs ("Over My Head," "Don't Stop," "You Make Loving Fun," "Little Lies"). Some of those are brilliant - personal favorites are "Say You Love Me," "Hold Me" and "Everywhere." But on *Bare Trees,* McVie contributed the rockin "Homeward Bound," arguably the album's best song.

Had she continued in that songwriting direction, and had Kirwan and Welch been able to get along and keep it together, Fleetwood Mac would have had a whole other profile.

That's not to condemn the Buckingham-Nicks version, or to say Kirwan-Welch would have been "better." Kirwan had his share of personality problems with the entirety of the band, and also battled substance abuse. The pressure of being the sole American-based constant during a stunningly traumatic period of the band's history took its toll on Welch, who resigned and was ultimately replaced by Buckingham-Nicks.

And the rest, of course, is history.

But *Bare Trees,* in retrospect, holds up as a superb album. It's of its time and above, and right down to the odd little poem read by "Mrs. Scarrott" to conclude the album. It's a terrifically eccentric British touch to an album that was a must when I was in high school and fortunately remains a key touchpoint now.

***

No. 162. *Heaven Tonight,* Cheap Trick (1978) – The first Cheap Trick album I bought. Everything I'd read about them was accurate. I thought they were the next Beatles. Not for the first time, I was wrong. I can still make a case. Favorite songs: "Surrender," "On Top of the World," "Heaven Tonight"

No. 161. *Whatever,* Aimee Mann (1993) – It took this to convince me how great Aimee Mann was. And then she got better. Favorite songs: "I Should've Known," "Could've Been Anyone," "Say Anything"

***

No. 160. *The Gold Experience,* Prince (1995) – His best. I can listen to each track any time and enjoy it fully, even the ones that come off as risque or misogynistic or both. Favorite songs: "Endorphinmachine," "Shy," "Gold"

The Prince album I consider it vital to listen to beginning to end is *The Gold Experience.*

I know, I know. Some of you were expecting *1999, Purple Rain, Sign of the Times.* Heck, the CD of *Lovesexy* was originally issued as one track, so we know how Prince wanted us listening to it. (That move annoyed me so much I returned the CD, bought the 12-inch single of "Alphabet St." and never gave it a second thought.)

Something about *The Gold Experience* hit me at the right spot at the right time. And of course, that's a lot of what music's all about to begin with.

For me, *The Gold Experience*, above all Prince albums, hangs together as one piece. And I find it -- as laughable as this might sound considering the name of the first song on *The Gold Experience* is "P Control" -- an uplifting experience.

At the time I was digging into songs like the Aerosmith-like "Endorphinmachine" and the gorgeous pop of "Dolphin" and the absolute majesty of "Gold" (probably my favorite Prince song ever), a friend was reading Betty Eadie's *Embraced By the Light,* a first-person narrative of a near-death experience. My friend was sharing details of the book with me, and I began hearing references to the themes of the book in lyrics from *The Gold Experience,* particularly "Dolphin" and "Gold."

But then I read the liner notes to *The Gold Experience.* (It just showed how much things had changed between the vinyl album days and the compact disc days. In the album days, I would have had the liner notes memorized, the way I memorized details from the *Sgt. Pepper's Lonely Hearts Club Band* album sleeve. But with the CD, I hadn't even taken the booklet out, afraid of how much work it would take to slide it back in.)

It turned out -- at least the liner notes claimed -- that Prince had read and been influenced by *Embraced By the Light.*

I decided to make it my goal to be sure everyone knew how brilliant the album was, starting with my female friend who'd been reading Betty Eadie.

She didn't get past the first song. Too offensive.

So I learned to tape the album for some folks *without* the first song. And I'd like to think it made a difference for at least a few people.

(There's another longer version of the song by Prince. [It's actually better as well, and its name is "Pussy Control," but that's beside the point.] The first verse of that version is an apology/explanation for use of the word. It's kind of like the original version of Black Eyed Peas' *Let's Get It Started.* They didn't get their Grammy for "Let's Get Retarded," which is the same song except for "Let's Get It Started" with a first verse requesting we not be offended by use of the word.)

***

No. 159. *The Third Reich 'n Roll,* The Residents (1976) – A total deconstruction of rock and roll. Each side is a full-length suite of avant garde, with frighteningly recognizable fragments. Every time the outchorus of "Hey Jude" melds into "Sympathy for the Devil," I get chills.

I've had people unnecessarily try to "protect" me from music at a few points in my life. The friend who schooled me on Neil Young's history as I worked backward from *Decade* refused to lend me his copy of *Tonight's the Night,* although when I finally heard it, it became my favorite Young album (and one of my 10 favorites ever). A couple of years later, a record store owner who was helping me fill in gaps in my historical knowledge thought The Residents would be too strange for me.

Given what he knew of my tastes, he was right. But I came to love The Residents for reasons similar to my love for *Tonight's the Night.* Neither is an easy listen. Young comes from a true dark emotional place. The Residents come from a true dark intellectual place. Their work, to me, illuminates some of the darker traits of both pop music and the American dream, if it isn't too pretentious to make that statement.

Bastardizations of 1960s pop cover two sides of the band's *The Third Reich N' Roll* album, the first thing of theirs I heard. (And it was exactly the right thing to introduce me to their work.)

Tribal sounds, which move into electronics, which move into vocal approximations of what the songs might sound like to someone who doesn't speak English - it all combined to fascinate my ear and engage my brain. Probably the most magical moment - at once moving, exciting and a little frightening - was the close of the second side, where the band's disjointed vocals kind of resemble the outchorus of The Beatles' "Hey Jude." Then, slowly mixed up from the background, came the "Whoo-hoo"s I recognized as being from The Rolling Stones' "Sympathy for the Devil."

Pretty easy to tell what these guys thought of the 1960s.

And digging deeper into the group was even more fascinating. The group has never revealed the identities of the people behind the music. They made public their inner battles and conflicts, but only in a very oblique fashion. Take a look at some of the history by following links on their labyrinth Web site.

They've made an art out of being a band. And they continue to this day. As with all acts, my interest in what they're doing ebbs and flows. But they may be the most truly artistic act I follow.

All that said, like my friend the record store owner, I wouldn't recommend The Residents to a lot of people. It's truly music you must listen to rather than have on, and it insists that you think about it during and after your listening periods.

It's not easy, but sometimes it's OK to be challenged.

***

No. 158. *Fables of the Reconstruction*, R.E.M. (1985) – Or is it *Reconstruction of the Fables?* Hard to believe this was a hit just like Whitney Houston and Miami Sound Machine when it came out. Singer Michael Stipe's mushmouth had me listening to this album altogether too

215

often. Favorite songs: "Feeling Gravitys Pull," "Can't Get There From Here," "Green Grow the Rushes"

Thirty years is a long time to be around.

That was my first thought upon hearing about the breakup of R.E.M.

My second thought? "When was the last time they mattered to me?"

I've always admired R.E.M., but as for having been a big fan of their music - well, not really. I was also always at kind of a loss about how they became so huge. Wasn't it just me and a handful of people arguing about the quality of *Murmur* one minute, and then the next they'd signed to Warners and were on MTV with high-production videos and selling out arenas around the world?

I remember covering a sporting event at the Met Center in Bloomington and being among those sitting at tables near the basketball court. As workers cleaned out the seating area of the arena, they also took charge of the public address system. As I wrote about the game I'd just covered, I was amused as "Radio Free Europe" blasted through the speakers. I'd never expected the biggest FM station in Minneapolis to be playing R.E.M. Imagine how I felt five years later.

I saw them on the *Lifes Rich Pageant* tour in 1986. Already by then they seemed to have raced past my affection and into the hearts of a fickle pop/popular audience. I remember a friend at the show being dismayed as the band slopped its way through "Superman" to the adulation of much of the crowd. R.E.M., that friend thought, was suddenly playing to a crowd that didn't understand them the same way we did.

But to the point. "When was the last time they mattered to me?" (A friend echoed that thought in a fashion on my Facebook page, responding to my post about the breakup by writing, " I...didn't know they were still together.")

So I looked over the discography just to see which of their albums was the last I really, really liked. And I landed at 1994's *Monster*, the one with

"What's the Frequency, Kenneth?" The loud one. The one that sounded like a rock band. The perfect antidote to "Losing My Religion." (Which, by the way, remains my favorite R.E.M. song.)

Subsequent albums were hailed (by someone) as a "return to form." This time, whichever writer was working would insist, they mean it. They're serious about being what they were.

But who wanted what? A portion of the audience wanted *Automatic for the People,* and would have loved 12 re-writes of "Everybody Hurts." Some wanted more of "The One I Love," one of the most misunderstood songs in their catalog. The people who *really* didn't get it wanted a bunch of "It's the End of the World As We Know It (And I Feel Fine)"s.

And then there were people like me, who respected what the band did when it took over the world, but (like Woody Allen film fans) liked the earlier stuff better. *Murmur, Reckoning, Lifes Rich Pageant* - each had their defenders.

For me, the winner was *Fables of the Reconstruction/Reconstruction of the Fables,* the first album of the band's that I really delved into, and the one that houses my second-favorite R.E.M. song ("Can't Get There From Here"). I just always seemed to swim against the popular tide with them.

My interest slowly disintegrated, to the point where I didn't even realize they'd put out *Collapse Into Now* until months after its release.

What will I miss? There always seems to be a level of comfort in knowing that there are performers of some longevity in a given field. I may have stopped watching David Letterman's show, but it made me happy he was still out there. R.E.M. making albums was kind of in that class - I suppose until I didn't realize they were still there anymore.

***

No. 157. *International Pop Overthrow,* Material Issue (1991) – This slice of genius out of Chicago gave birth to an ongoing music festival of the same name. One of the best power pop albums ever. Favorite songs: "Valerie Loves Me," "Diane," "Very First Lie"

No. 156. *American Stars n Bars*, Neil Young (1977) – By this time, I'd have bought an album of Neil Young reading a phone book. But he put out this, a collection as disorganized as its cover. But I listened, and kept listening. Favorite songs: "Hey Babe," "Will to Love," "Like A Hurricane"

***

No. 155. *Brain Salad Surgery*, Emerson Lake and Palmer (1973) – And we didn't even mind that the epic piece was so long it had to be split over two sides. The arrogance of these guys was almost comical. Their brilliance was inarguable. Favorite songs: "Karn Evil 9," "Still … You Turn Me On," "Benny the Bouncer"

I may have understood Keith Emerson less than any music figure of prominence from my teens.

Emerson's talent was undeniable. He was particularly the player whose contributions were most important in making Emerson, Lake and Palmer what they were.

For better or worse. When I was discovering music, I adored Emerson, Lake and Palmer. That appreciation of Emerson, Lake and Palmer led me to The Nice, and Emerson's bombastic style and skill came into even clearer focus.

But just a few years later, punk rock and New Wave came along and made me temporarily abandon prog rock as too pretentious and elitist. It took me a while to realize I could love all kinds of music, just because I loved it. My tastes did not have to line up in a neat grid.

The rediscovery and delight I found later in *Brain Salad Surgery* was a textbook example of that love. Was it indulgent and overdone? Possibly. It was also etched permanently on my brain, which doesn't happen to all music. Clearly I'd been delighted by the album, because I was again.

Keith Emerson, whose sense of humor and the absurd I never appreciated until reading interviews with him later in his life, was a large and important part of my love for it.

***

No. 154. *Skylarking*, XTC (1986) – Every XTC album is really a concept album. This one is a little more obvious. "Dear God" was originally not on the album. I don't find it as trite as its author. Favorite songs: "Dear God," "Earn Enough For Us," "Season Cycle"

No. 153. *Tea for the Tillerman*, Cat Stevens (1970) – Great artists generally have at least one amazing five-year stretch in them. This was the start of his. Favorite songs: "Where Do the Children Play?", "On the Road to Find Out", "Father and Son"

No. 152. *Innervisions*, Stevie Wonder (1973) – The reason there are four hit singles on this album is because they stopped putting out songs from the album as singles. Every one could have been a hit. And this starts the tradition of horrible Stevie Wonder albums covers. Favorite songs: "Higher Ground," "Living for the City," "Don't You Worry 'bout a Thing"

No. 151. *Black Ribbons*, Shooter Jennings & Hierophant (2010) – The Stephen King-as-DJ sub-story in this album can be hokey at times, but it can also be chilling. "All of This Could Have Been Yours" may be my favorite song of this century. Favorite songs: "All of This Could Have Been Yours," "Triskaidekaphobia," "Wake Up!"

No. 150. "*Layla and Other Assorted Love Songs*," Derek and the Dominos (1970) – The best recorded advertisement of the creative benefits of cocaine. Of course they had to flame out. I also bought the *Layla Sessions* album, which featured close to 2 1/2 hours of jams. I listened to it more than a lot of Clapton albums. Favorite songs: "Layla," "Bell Bottom Blues," "Why Does Love Got to Be So Sad?"

No. 149. *Trouble in Paradise,* Randy Newman (1983) – I didn't believe he really loved L.A., and continue to hold that position. It makes the song better. More commercially accessible than anything else he's done. And getting Paul Simon to sing on a song that makes fun of songs like Paul Simon writes is genius. Favorite songs: "Christmas in Capetown," "I'm Different," "The Blues"

No. 148. *The Stranger,* Billy Joel (1977) – If you knew him before this (and I did), you knew this one was going to be the album that turned it around and made him a superstar. When he started issuing his later nonsense, I'd go back to this album to remember what he had in him. Favorite songs: "Scenes from an Italian Restaurant," "Only the Good Die Young," "Vienna"

No. 147. *The Who Sell Out,* The Who (1967) – I wish the radio parody with the commercials had been throughout the album, as it was on the reissue. This really was art rock, and remains very clever. Favorite songs: "Mary Anne with the Shaky Hand," "I Can See For Miles," "Rael (1 and 2)"

No. 146. *Close to the Edge*, Yes (1972) – I have this too low. Of all the albums I've revisited with this project, this is the one I've grown to appreciate much more. I still don't think it's their best album (many do), but it's closer than I thought a year ago. Favorite songs: "Close to the Edge," "And You and I," "Siberian Khatru" (it's a three-song album)

No. 145. *Underdog Victorious,* Jill Sobule (2004) – Sobule tells stories effortlessly, giving listeners a feel of the familiar ("Strawberry Gloss"), the exotic ("Tel Aviv" and "Joey") and the hilarious ("Under the Disco Ball"). Part of the stretch where, for me, she could do no wrong. Favorite songs: "Cinnamon Park," "Tel Aviv," "I Saw a Cop"

No. 144. *Good Old Boys,* Randy Newman (1974) – If you listen to this album and are convinced Newman lived his entire life in the South and this was autobiographical, you'd be just like teenage me. He didn't, and it's gorgeous. Favorite songs: "Louisiana 1927," "Rednecks," "Marie"

No. 143. *Volunteers*, Jefferson Airplane (1969) – The last album by the original band. Epic. This is so tight, arguments at the time of their importance are less ridiculous than they seemed in retrospect. Favorite songs: "We Can Be Together," "Volunteers," "Wooden Ships"

No. 142. *Stevie Wonder's Original Musiquarium I,* Stevie Wonder (1982) – A best-of that included four new songs, and alternate (sometimes better) versions of the hits. It wasn't hubris. It was just Stevie. Favorite songs: "Living for the City," "Master Blaster (Jammin')," "Boogie On Reggae Woman"

No. 141. *Odds & Sods,* The Who (1974) – They were so prolific, they needed collections like this just to satiate fans who didn't want to mess with all the 45s. I'm happy "Long Live Rock" managed to rise above its being dumped in this package for fanatics. Favorite songs: "Glow Girl," "Pure and Easy," "Long Live Rock"

***

No. 140. *The World is a Ghetto,* WAR (1972) – I'm not sure why WAR was my favorite group at the time. I can't imagine I grasped what they were doing. But they laid a great foundation. An underrated band. Favorite songs: "The Cisco Kid," "The World Is a Ghetto," "City, Country, City"

When I interviewed Lonnie Jordan as the 21st century version came to my area, I related to him that as War emerged in the early 1970s, my peers had no idea how to classify the band. Some called them R&B, some called them funk. Others thought they were a soul band, and the ones who just heard them on the radio thought they were a top 40 act.

War was my first favorite band. It set me apart from most of my peers early on, a place I got used to as my life went on.

I always considered War jazz. For example, if you heard "The World Is a Ghetto" on the radio, you only heard about 40 percent of its 10-minute plus running time. The song in its album form is a true, loose workout, full of improvisation, a good indication of the rest of the album with which the song shares a title.

Jordan empathized.

"We just called it 'universalist music.' We had difficulty being labeled. We had a hard time in the record stores. We just couldn't seem to find where we should be at. I think it also hurt us when it came to getting awards. People never seemed to know what category to put us in, so they'd overlook us.

"Ultimately, we got to the point where we thought we weren't going to worry about it, we'd just let the fans decide. And as a result, we've got what I call a real salad bowl of people in the audience -- all ages and all colors."

The World is a Ghetto was, I think, the fourth album I ever purchased (behind *Chicago V* and The Beatles' *1962-1966* and *1967-1970* collections). I bought it as soon as I saw it, after hearing the title cut on the radio. (I still vividly remember the red-and-white "$3.99" price sticker. I used to trim the shrink wrap and put the price sticker inside the album sleeve. I was always a little self-conscious about that.),

Every once in a while I will pull out a copy of *The World is A Ghetto.* It held up when I spun through the reissue.

The attraction with the reissue is four new tracks - a couple of studio jams, an alternate take and a rough early version of the title cut. One of the jams is a substandard 12-bar blues walk-through, but the other shows exactly what I loved about War. It's a undefinable combination of funk, pop, rock, Latino, jam band -- take your picks. But it flows naturally, effortlessly and beautifully, like a couple of the 10-minute tracks on the album proper.

As I listened, I felt a lot of pride for that 13-year-old me who bought that album and for about a year said War was his favorite band. There was no reason for me to love that music as much as I did and do. It differed immensely from the heavy metal and pop metal and top 40 stuff my friends were listening to, and part of the reason I abandoned War and Chicago as time went on was not just my perception of a decrease in the quality of their efforts, but the peer pressure over not listening to the same stuff my friends were listening to.

Some of my teenage taste was abhorrent. My unabashed (and continuing) love for Uriah Heep is a great example of that. But the kid who liked *The World is a Ghetto*? That kid had good taste.

***

No. 139. *The Six Wives of Henry VIII,* Rick Wakeman (1973) – Even when the punks were complaining about prog rock and I was supposed to be on their side, I always had a weak spot for stuff like this. There are really a gorgeous collection of melodies here. Favorite songs: "Catherine of Aragon," "Catherine Parr," "Catherine Howard"

No. 138. *Security,* Peter Gabriel (1982) – Somewhere around this time, I learned Gabriel wouldn't let his drummers play cymbals. It changed the sound incredibly. I didn't call it "world music," although it was. I just called it "good." Favorite songs: "I Have the Touch," "Lay Your Hands on Me," "Kiss of Life"

No. 137. *The Best of The Guess Who,* The Guess Who (1971) – This was the first album I remember feeling fully aware that every song was excellent. I like having more by them, but if you're pressed for time and space, this is really the only one you need. I like this so much that "American Woman" isn't even one of my three favorite songs on it. Favorite songs: "No Time," "No Sugar Tonight/New Mother Nature," "Hang on to Your Life"

No. 136. *Fegmania!,* Robyn Hitchcock (1985) – I dove into Hitchcock fully after first hearing him. He was still solidly doing pop (albeit weird pop) at the time. Favorite songs: "Another Bubble," "My Wife & My Dead Wife," "Heaven"

No. 135. *The Rutles* (1978) – A timeless classic. I have a feeling even Neil Innes, who wrote all the songs, would be amused that this is ahead of two Beatles albums and six of their solo albums. Sadly, "Get Up and Go" is not on the original album. Favorite songs: "Hold My Hand," "I Must Be in Love," "Let's Be Natural"

No. 134. *Fleetwood Mac,* Fleetwood Mac (1975) – Their warmest album. I'm not sure they were ever this happy and optimistic again. So, of course, the music got better. And the world realized Lindsey Buckingham was a genius. As his eccentricities grew, so did my appreciation. Favorite songs: "Monday Morning," "Blue Letter," "Over My Head"

***

No. 133. *Nilsson Schmilsson,* Nilsson (1971) – A little cheekiness with your pure pop. Later, he stopped caring, and while his talent remained obvious, it didn't always show through. This. though, was fantastic fun. Favorite songs: "Gotta Get Up," "Coconut," "Jump into the Fire"

"One" was written based off a busy signal. That's where the keyboard rhythm at the beginning of the Three Dog Night song comes from.

That's one of hundreds of fun and fascinating pieces of information in the film *Who Is Harry Nilsson?* The documentary is about a singer-songwriter who never really got the fame and riches he deserved – and is probably best-known for a couple of songs he didn't write.

Harry Nilsson is one of my favorite performers. But even at that, I didn't realize how many of his albums I owned (around 20, by my count, although there are discographies that apparently include every session at which the man ever exhaled) until I saw the montage of covers in the documentary.

He wrote "One," made a hit by Three Dog Night. "Cuddly Toy" and "Daddy's Song" by The Monkees. The theme to *The Courtship of Eddie's Father.* His songs have been recorded by John Lennon, Ringo Starr, Blood Sweat and Tears, Rick Nelson, Aimee Mann, Andy Williams, The Turtles, Jellyfish, Liza Minnelli and dozens more.

But there are two songs he's best known for performing. "Everybody's Talking" won him a Grammy. It was used in the film *Midnight Cowboy.* It was written by folk songwriter Fred Neil.

Nilsson's other well-known song is "Without You." It won him another Grammy. Some of you might know it from Mariah Carey's version of it. It was written by Pete Ham and Tom Evans of the group Badfinger, although its authorship has been called into question and is one of the saddest parts of another tragic story. (Some advice: Unless you're ready, willing and able to wallow through some amazingly sad stuff, steer clear of any biographies of Badfinger. You've been warned.)

But there's much more to Nilsson than that handful of songs. There's two decades of songwriting and singing and living hard and not outliving most of your friends, dying at 52 with a lot of living left to do.

But at least he did some of his living on tape. So I'm watching the documentary and seeing clips of Nilsson lip-synching on Hugh Hefner's Playboy TV show. In color. With girls in miniskirts and shag haircuts bobbing their heads beside him, and the camera over Hefner's shoulder as he "sings."

I thought my head would explode out of nostalgia. I remember watching those shows with my dad when I was a kid. I didn't understand them at all, but dad seemed to like them. And the music stuck with me.

The documentary does a brilliant job of showing the rise and fall and further fall of the guy whose 3½-octave voice seemed poised to dominate pop music at the turn of the 1970s. He was friends with The Beatles, and in *Nilsson Schmilsson* produced a top-to-bottom solid album, including "Without You" and "Jump Into the Fire."

(My mother is still haunted, I'm sure, by the drum rhythm that starts about four minutes into "Jump Into the Fire," given how much I played along to this song as a high school-aged drummer.)

But Nilsson, the film shows, could not stand fortune. Even after finding a sympathetic and respected ear in producer Richard Perry, Nilsson broke up the working relationship. When he and Perry went to a posh eatery to work out some difficulties during the recording of *Nilsson Schmilsson*, Perry reminded Nilsson of a promise that things would be done the producer's way. "I lied," the singer admitted.

There comes a point when things turn bad and don't get better for Nilsson. He does a disastrous film with Ringo Starr, *Son of Dracula.* It's easier to find Nilsson's wonderful "Daybreak" song from the soundtrack than it is to find a copy of the film. (I'm still looking.)

Recording the *Pussycats* album with John Lennon as producer, Nilsson shreds his beautiful voice. One talking head recounts Nilsson describing blood on the studio microphone from Nilsson's singing.

He ultimately winds up being bought out from his RCA Records contract. And then insult adds to injury when he discovers his trusted business manager has stolen millions of dollars from him.

It's a depressing story, but made with joy. And it has volumes of entertainment value. My favorite part? Eric Idle (Monty Python) recounting meeting ex-Beatle George Harrison at Nilsson's gravesite after Nilsson's funeral and, at Harrison's suggestion, leading an assembled group in singing Nilsson's "You're Breaking My Heart."

"You're Breaking My Heart" was from the *Son of Schmilsson* album, pieces of which I (in probably a perverse way typical of my taste) preferred to *Nilsson Schmilsson*. And *Son of Schmilsson* also included a song that I regularly would play and convince listeners it was actually by someone else.

Honestly, to this day, I can play this song for people and tell them it's a great lost Paul McCartney song, and a lot of them will believe me. It's actually Nilsson's "The Lottery Song," and it's the prettiest thing you'll hear today. Go find it.

***

No. 132. *Live at the Portland Arms*, The Soft Boys (1983) – "Unplugged," before we called it that. What sounds like a small yet appreciative crowd is treated to lunacy all the way through, including them hilariously massacring Elvis Presley's "All Shook Up." Favorite songs: "Human Music," "I Like Bananas (Because They Have No Bones," "That's When Your Heartaches Begin"

No. 131. *Deja Vu,* Crosby, Stills, Nash and Young (1970) – This album is too often criticized for what it isn't than what it is. It is an attempt at American Beatles (never mind that Nash is English and Young Canadian). It is successful, if disjointed. They never really were a "group" group. Favorite songs: "Carry On," "Woodstock," "4 + 20"

No. 130. *Girlfriend,* Matthew Sweet (1990) – Boy, did this come out of nowhere. Friends and I listened to previous albums of Sweet's, trying to find a hint of how tight and tough this album turned out to be. Favorite songs: "Divine Intervention," "I've Been Waiting," "Girlfriend"

***

No. 129. *Sgt. Pepper's Lonely Hearts Club Band,* The Beatles (1967) – I go back and forth on this regularly. It's a new Beatles, a whole other band, but there may be a bit too much McCartney on here for the tastes of some. (The

226

second album named *Sgt. Pepper* on the list. See also No. 257.)
Favorite songs: "Fixing a Hole," "Lovely Rita," "A Day in the Life"

(2007)

Forty years ago, The Beatles unleashed *Sgt. Pepper's Lonely Hearts Club Band* on the world.

A generation cringes now. It's just time enough now for Baby Boomers -- who think everything they've created culturally is the best that ever has been and ever will be created -- to slam the greatness of *Sgt. Pepper* over the head of unsuspecting Generation Xers and Generation Nexters.

I'll admit I (barely a Boomer -- I got in at the tail end) am guilty of making that assertion regarding The Beatles in general.

But *Sgt. Pepper* (which was released in Great Britain on June 1, 1967, and in the U.S. a day later)? I've never said that, never thought it, never believed it for a second.

Here's the heresy: *Sgt. Pepper* is far from The Beatles' greatest album. It's barely in their top 10 best albums.

What made *Sgt. Pepper* revolutionary was it being the first true shared listening experience by a burgeoning youth culture. It played a key role as soundtrack at a time when the world was changing faster than most could keep up with. Arguably, the last time that culture had a true shared listening experience was Michael Jackson's *Thriller*.

The baroque stylings and psychedelia of *Sgt. Pepper* changed music, for better or for worse. Some still curse the idea of concept albums and attendant self-indulgence, feeling the best use for pop music is in disposable three-minute nuggets. The Beatles, these folks will argue, destroyed music by expanding it into places that shouldn't be traversed by those not named John Lennon and Paul McCartney.

But *Sgt. Pepper* doesn't strike me as a *great* album, and I've always declined to mention it in the same breath as its contemporaries, The Beach Boys' *Pet Sounds* and The Zombies' *Odessey and Oracle*. *Pepper* is good,

227

not great. ("A Day in the Life," however, is one of the most stunning things I've heard, to this day.)

In the unlikely event you're under the age of 20 and reading this, keep one thing in mind: You don't have to believe art produced in the 1960s is the best ever, even if all of your elders insist on it. Make up your own mind. I'd suggest starting with "The White Album" and the movie *Z*. That ought to stir up your mind a little bit. Meanwhile, I promise to go back to Radiohead's *OK Computer* and Green Day's *American Idiot* to see if I can figure out what all the fuss is about.

***

No. 128. *Raspberries* (1972) – I was young enough and loved the 60s British sounds here so much that I didn't know I wasn't supposed to like this if I wanted to be "cool." "Go All the Way," which has one of the five greatest song openings in rock history, is cool enough for me. Favorite songs: "Go All the Way," "Come Around and See Me," "Don't Want To Say Goodbye"

(2005)

By the early 1990s, a veteran of so many live concert music performances that I could hardly count how many I'd attended, I decided to narrow my scope, and anticipated seeing just two more performers in concert before I bowed out.

(I didn't imagine then that in 10 years time, I'd be averaging as many shows in one year as I used to attend in three.)

By the early 1990s, I was most interested in seeing Tony Bennett and Prince. (I never got around to seeing Prince, but have seen Tony Bennett three times and wouldn't hesitate to go again.)

There was a band that would have made my list, but their reunion was so unlikely, I didn't even imagine the possibility.

Then hell froze over.

The Eagles announced their reunion in 1994 with a press release headlined "Hell Freezes Over." The headline was a wink at the improbability of the cash grab -- errr, ummm, reunion. But there was a reunion out there even more unlikely, rumored as much (although certainly not in as high a profile) as The Eagles'.

The Raspberries, probably the greatest American power pop band ever (best known for their 1972 hit "Go All the Way"), broke up in 1975, and band member Eric Carmen (author of most of the hit singles) launched a solo career. He had top five singles with "All By Myself," "Never Gonna Fall in Love Again," "Hungry Eyes" and "Make Me Lose Control."

Rumors about a Raspberries reunion had been loud since 1999, when some of the band members got together and planned a tour and an album. Carmen backed out at that time, and the remaining members recorded a six-cut CD but didn't tour.

But late last year, Carmen realized his concerns about ruining fans' memories of and respect for the band could be allayed. And after a pair of dates in their home base of Cleveland, they played House of Blues in Chicago.

How significant was this date? Chicago Reader summed it up for many of the believers: "For those who regard power pop as a religion, (this is) a moment on par with the Second Coming."

I never imagined I'd be able to see them. But after paying $58.62 for a ticket with a face value of $43.50, I was ready.

In the early 1990s, as I was discovering the wonders of online services, I came across a bulletin board discussion area focusing on power pop. I posted a note about The Raspberries' magnificent combination of The Beatles, The Who and The Beach Boys. Within a couple of days, I received an e-mail from someone asking where they could get hold of Raspberries recordings.

At that time (although it's essentially the same now), the band's recordings were unavailable. And while now one could suggest a number of places to download files or quickly burn a CD or two, the technology at that time wasn't quite so available.

The problem was compounded when I eventually realized I was exchanging e-mails with a man in Brazil.

The easiest way to bridge the communication gap was to simply tell the man I'd tape the four albums I had and mail them to him. (Which turned out to be more difficult and expensive than I'd expected, but that's another story.)

Upon receiving the package, the Brazilian vowed I was his friend for life and welcome to visit anytime I wanted.

I wish I could remember his name.

As I looked around the House of Blues at this odd combination of middle-aged power pop fans and people who weren't even born when Eric Carmen's solo career was on its last legs, all waiting to hear songs that were at least 30 years old, I thought, "I guess I can't make jokes at the expense of people going to Rolling Stones shows anymore."

The show started with the band's logo projected on a screen in front of a closed curtain. The next two slides in the video presentation said, "They said it could never happen," then, "They were wrong."

As a collage of video clips, home movies and still photos was projected with excerpts of the band's hits, I suddenly thought of my Brazilian friend. And as the sound collage merged seamlessly into live music ("This isn't the original recording," I thought, unaware that the band was playing live behind the curtain), I remembered how in one of his e-mails, he described being driven to tears at being able to hear music he hadn't heard for so long.

And for a moment, seeing the real Raspberries on stage at Chicago's House of Blues -- as I wiped an unexpected tear off my right cheek -- I knew exactly how he felt.

***

230

No. 127. *Never Mind the Bollocks, Here's the Sex Pistols*, Sex Pistols (1977) – There was no way the band or the album could live up to the billing. And then they did. In my circle, declaring you liked this album was drawing a huge line in the cement. Favorite songs: "God Save the Queen," "Anarchy in the U.K.," "Pretty Vacant"

There was a time Sid Vicious wasn't fit for prime time.

His bandmates, The Sex Pistols, weren't ready either. They were too much noise, too lower-class British, too vulgar. They looked unkempt and uncouth, and their music was grating.

Except to me. There weren't many in my peer group who liked the Pistols. But what they heard as "punk" I heard as faster and more poorly recorded metal, with lyrics I struggled to understand, often because of their very British-ness.

I first saw the Sex Pistols on a show featuring "young talents." Both Andy Kaufman and Steve Martin were part of the show. I can find no record of the show, but I suspect it was summer 1977. The show was pedestrian until the Pistols showed up with all their filth and fury, causing an immediate schism between me and my father.

I didn't immediately become a Pistols fanatic, but I liked what I heard, eventually picked up the album and enjoyed it, and following the band through all their insanity via assorted music press became a favorite hobby.

Sid Vicious died in February 1979, overdosing on heroin at age 21. But he never really died. The Sex Pistols legend grew even after they broke up, after Vicious died, after singer Johnny Rotten formed a new band.

It's not as though they were ever in the mainstream. Their one album, *Never Mind the Bollocks, Here's the Sex Pistols,* didn't even break the top 100 in American charts.

But the mythmaking continued. *The Great Rock n Roll Swindle* was a fantastic film that maybe kind of told a little bit of the Pistols' story, and it included a clip of Sid performing "My Way" in a beautiful theater. And this is where we bring things to today.

Acura is using Vicious' recording of the classic Frank Sinatra/Paul Anka tune in its ads. (There are a number of cuts, but the two-minute one is the craziest.) The first time I saw it, I ran through the emotions of bemused, perturbed and sad, right around to amazement. Almost immediately, I posted on Facebook:

Interesting how Sid was relegated to late night TV when this was new (1978, and certainly no small part of that was because of Sid shooting the audience) and now it runs as background music for a car commercial. Warning: He curses and shoots the audience and, well, he's very Sid-like.

And I posted a link to the clip. Yes, he does shoot the audience.

The first time I saw the clip and heard the song was in *Mr. Mike's Mondo Video,* a compilation of freak show kinds of things designed to bemuse and outrage, hosted by Michael O'Donoghue. The show ran late night on NBC in early 1979, in place of *Saturday Night Live* for a week.

The reactions then were almost the same as now. I found it funny. (For me, the shooting was canceled out by Vicious casually tossing the gun away. See? He only did it because somebody told him to!) Others were offended by the desecration of the song, the unmusicality of Vicious, and his very existence.

I'm not certain to whom Acura is trying to appeal with this ad. Aging punks (they're in their 50s now). Young hipsters who will be taken aback by the angry old music? Sex Pistols fans?

I'm still seeing online debates about Vicious and whether this is music or trash. You know what you think when you hear it. I've always loved it, and never thought I would find too many others who did. But the point of the ad is will its presence sell cars?

Not to me, anyway. But I still like hearing the song.

***

No. 126. *Hot Rocks 1964-1971,* The Rolling Stones (1971) – A necessary primer on The Rolling Stones. Their discography was plenty confusing, and this helped straighten things out. It also made Mick Jagger seem larger and scarier than life. Side three is vital. Favorite songs: "(I Can't Get No) Satisfaction," "Jumpin' Jack Flash," "Honky Tonk Women"

There's a thin line between lovable rakish rogue and royal pain in the backside.

Rolling Stones guitar player, songwriter and all-around innovator Keith Richards stomps all over that line with his book *Life,* and perhaps your reaction to the book says more about you (or me) than it does about Richards.

If you were to pick a member of The Rolling Stones least likely to write a memoir, it would be Richards. When the impending book was announced, the jokes about Richards not being able to remember anything to put in autobiography were as funny as they were predictable.

And in some cases, that assumption is apparently correct. Richards breezes through much of the 1970s and 1980s (they recorded some albums, he did heroin, he and Rolling Stones singer Jagger became estranged), but has room to detail stories of pets, and even include a recipe.

Richards does make some invaluable contributions in clarifying some of his life legends. No, he never had his blood swapped out as a cure for heroin addiction. He fell seven feet from a spot on a tree where many people had previously sat - he wasn't up climbing for coconuts.

And the reason he believes he's outlived so many heroin addicts? It has nothing to do with him being a human cockroach, or his having superhuman consumption and coping capabilities (although he may be and have that). Rather, it's that he spent his addiction time trying to "maintain." He never looked for a bigger and better high. With heroin, he looked for constancy.

There are some other important sections in *Life.* In one section, Richards explains open guitar tuning and its uses and advantages so brilliantly and succinctly that musicians might be tempted to copy those pages and hand them to anyone confused by what open tuning accomplishes or how it's done.

Elsewhere, he describes how "Jumping Jack Flash" and "Gimme Shelter" were essentially recorded acoustically, and simply and expertly explains how it was done. And he gives an explanation for why the band continues to tour and trot out mostly its classic catalog: If people want to see the band, the band wants to play. If people are paying a lot of money to see the band, presumably they want to hear the hits.

So for the most part, harmless and entertaining stuff. Certainly everyone has the right to tell their story their own way, and Richards comes off as a charming minstrel, wandering through life and living an existence many of us would doubtless choose if given the option.

But he also comes off as someone absent of reflection. Richards' attitude seems to be, "I'll do what I wish, you do as you wish, just don't let me down."

Or rely on him too much, apparently. Richards reminds us he never missed a show - even after his infant son's death. But he bristles at Jagger's takeover of the band's business end, without fully acknowledging there would be no Rolling Stones without the singer assuming those duties.

And he brushes over the long delays - in recording and particularly at concerts - caused by his narcotics-induced fogs. Guns N' Roses singer Axl Rose at his most tardy would still have been put to shame by the Keith Richards of the 1970s.

Many people were damaged by Richards' behavior, or just by being around the man. There's no expectation of Richards taking any responsibility for the behavior of those around him. After all, even though he had his share of weapons, including knives and firearms, there's never been a claim that Richards kept anyone around him via threat, or that he demanded anyone around him try to keep up with his pace and intake.

And it's probably silly to look for reflection or regret in a tome designed to celebrate the *Life* of one of the most notorious death-chasers in rock music history.

It's only rock n' roll, and that's fine. But it could have been much more.

***

No. 125. *London 0 Hull 4,* The Housemartins (1986) – Another one of those British groups that came from nowhere and made one brilliant album. Probably placed a little too high. Favorite songs: "Happy Hour," "Flag Day," "Sheep"

No. 123. *Southern Rock Opera,* Drive-By Truckers (2002) – Every time I think concept albums are an outdated idea, something comes along to change my mind. This ambitious opus, with nods to Lynyrd Skynyrd and their tragic conclusion as well as Southern culture in general, changed my mind when this came out. It had to be changed again a few years later. Favorite songs: "Shut Up and Get on the Plane," "Days of Graduation," "Ronnie and Neil"

No. 123. *Nevermind,* Nirvana (1991) – Like the Sex Pistols' album, it's easy to forget what a blast, what a culture-changer this album was. Favorite songs: "Smells Like Teen Spirit," "Come As You Are," "Stay Away"

***

No. 122. *Introducing The Beatles*, The Beatles (1964) – How many copies of this album do I own? How many are counterfeits? The colors on the cover generally indicate when it was released. The newest copy I own probably came out sometime in the 1980s. The music is great, although they were still clearly feeling their way. Favorite songs: "Anna (Go To Him)," "P.S. I Love You," "Twist and Shout"

(2014)

It's nothing short of fascinating that my memory of The Beatles' 1964 arrival in the United States marks the point where the world changed from black-and-white to color. Particularly since color television didn't arrive in my house until two years later. Even the color photos of the group on the set of *The Ed Sullivan Show,* the ones with the blue set's arrows painted white and appearing brownish under the television lights, are disarming to me.

But that was part of the deal with being a small-town 5-year-old in a cozy family setting, rabbit ears atop the television pulling in KGLO from Mason City, Iowa, 90 miles away.

The night of The Beatles' appearance, KGLO didn't even have any programming on before the Sullivan show. So my 2-year-old sister and I sat patiently waiting for Ed to introduce us to the band.

And he did, and they did, and my world was never the same.

Who knows when each person's moment of "that's what I want to do" comes in their life? Many of us may not even recognize it when it does. I've often said in my adulthood that music is my best friend. It comforts me, consoles me, amuses me, enrages me, makes me feel there's a reason to be alive, and it's always there when I need it. Who's to say it wasn't that moment 50 years ago where I realized what I wanted to do, what brought the most peace to my mind and life, was deceptively simple three-minute pop songs?

That wasn't what it was about in 1964, of course. What it was about then was the joy of something I'd never seen before, a willingness to commit to whatever the music moved your body and soul to do. That's what The Beatles were doing when they shook their shocking mops of hair. (How cool were those, by the way? To this day, as dated as they might appear, the lads all look spectacular.) That's what the audience members were doing with their screams.

It's no small wonder considering that kind of introduction that my disappointment was overwhelming when I eventually realized music alone couldn't bring about world peace and utopia.

But realizing that call to love of music and realizing that ultimate disappointment was a long way off in February 1964. What was important then was a launching into a wonderful world with art that spoke to me personally in a way no other art ever had, or would, or could.

236

At some subsequent point – my heart tells me the next day, my head tells me there's no way that was possible, my family has no memory of the moment at all – my mother brought home a copy of *Meet The Beatles,* the album that sold 5 million copies and spent 11 weeks at No. 1. The record belonged to the family, but there was no question it was mine. It was left to me to figure out what was going on within and without the record.

What were they singing with those odd accents? Why could you hear five instruments when there were only four people in the group? Why did the album notes make cryptic references to the performers singing "double-tracked"? (It took me a long time to grasp what could be done in a recording studio, most specifically that a person could easily sing accompanying themselves thanks to the miracle of magnetic recording tape. Apparently before I grasped that, I thought The Chipmunks were a real band.)

And those photos. Did these guys always dress alike, and groom alike? And what the heck was going on with the cover photo? Why were there disembodied heads with light only on one side? Were they so poor they couldn't afford more light? And why were there three on top, and Ringo Starr on the bottom right? Was that some kind of statement about his significance? Couldn't the photographer have lined up all four of them in a neat row?

(Imagine what I thought a couple of years later when I saw the cover for *Rubber Soul.*)

What made The Beatles stand out then is what makes them stand out now. They were not willing to be fully drawn into any expectations, that of their record company employers or that of their audience. They were determined to grow, and not repeat themselves.

They were that rarest of things, a wildly popular artistic conglomeration that was focused on art. They may not have realized it, they may not have been doing it entirely consciously, but they accomplished it.

Ultimately, that's the greatest gift we received 50 years ago.

And hey, if all that happens is you listen to the music and it takes you to a place where you smile, are happy and forget about your woes for a few minutes, that's a win, too.

Yeah. Yeah. Yeah.

***

No. 121. *Apostrophe (')*, Frank Zappa (1974) – For years, this was my sole Zappa album. There were better ones to be had, but this was plenty good. "Uncle Remus" is a devastating track. Favorite songs: "Apostrophe (')," "Cosmik Debris," "Uncle Remus"

No. 120. *Can't Buy a Thrill*, Steely Dan (1972) – The hits sounded strange on AM radio. (Donnie Osmond, Dawn and Vicki Lawrence all charted ahead of "Reeling in the Years.") They set the stage for a decade of important albums. Favorite songs: "Reeling in the Years," "Midnight Cruiser," "Dirty Work"

No. 119. *Mind Games,* John Lennon (1973) – History writes this as a vacant period for Lennon, but that's not what I was experiencing. The title track is my favorite solo Lennon song. Favorite songs: "Mind Games," "Tight A$," "I Know (I Know)"

No. 118. *Born to Run,* Bruce Springsteen (1975) – It may have been hype that brought him to the masses, but there was quality to back it up. This is the template for his most successful efforts. Favorite songs: "Born to Run," "Jungleland," "Meeting Across the River"

No. 117. *The Big Express,* XTC (1984) – It was a but of a change of direction, but didn't really hint at the ornate stuff that was to come. It was still abrasive in the ears of people who needed to hear it abrasively. Favorite songs: "Wake Up," "Shake You Donkey Up," "You're the Wish You Are I Had"

No. 116. *Argybargy*, Squeeze (1980) – My first Squeeze album. It probably shouldn't be this low. A number of "New Wave" bands were putting out infectious albums like this at the time. I could have lived there forever. Favorite songs: "Another Nail in My Heart," "Farfisa Beat," "Wrong Side

238

of the Moon"

No. 115. *Repercussion*, The dB's (1982) – The more odd of their first two albums, the first side nevertheless totally nails it. "Amplifier" should be a famous anthem. Favorite songs: "Living a Lie," "Amplifier," "Ask for Jill"

No. 114. *Q: Are We Not Men? A: We Are Devo,* Devo (1978) – In addition to this being plain good, thoughtful music, I owe it for giving me a pathway to even stranger stuff. I may have never listened to Velvet Underground or The Residents without Devo. Favorite songs: "Uncontrollable Urge," "(I Can't Get No) Satisfaction," "Jocko Homo"

***

No. 113. *Velvet Underground and Nico,* Velvet Underground (1967) – You either get it or you don't, and you likely have trouble understanding the opinions of those who feel differently from you. I'll admit it took me a while to grasp it, and it was "Venus in Furs" that led me in. Favorite songs: "Femme Fatale," "Venus in Furs," "All Tomorrow's Parties"

In the 1970s, as I was learning about Neil Young, a friend and Young fan helped me along by lending me the man's early work that I'd missed. But the album he held back was *Tonight's the Night*. He didn't think I'd like its bleak and morose nature.

Instead, the album grabbed me immediately. Its bare emotion attracted me. Like listening to Bob Dylan's *Blood on the Tracks* for the first time.

It's no accident, I think, that those two albums are among my favorites ever.

Now, rewind 45 years back from now. It's fascinating to wonder what people thought in 1967 when they first heard *The Velvet Underground & Nico*. If lyrics had ever been quite this explicit, those efforts are lost to the ages. Writers talked about some of the topics explored on the Velvet Underground album, but Lou Reed turned explicit as he wrote about heroin, waiting for a drug dealer, and sadism and masochism.

Predictably, in 1967, few people heard the album. "Heroin," "I'm Waiting for the Man," "Femme Fatale" and "Venus in Furs" weren't exactly radio fare. (Even though they probably should have been.) The right people eventually found the album, building Velvet Underground's reputation and leading to the theory that everyone who heard *The Velvet Underground & Nico* formed a band.

While it's regularly on lists of the greatest albums ever made, it's a difficult sell. It's not filled with sweet melodies or rockin' tunes. It defies you to put it on as background music. It's frank, stark, and in your face. There's nothing pretty about it. Even music connoisseurs have trouble digging into it.

My college roommate appreciated all forms of music. A few years after school, I was visiting him and thumbing through his piles of CDs. I found one stack that confused me. It included, among a handful of other discs, *The Velvet Underground & Nico*.

"That's the pile I'm selling," he said.

I was stunned he didn't share my appreciation. He said it just sounded like noise to him, which was easy enough to understand. Viola was a key instrument. Drones were present everywhere. Songs were one and two chords. Lyrics were stark. And when it came to vocals, Lou Reed was a lot closer to Bob Dylan than Paul McCartney or John Lennon.

Knowing my ex-roommate's tastes, I played about half the album, focusing on the more melodic pieces ("Femme Fatale," "Run Run Run," "There She Goes Again"), steering clear of the drones and the songs where Reed was more prominent. He promised to listen again, and I hoped the frosting of the softer songs would help him into the more difficult pieces ("Heroin," "All Tomorrow's Parties," "Venus in Furs," the latter of which being a song I can listen to just about any time).

I don't know if he ever did get back to it. I do know, however, that it's not an album to recommend lightly. I don't know anyone personally who likes Velvet Underground as much as I do, and I can't think of a single person to whom I've recommended *The Velvet Underground & Nico* that has come back and thanked me.

No. 112. *Daryl Hall and John Oates* (silver album) (1975) – Any number of bands in the 1970s had fantastic hits that far outshone the rest of the album. On this one, "Sara Smile" was just part of the package to my ear. Truly blue-eyed soul. Favorite songs: "Camellia," "Gino (The Manager)," "Grounds for Separation"

No. 111. *Rubber Soul*, The Beatles (1965) – I'm speaking here of the original U.S. album, which ended up leaning lighter in tone. I could pick three different favorite songs off the album tomorrow and it would still be accurate. Favorite songs: "The Word," "It's Only Love," "Run for Your Life"

***

No. 110. *All Things Must Pass,* George Harrison (1970) – This is sprawling and amazing, and it's haunting to consider how The Beatles might have incorporated these songs had they stayed together. And anyone with the nerve is 1970 to rhyme "Jesus" and "visas" was plenty impressive for me. Favorite songs: "Wah-Wah," "What Is Life," "Awaiting on You All"

Who wins the title for best videos, post-Beatles career?

Bet you didn't even know that was a category, did you?

In 1976, George Harrison was running at a weak No. 4 in the Tim's Favorite ex-Beatle Derby. I found *Living in the Material World* boring, especially the second side. "You" was my favorite Harrison song, until a few years later when "Blow Away" came out. But the *Extra Texture* album made me slide George into the group of performers whose albums were not purchased unless I heard at least one more song that I really liked.

And in early 1976, Harrison had been found guilty of "subconscious plagiarism" in a case that (correctly) pointed out the similarities between "He's So Fine" and "My Sweet Lord."

Again, as I look back now, I have no idea why it meant so much to me at the time, but I was appalled to think that Harrison stole his best-know song from an *oldies* act.

But it meant something. I was still rooting for George, but he was making it difficult.

On Nov. 20 of that year, Harrison was a guest on *Saturday Night Live*. The show aired a couple of pre-produced Harrison film clips: "Crackerbox Palace" and "This Song."

"Crackerbox Palace" was OK, but bothered me. It seemed Harrison had fallen into this odd trap of songs that were always too slow. The tempos made even bright songs into dirges. And that was the trouble with the previous album. Even "You" sounds like the only reason it's moving forward as well as it does is because the drummer is forcing everyone else to keep up.

What happened to the guy who turned in the upbeat songs on *Let It Be*? The guy who woke us up with "For You Blue" after "The Long and Winding Road" put us to sleep? The guy who wrote "While My Guitar Gently Weeps" and "I Want To Tell You" (the song that, along with "Got To Get You Into My Life," makes me wonder what *Revolver* would have sounded like if they'd recorded it in Memphis, as they once pondered)?

And then later in that *Saturday Night Live* episode, George Harrison earned his lifetime artistic pass with me.

That opening riff -- really kind of a soul riff, although I couldn't have realized it then and can just barely describe its feel even now -- made me sit up straight.

I'm almost certain that by this time, I associated that Tom Scott saxophone with that really slick sound I heard on all the "California" records of the time. But its presence here would essentially mock it.

Does anybody know what I mean when I say "California" records? It's that stuff that's tight and professional and a little sterile and a little too precise. I guess some people call it "yacht rock," but to my mind and taste, "yacht rock" is far too placid a description for some of those cocaine-fueled California records. I just recently learned, to my horror, that an upcoming album on this list is actually that dreaded "yacht rock" -- Poco's *Legend*. The songs were so good, I never realized what the arrangements did to them.

"This Song" is, first of all, "Crackerbox Palace" with some "California" shoved straight into the heart of it, to the betterment of the tune.

And it doesn't take long getting into the video before you realize this is going to be a middle finger to everything about the plagiarism case. Harrison's ability to so quickly format such a fantastic response is truly a supreme artistic accomplishment.

Just the way Harrison walks into court is funny. His hair was flying just the right amount of 70s modicum, and he was still impossibly thin.

Then comes the staging of the video, a courtroom scene with some clever jokes, some visual similarities to Monty Python, a hipper concept for video promotion and along with everything else, a top-notch song.

It was a song whose best joke is so fantastic I can never repeat it vocally to anyone. I try to match the rhythm and cadence of Monty Python's Eric Idle, but I can't come closer. All that means, though, is I'm always hearing the falsetto "Could be 'Sugar Pie, Honey Bunch' – No, sounds more like 'Rescue Me'!" for the first time.

It's even taken me this long to realize there are two versions of this, although I knew it. It one of those cases where I have two different versions of a song in my head, and it takes me a while to realize why.

(There are duplicate versions in my head of a number of songs, including Three Dog Night's "Joy To the World," Johnny Rivers' "Rockin' Pneumonia," Steely Dan's "Reeling in the Years" and Jethro Tull's "Locomotive Breath." The latter two are quadrophonic mixes that ended up in my head somehow, and the first two are differences between the 45 version and the album version.)

Why it's so hard for me to simply register that the 45 version of "This Song" just has that little bit snipped out. Maybe because even then I thought, "They can't possibly be editing an ex-Beatle's song to fit radio formatting, can they?"

With "This Song," there's the 3:45 version as featured in the video (which was also the 45, which was also the version with which I was most familiar), and a 4:14 album version. The cut is at 3:15. With the video and 45, a tasty guitar solo and some scatting from Harrison are excised. Too bad. They're the pieces that push the song from great to overwhelming.

Like I said, at this point, it became my favorite Harrison song.

***

No. 109. *Houses of the Holy,* Led Zeppelin (1973) – We knew it wasn't as good as the one before it. My appreciation has grown as I've aged. Still, bad cover. I tried to keep my paper band around the album intact. Favorite songs: "The Song Remains the Same," "No Quarter," "The Ocean"

No. 108. *Blonde on Blonde,* Bob Dylan (1966) – I steered clear of this one for a long time, understanding that double Dylan could hurt my tiny teenage brain. I was right, but it was OK. I caught up. Favorite songs: "Rainy Day Women #12 & 35," "Visions of Johanna," "I Want You"

No. 107. *Help!,* The Beatles (1965) – This ranking is for the original U.K. album. When I finally acquired it via import in the late 1970s, I understood better what a horrible job had been done in eviscerating those albums for the U.S. market. Favorite songs: "The Night Before," "You're Going to Lose That Girl," "Help!"

No. 106. *In Utero,* Nirvana (1993) – It was loud and obnoxious and a little scary, and for a minute when it was the most popular album in the country, it seemed they might have succeeded where the Sex Pistols fell short in changing the entire sound of music. Favorite songs: "Serve the Servants," "Heart-Shaped Box," "All Apologies"

No. 105. *Talking Book,* Stevie Wonder (1972) – This started what became close to a perfect decade for him. To this day, those swirling keyboards make my head swim. In a great way. "You Are the Sunshine of My Life" is so timeless, I can't believe it was written during my lifetime. Favorite songs: "Maybe Your Baby," "Superstition," "You Are the Sunshine of My Life"

No. 104. *Some Girls,* The Rolling Stones (1978) – After meandering through the middle of the 70s, this kicked back with a vengeance. The extended "Miss You" was one of the greatest dance mixes ever. This is funny and sassy and they're on top of their game, for the final time. Favorite songs: "Miss You," "Some Girls," "Shattered"

No. 103. *Gaucho*, Steely Dan (1980) – I appreciate this far more now than I did when it was released. It was too dark and too laid back for me at the time. It's grown on me. Favorite songs: "Babylon Sisters," "Hey Nineteen," "Time Out of Mind"

No. 102. *Arizona Bay*, Bill Hicks (1993) – Released after his death, it cemented for me his brilliance. With the mood music, he created a piece that stood up to repeated listens, and showed what might have been and what was lost when he passed. Favorite songs: "Step on the Gas (L.A. Riots)," "Hooligans," "Elvis"

***

No. 101. *Rhythm Nation 1814,* Janet Jackson (1989) – The best thing with which anyone from the Jackson family was involved. And she was far ahead of her time (or expanding on a noble concept) with its all-accepting message. Oh, and every time I hear the title cut and "Black Cat," I want to turn the volume to 11. Favorite songs: "Rhythm Nation," "Miss You Much," "Black Cat"

(2007)

This is only a big deal to me. That said, it *is* a big deal to me, so I appreciate any indulgence.

I've been putting together year-end favorite albums lists for years. The first one that was published was in 1985. (My pick that year, for the historians, was R.E.M.'s *Fables of the Reconstruction.*)

I've gone back through the years and made a handful of adjustments in the lists. But I've always noted those changes in some spot I considered public and definitive, and I've adjusted my thinking on how to handle albums I don't get to until after I've already completed my year-end review. (Right now, my policy is to add those albums in a list at the end of each given year, with text that says something along the lines of "If I'd heard this last year, it would have made my list.")

(Again, I know this is only a big deal to me. But it's something I think about, probably more than I ought to.)

There's been once since 1985 that I chose to not name an album of the year. In 1990 (reflecting albums released in 1989), I didn't list a No. 1 album - I listed a tie for No. 2.

I have no idea why, in retrospect. It seemed at the time like such a bold statement for me to make. "Nothing is great enough for me to christen as *my* album of the year, so I will withhold this honor."

Imagine the disappointment of the artists who released albums that year.

I also suspect I stole the idea. *Trouser Press* magazine, my mainline into the music I loved in the late 1970s and early 1980s, one year declined to name a No. 1 album. I thought that was cool.

Still not sure why.

I've been going through old albums recently, and pulled out Janet Jackson's *Rhythm Nation 1814.* It's an album I always liked. When I was putting together my list of best albums of 1989, however, I didn't feel right putting *Rhythm Nation 1814* at No. 1.

Still not sure why.

So I left my No. 1 spot empty, and shared the No. 2 position between *Rhythm Nation 1814* and Faith No More's *The Real Thing.*

No longer.

I am now changing *Rhythm Nation 1814* to the No. 1 spot from the year.

I'm making myself feel better about it by saying I'm not really replacing anything, I'm just finally making a decision - a quarter-century too late.

Rhythm Nation 1814 is an audacious effort. It's socially relevant, a bold artistic statement from a woman who could have been viewed as a pawn of producers Jimmy Jam and Terry Lewis. She had no business attempting something so bold, and no one had any business expecting her to be anything more than a lightweight dance music queen.

Kind of the same thing I thought about Madonna when her career started.

I realized as I listened to *Rhythm Nation 1814* again how great and diverse it is musically. There's dance, pop, ballads and some kickass rock. In fact, I'm able to find in *Rhythm Nation 1814* what so many find in her brother Michael's *Thriller* album. For me, *Rhythm Nation 1814* is a solid collection of songs that additionally builds to a greater whole.

***

No. 100. *King of America*, Elvis Costello (1986) – The last time he truly surprised me. At the time, it seemed he might surprise me every two or three years. Favorite songs: "Brilliant Mistake," "Indoor Fireworks," "American Without Tears"

***

No. 99. *Sandinista!*, The Clash (1980) – Smart critics at the time called it their *White Album*, which makes more sense to me now than it did then. Then, I was excited about six sides of Clash music, even though I had no understanding of dub. Favorite songs: "The Magnificent Seven," "Police on My Back," "Washington Bullets"

I'd like to go back in time and ask myself what I was hearing in *Sandinista!*

I vividly remember walking into my neighborhood record store and spending $9.99 plus tax for the three-album set. (I am old enough that I vividly remember my neighborhood record store.) At the time, The Clash had released the double album *London Calling* and the 35-minute 10-inch EP *Black Market Clash* less than a year previous, so a fresh triple set was making me think (long before they were declared as such) that The Clash might be the only band that mattered.

Critics at the time and now who take issue with the bloated nature of the album may be missing the point. What I hear now is an album broken into pieces largely of like styles, save for one or two songs, four or six minutes per side. It's in those moments that the band places its style experiments, starkly contrasting with the remainder of the side. Sick of the reggae/dub stuff? You can't be if one of their rocking or popping or comical songs suddenly shows up. Certain songs may have felt like they overstayed their welcome at the time, but would fit in perfectly now on a trip-hop playlist.

I remember stomping around downtown Rochester and angrily insisting that "Hitsville U.K." could be a hit single if only one of those stupid radio stations would play it so people could actually hear it. In retrospect, the only thing I can guess is I must have thought anything with a Motown bass line could be a hit single. It's almost the same with "The Sound of Sinners."

I also wonder in retrospect how much of my appreciation of the album came from me crawling up inside it for consolation after John Lennon's murder. I remember ending a three-year moratorium on concerts in Jan. 1981, mere weeks after Lennon's death, and seeing Squeeze and Elvis Costello in concert and realizing music hadn't died for me just because Lennon did.

Whatever the reason, it's fascinating to revisit and hear how busy and complex it is, and realize I was getting something out of it.

***

No. 98. "Hey Jude/The Beatles Again," The Beatles (1970) – As I tried to gather up all their tracks as a teen, this was vital because of how it gathered cuts previously unavailable on album. In addition, this holds up well with repeated listens. Favorite songs: "Revolution," "Hey Jude," "The Ballad of John and Yoko"

"Out of print" was among the most difficult concepts for me to grasp in my early teens. I was surrounded by stores overflowing with books and records. There was an entire business sub-culture devoted to selling *used* versions of these items.

How could this stuff be impossible to find?

I was to learn. I began searches that would take two or three years to find a specific pressing. I would run into newcomers to the record pursuit and nod sagely and sadly as they described their determination to find a grail whose existence couldn't even be proven. It might have been out there, but those of us who were looking hadn't found it yet.

And with some acts, I didn't realize how fortunate I was to be exactly where I was in time. And this is where the album *The Beatles Again* comes in.

You might not even be aware of this album. Or you might know it as "Hey Jude." To my friends and me, the content was far more important than the name.

There was a tremendous divide among my friends who liked The Beatles, and I was more likely to be on the opposite side. As we young teen males perused the work and tried to establish our toughness and coolness, we generally weren't allowed to admit to liking "soft" songs. There'd better be guitars, drums, speed and anger. (One of the key reasons Elvis Costello originally appealed to me.) I was the first among my peer group to own both of The Beatles' double-album sets, *1962-1966* and *1967-1970*. More than one friend told me they would have bought the blue *1967-1970* set and waited on the red *1962-1966,* if they'd have bought it at all. But the red album had both "She Loves You" and "Can't Buy Me Love." Those were (and are) two of The Beatles' greatest songs, and I needed them in my life as much as I needed "Hey Jude" and "Revolution."

We all started to work our various ways through various bands' catalogs as we tried to catch up. And one of the first of the "original" Beatles albums to come into my life was *The Beatles Again/Hey Jude.*

A friend had the album before I did. We sat in his bedroom and listened, and I marveled at the distinct songs on the album, from the previously mentioned "Can't Buy Me Love" to the previously mentioned "Hey Jude" and "Revolution." I didn't realize it at the time, but the album – actually simply a selection of Beatles recordings that had never been released on Capitol Records – was really a cross-section of The Beatles' history, more anthology than greatest hits.

Oh, it could have passed as a greatest hits album. I was smart enough even at the time to realize "Hey Jude" and "Revolution," which came out in 1968, had combined to provide one of the greatest values ever for a 7-inch vinyl record. "Can't Buy Me Love" (1964) was among my favorites in the early blitz. I remembered friends who (probably inherited or poached from siblings) had the singles of "Lady Madonna" and "The Ballad of John and Yoko." (Yes, I lived quite intensely through the shock, disgust and scandal of John Lennon singing "Christ" on a record.) I knew "Don't Let Me Down" and "Old Brown Shoe" due to their inclusion on *1967-1970*.

So *"he Beatles Again/Hey Jude* was a twisted little record. It was one Allan Klein had organized to get The Beatles income at the newly negotiated increased royalty rate. Songs that had never been scooped onto a Capitol Records album were piled on to this. (In a cruel twist, there were several other songs that ended up stranded in strange places, making it impossible to collect The Beatles' discography without dozens of duplications.)

But bless them for this one, at least. It leans slightly Lennon, which matches what my gut has always been, even if my head often prefers McCartney. But best of all, it's a perfect example that, from 1964 to 1969, these guys covered a lot of ground, and never repeated themselves. It remains an album I can hold up and say, "If your favorite can do something this grand, then good for the world, because not a lot of people can do something this great."

I love everything about this album, even the things that are wrong. And it starts with the cover. The spine says *Hey Jude"* But you look on the inside, and original printings say *The Beatles Again*. And I didn't realize it at the time, but even the cover photos are allegedly reversed – the back photo is actually supposed to be the front. (Which still doesn't make sense to me. Why would you pick that photo over the actual cover used, yet another group shot of The Beatles, clever in its simplicity?)

And why does the album start with the old songs? Why would "Hey Jude" *start* the second side? And even trying to logic it away by thinking the songs were placed in chronological release order, why would "Revolution" be at the end of the first side when it was really the B-side of "Hey Jude"?

Why are "The Ballad of John and Yoko" and "Old Brown Shoe" separated by a song that was on the charts earlier?

All of these things can be explained, of course. And none of them are as life-shatteringly important as I felt they were at the time.

I like to routinely express disappointment at compilations, particularly compilations of performers whose full catalog is at least as important, if not more so, than an easy skimming of their discography.

Then on the other hand, there are albums like *1962-1966, 1967-1970* and *The Beatles Again/Hey Jude.* These albums formed and solidified my love for the most important art of my lifetime.

It's possible to discern a theme for each Beatles album. For me, the theme of *The Beatles Again/Hey Jude* might as well be "Let's put together a pile of songs that Little Teen Timmy Cain will like."

How can I criticize them for that?

***

No. 97. *Meaty Beaty Big and Bouncy,* The Who (1971) – In addition to helping me understand what they were before I became familiar with them, this gave me a chance to show off and identify which member was represented by what word in the title. Favorite songs: "The Kids Are Alright," "Happy Jack," "Substitute"

No. 96. *Aja,* Steely Dan (1977) – This is very close to *Gaucho* on this list, because I view them as two parts of a fantastic whole. This album sounds so good, and the title track, which bored the then-impatient little punk rocker in me, I now find as subversive in its calm as any punk record that followed it. Favorite songs: "Black Cow," "I Got the News," "Aja"

No. 95. *Rumours,* Fleetwood Mac (1977) – The depth in this album was astonishing. That it was made by five angry, depressed and drug-addled people is a testament to their emotions and skills. Favorite songs: "Second Hand News," "The Chain," "Gold Dust Woman"

No. 94. *Them Or Us,* Frank Zappa (1984) – Probably Zappa's most stylistically convoluted album. There are a lot of topical references and inside jokes that may put off the casual listener. But the casual listener probably shouldn't be busting in to Frank Zappa double albums anyway. Favorite songs: "In France," "Stevie's Spanking," "Be in My Video"

No. 93. *Killer*, Alice Cooper (1971) – The band at their most frightening. We move past Dwight Fry screaming "I want to get out of here" to the Jim Morrison-meets-Wild West "Desperado," and the terrorizing "Dead Babies"/"Killer" closer. They weren't yet the cartoon they became. (And that was still a really good cartoon.) Favorite songs: "Halo of Flies," "You Drive Me Nervous," "Dead Babies"

No. 92. *Highway 61 Revisited,* Bob Dylan (1965) – This album, more than anything else he did, overwhelmingly influenced the popular music that followed it. Maybe his acoustic protests didn't get your attention. But if you could turn away after that rimshot gunshot that opens the album, you were incapable of paying attention at all. Favorite songs: "It Takes a Lot to Laugh, It Takes a Train to Cry," "Like a Rolling Stone," "Ballad of a Thin Man"

***

No. 91. *Empty Glass,* Pete Townshend (1980) – The halo on the cover, given the contents of the record and of the remainder of the cover, is fantastically comic. I wouldn't wish his issues at the time on anyone, but he turned it into the best album The Who never made. Favorite songs: "Rough Boys," "Let My Love Open the Door," "Gonna Get Ya"

(2012)

For a time in my adolescence and into young adulthood, one of the key musical figures was Pete Townshend.

As I wrote in a column about him 10 years ago, "Townshend was not just a great songwriter, in my book. He was articulating some of my thoughts. He wasn't John Lennon and Paul McCartney, composing music for the ages. He was Pete Townshend, writing songs for the here and now, continuing to say things in his music that some of us knew, but couldn't articulate."

For me, it started with *Who's Next* and *Meaty Beaty Big and Bouncy,* released consecutively in 1971. The first was one of the greatest rock albums ever, and the second was a greatest hits of the first five years of The Who. The dazzling brilliance and variety filled my brain, and left me scrambling to catch up and keep up. Which I did.

I followed Townshend through the decline of The Who and the ascendancy of his solo career, which exploded for me with 1980's *Empty Glass*, his breathtaking response to punk rock. Fewer were enthralled with 1982's *All the Best Cowboys Have Chinese Eyes,* but his wordplay, spoken-word stylings and ability to remain innovative still kept me around.

Then, just as Greg Proops said he did with Woody Allen post-"Annie Hall," I decided Pete Townshend's career had ended.

Not that there haven't been bits of the old Townshend popping up in his subsequent work. Just not enough to keep me interested, no matter how much I tried. And then came the whole child porn issue, which just leaves me baffled, even 10 years down the line and a large part of a biography later.

I've recently finished Townshend's *Who I Am,* an autobiography that's well-written (which I expected – he's a great writer of song and of stories), confounding (the details are like dice pouring out of a cup – I keep trying to catch glimpses of the other sides) and yeah, probably a little self-serving. (The way Townshend continually returns to the child porn discussion is often jarring, and sometimes gives a desperate feel of self-justification. Which, of course, is his right.)

The biggest problem I have with most biographies is I'm not particularly interested in starting my journey by reading about a child. Start with the adult – that's why I'm interested to begin with – and feel free to weave in details of the child, when appropriate. That's the way to grab my eyes. If you as a reader want every story to start exactly at the beginning, then we just look for different things.

So bluntly, my interest in Townshend is from the 1960s – as he was joining The Who – into the mid-1980s.

And my interest in him is far more in his art than in him. I never would have suspected that. But in his book, as he continues to go into details about his marriage and his indulgences and his boats and houses, I am bored. I am far more fascinated about details of his interaction with Jimi Hendrix, or his hearing choirs of music only in his head, or his band's work on the road.

Townshend was at the center of the most creative period of popular music in the 20th century. Yet, he seems to think everyone has already experienced that journey.

I'd recommend *Who I Am* to fans of Townshend, especially those who haven't read many of his interviews. But when I was first discovering the man, *Rolling Stone* magazine put out a book with a collection of stories done on The Who into the early 1970s. The book collected a number of Townshend interviews, including a lengthy piece where he first articulated his thoughts about the rock opera he was developing, which became *Tommy*.

I was hoping *Who I Am* would be more like that – a collection of brilliant thoughts and concepts from a brilliant man. I just set my expectations too high and too different from what he wanted to do.

***

No. 90. *She*, Willie Wisely (1996) – Clever and tight, but not too clever or too tight. While power pop, Wisely plays impressively with other styles. Given its time and the circumstances of its record, a particularly amazing production. Favorite songs: "Ready to Wear," "Lady of Love," "Go!"

No. 89. *Wish You Were Here,* Pink Floyd (1975) – Why was this such a disappointment at its time? Each piece fits, just as the pieces fit with *The Dark Side of the Moon*. Only this time, it's more sad. The people who set the misery of everyday life to music with *Dark Side* here revealed the intensity of their own misery. Favorite songs: "Shine On You Crazy

Diamond (Parts I–V)," "Welcome to the Machine," "Have a Cigar"

No. 88. *Plastic Ono Band*, John Lennon (1970) – However prepared you are, it's still a stunner to hear him sing "I don't believe in Beatles." The brilliance in its production is how few tricks there are. This is unabashedly honest. And maybe not many other people can, but I can sure hear the "wind" with which Yoko Ono is credited. Favorite songs: "Working Class Hero," "Look at Me," "God"

No. 87. *Imperial Bedroom*, Elvis Costello (1982) – I've always thought of this as his *Abbey Road*. The sounds come from everywhere, and polish up a cinemascopic collection of lyrics. "… And in Every Home" would have fit comfortably anywhere on The Beatles' album. Favorite songs: "Beyond Belief," "Kid About It," "Human Hands"

No. 86. *Sheik Yerbouti*, Frank Zappa (1979) – His broad step into broad comedy. It still contains some amazing musicianship, and most of the style parodies are great songs in their own right. He did the same thing two years later with an album that sits at No. 28. Favorite songs: "Flakes," "I'm So Cute," "Tryin' to Grow a Chin"

***

No. 85. *Pink Pearl*, Jill Sobule (2000) – Like Randy Newman, Sobule is at her best telling stories (true to life and presumably manufactured). For every smile, there's a twinge of sympathy. Even for Mary Kay Letourneau. Favorite songs: "Lucy at the Gym," "Heroes," "Mary Kay"

(Feb. 9, 2005)

I have a bigger love-hate relationship with Paul McCartney than almost any other entertainer.

Many times, his music has lifted my spirit higher than I thought possible. I can always find someone to blast the McCartney recordings I truly love (*Ram, Band on the Run, Venus and Mars, Back to the Egg, Flaming Pie, Run Devil Run*) and I can always find someone who will praise the stuff I like less (*Flowers in the Dirt, McCartney II, Wings at the Speed of Sound*).

255

(I still can't find anyone who likes *Press to Play.*)

McCartney played his song "Freedom" at the 2002 Super Bowl, and also wound up singing with FOX football commentator Terry Bradshaw. At that time, I wrote this:

Paul McCartney has made some horrendous mistakes in his long and storied career, he's fortunately made very few. The album *Press to Play* was one, the screenplay for *Give My Regards to Broad Street* another.

Perhaps the worst, though, was his Super Bowl "duet" on "A Hard Day's Night" with Bradshaw. McCartney was graceful, however, in not pointing out that Bradshaw massacred the lyrics.

That comment led to this e-mail from an angry reader (this is verbatim, all spelling and grammar errors intact - hey, when you're angry, you type fast):

"Am I really reading this right? You made the comment that Paul McCartney has made some really "horrendous" mistakes in his life.What kind of comment is that? This being from a writer from some small town newspaper.

E"xcuse me, bus hasn't Mr. McCartney been a member of a band that has sold the most albums / music in the history of music? If not, he's darn close. And was't his band (and bands) voted the most popular ever in the history of music? And I think Paul has made some pretty good social statements, too.

"I saw the Super Bowl half time interview and found it very amusing. Seems that Terry Bradshaw and crew have the highest rated NFL pre-game show. So what if he butchered the song. Mr. McCartney did not wreck the song.

"I'm sure you did not make a few mistakes in your life. I guess that's why you are writing for the Decatur Herald instead of the Chicago Tribune or New York Times.

"That is about the worst comment I have ever seen a journalist write.

"Get a life."

For the record, I've made a lot of mistakes, including paying list price for McCartney's *Pipes of Peace* album.

Now, I suppose it would be extremely ungracious of me to point out that the most recently written song among McCartney's selections for that Super Bowl halftime show at Sunday's Super Bowl ("Live and Let Die") is 32 years old.

But it's still telling that McCartney - the "tame" entertainment choice after last year's free-for-all - came under fire for performing "Get Back," with its lines about "California grass" and cross-dressing.

Maybe the post-Super Bowl episode of *The Simpsons* summed up our collective confusion over what we want from entertainment. Homer Simpson and neighbor Ned Flanders combine on a halftime show that recreates the Biblical flood, and are faced with a wave of criticism, including a "woman on the street" who's interviewed and complains she's trying to raise her son as a secular humanist, and it's impossible with entertainment like the Simpson/Flanders show.

Somebody's always going to be angry about something.

Singer-songwriter Jill Sobule wrote a song for her 2000 album *Pink Pearl* (my album of the year for 2000, by the way) called "Heroes." In the song, Sobule details the shortcomings of any number of heroic historic figures, including William Faulkner, Dorothy Parker, Orson Wells, Pablo Picasso, Babe Ruth, Bob Dylan, and "that guy in *Seven Years in Tibet.*"

The song includes the line "Paul McCartney jealous of John, even more so now that he's gone." In a 2002 appearance in Peoria, Sobule introduced the song by asking if people had seen the McCartney-Bradshaw duet, and added, "Didn't that just make you sad?"

After the show, I told Sobule what I'd written about it, and she laughed. Then I told her about the e-mail, boiling it down to, "Paul McCartney was great, he was in The Beatles, you live in Decatur and you suck."

Sobule laughed again, then said, "You know, I suppose that's probably true."

And I thought she liked me.

***

No. 84. *Tommy*, The Who (1969) – The first (but not last) time they were transcendent. I never had trouble understanding the story. I also never lit a candle while it was playing to reveal my future. "See me, feel me, touch me, heal me" is among the greatest lyrics ever. The Broadway show and film are totally different and inferior entities. Favorite songs: "Christmas," "I'm Free," "We're Not Gonna Take It"

No. 83. *Randy Newman's 'Faust'* (1995) – Now here's a concept piece that floats around, confusing with the presence of James Taylor and Don Henley, and baffling with a title that doesn't match the popular thought of what the album might be. It's a combination of *Faust, Paradise Lost* and *The Devil and Daniel Webster.* Oh, and it ends with a love song to Las Vegas. Favorite songs: "Glory Train," "Feels Like Home," "Happy Ending"

***

No. 82. *Dog Problems,* The Format (2006) – A spectacularly tight concept album about relationship woes. ("Dog Problems" are what you have when you break up.) This paved the way for the band fun., but The Format was more fun. Favorite songs: "Time Bomb," "She Doesn't Get It," "Inches and Falling"

December 2006

Every once in a while, an album comes out of nowhere, making you wonder where it came from, what facilitated its creation and how it could possibly ring so true.

That's the case with *Dog Problems* by The Format, an Arizona-based band.

The album has been greeted with overwhelmingly positive reviews as writers struggle to accurately describe the sounds in this pop offering.

Beatles. Beach Boys. The Zombies. Supertramp. Queen. Raspberries.

Dwight Twilley. Barenaked Ladies. The Shins. Sufjan Stevens.

Pet Sounds. Abbey Road. Band on the Run. The Soft Bulletin.

Those comparisons are all accurate, but *Dog Format* is both less and more than any combination of the above.

The album is about the disintegration of a five-year relationship.

Singer Nate Ruess and his girlfriend bought a dog after each of their break-ups. (Hence the title. One of the dogs ran away and is referenced on the song "Snails.") The album's 12 songs deal with the affair in retrospect, with all of the guilt, accusations, recriminations and regret in place.

And it's all wrapped with a clever, melodic bow. That's where the *Pet Sounds* and Zombies comparisons come in. It's not necessarily that The Format sounds like that album and band. It's that the style is similar, the feel is the same.

This is a cerebral effort, but many listeners will simply get an hour of enjoyable pop music out of it. And that's fine.

Like The Beach Boys and The Zombies before them, early-20-somethings Nate Reuss and Sam Means have created a mature album that deals with timeless issues of love gained and lost. Yet they didn't forget to have some fun in the meantime, creating catchy melodies that often bury the lyrics' bleakness.

There are details so personal yet so perfect, it's sometimes painful to listen. ("This is the sound of my heart breaking, and I hope it's entertaining," Reuss sings on the title track.) Reuss and Means have an eye for specific details that let listeners know what they're saying, even without necessarily experiencing it.

In the album's first song, "Matches," the singer discovers a jacket he never wore, but recalls "it once kept you warm." He finds matches in the pocket, but at by the end of the song, he finds he "made a wish, but the match never lit." Musically, a calliope plays in the background.

This isn't your standard-issue emo album.

"Time Bomb" is a hit single is a parallel universe, the centerpiece of the album, the place where the concept is cemented. The boy complains that the girl - who at one point we're told has attempted suicide - "swore 'together forever'," but she clearly has "no concept of time."

Later in the song, she returns, and he observes, "You're just in time to wreck my life."

But it's not as though the album is dour. Many could listen to "Time Bomb" and not gather the bitterness. The juxtaposition of dark lyrics and upbeat music adds to the depth.

So does a sense of humor. The title track owes more than a little bit to Queen; Reuss has the vocal chops to at least echo Queen singer Freddie Mercury, if not match him. And Reuss also has the love of the studio to sit and overlay vocal track upon vocal track to mimic Queen's (and/or The Beach Boys') falsetto choir sound.

In fact, in a clever, low-budget video for the track, the Queen joke is played out hilariously. The lead "character" in the video is a hand. That's right, a hand, making movements in sync with the vocal. (Atop the second knuckle is a small replica of Reuss' trademark hat.) When the song builds to its Queen-like choir peak, three more hands appear - looking like a poor man's version of the famous shot of the group that opens the "Bohemian Rhapsody" video.

(And in a comic but eerie callback to the girl's suicide attempt, in one shot in the video, there's a Band-Aid on the wrist of the "singer.")

Yet The Format's album is definitely modern. In the title track, Reuss takes a shot at the MySpace generation, singing, "But boys in swooping haircuts are bringing me down/Taking pictures of themselves."

In "Inches and Falling," there's a more-than-passing reference to "Playground in My Mind," a coy hit from 1973 known best for its chorus of "My name is Michael, I've got a nickel." Yet the sing-songy tone of The Format song masks a deeply cynical set of lyrics, where a pilled-up singer accuses his departed lover of looking for someone else who "can treat you wrong."

And by the end of the album, the singer has found the ultimate in anger, despair and revenge. "If she seems as lonely as me, let her sink, let her sink, let her sink."

Concept albums aren't cool, and they may even be an anachronism in today's iPod, single-song, downloading culture. A number of The Format's songs work as individual tunes ("Time Bomb" in particular), but the album has a powerful impact as a unit.

Dog Problems was a gutsy chance for the band to take. It's a gamble that pays off again and again, especially for the listener.

***

No. 81. *Stands for Decibels*, The dB's (1981) – I was so overwhelmed by the brilliance of this album, I was stunned to realize they weren't a huge chart success. It didn't make me like them any less. It might have made me like them more. Favorite songs: "Black and White," "Tearjerkin'," "Big Brown Eyes"

No. 80. *Big World,* Joe Jackson (1986) – This hit the music lover in me with the melodies, the disgusted cynic with the lyrics, and the absurdist in me with its methods. It was recorded live, and it has three sides on two albums, a concession the record company made so Jackson could release the same songs on vinyl and on CD. He cuts across styles effortlessly. Favorite songs: "Wild West," "We Can't Live Together," "The Jet Set"

***

No. 79. *Legend,* Poco (1978) – Almost a country yacht rock album. By this time, even their label had given up on them. Fans from 10 years earlier might not have recognized or approved of the hits. Those hits were fantastic nevertheless. Favorite songs: "Heart of the Night," "The Last Goodbye," "Legend"

The most drastic intense discussion I've had came interviewing Don "American Pie" Maclean. He was ill, and ultimately wound up postponing the show to a later date. He may have been extra feisty as a result. And I admit to being a little irritated with Maclean after seeing him perform 10 years earlier.

Not with his performance, which was fine, but with the arrogance of his between-songs lectures to the audience. He admonished us to hang on to our publishing (thanks for the tip), and made it clear he didn't have to be there playing for us, he played because he wanted to. He blasted grunge music (which definitely dates the story), saying it wasn't music. He was proud he'd protected his copyrights, and pointed at a 4-year-old hoisted on a man's shoulders and said, "I love seeing that, because she'll be a fan in a few years and buying CDs and putting money in my pocket."

Nothing quite like a little summer sunshine.

During our interview, Maclean kept on talking about hanging on to his copyrights and how much business savvy he had, and he repeated the whole routine about doing it because he loved it, because he had so much money because he was so smart.

We were both a little edgy during the conversation. Somehow, I irritated him. I was trying to be honestly complimentary to his music. He couldn't even take that. When I said his song "Dreidel" was one my favorites, he dismissed me by saying, "Ahh, it was a lousy recording."

Out of frustration, I ultimately wound up saying, "Don, it occurs to me that if you'd have spent as much time and energy on your music as you have on your business, we might be talking about your new album, or we might not be talking at all, because you'd be playing a bigger venue."

To his credit, he didn't curse at me and hang up. (I probably would have hung up on me at that point.) We continued to intensely discuss the nature of business versus art. At one point, he called me "foolish and naive." At one point, I told him something he said "may be the biggest pile of crap I've heard all year, and I've heard a lot of nonsense."

So intense discussions will happen. But I never expected what I wound up with talking to Poco guitar player Rusty Young.

Young was talking about what it's like to still be on the road after more than 35 years.

"We enjoy it much more than we did 20 or 30 years ago," He said. "We were always fighting for a hit single, trying to get the album to sell. We don't have that kind of pressure any more."

I have a couple of reference books at my desk, and quickly pulled them out to point out that "Keep on Tryin' " (1975) and "Rose of Cimmaron" (1976) got plenty of airplay where I was. "Yeah," Young said, "but you've got to be in the top 20 before it's a hit." (Their single "Crazy Love" and "Legend," the 1978 album it was on, both made the top 20.)

It was only after we hung up that I was struck with the insanity of me trying to convince Rusty Young that he'd had hits "where I came from." It probably meant about as much to him as it means to me when somebody tells me David Hasselhoff is wildly popular in Germany.

***

No. 78. *Hotel California,* Eagles (1976) – Pardons every excess which they ever committed, or of which they were ever accused. The closing solo(s) of the title cut is a lesson on how perfect pop and rock were constructed in the mid-70s. Favorite songs: "Hotel California," "Wasted Time," "Victim of Love"

There are a few artists with whom I have … oh, let's say *complicated* relationships.

They all seem to be artists I encountered early in my life and the few among those that stuck around in some way, shape or form for a half-century or so. Paul McCartney is one. Jeff Lynne is another. Rod Stewart. Pete Townshend.

263

And certainly Don Henley.

Now let me be clear about all of the acts mentioned. I adore them. They combine for about three dozen of the entries on my 365 favorite albums list. But each of them have also gone through periods -- *lengthy* periods -- where my reactions to their work was either "What the hell are you doing?" or "What the hell is the matter with you?"

At first, Don Henley was just this guy in Eagles. (And by the way, is they The Eagles now, or the Eagles, or just Eagles? They insisted on no article "the" early in their career, and then by the 1990s, best-of collections were coming out saying "The Eagles." That after their ongoing and kind of painful efforts to avoid any use of it: *Their Greatest Hits, The Best of Eagles, The Legend of Eagles.*)

Then, as it felt like their albums were piling up high with diminishing returns, along comes their fourth album. The last voice you heard when listening to *On the Border* was Henley singing the execrable "Best of My Love." When your music was too wimpy for me, a born sucker for wimpy pop, there was something seriously wrong. (Of course, in this case, as it often is when I found something "seriously wrong" with a recording, it sold like crazy. "Best of My Love" was Eagles' first No. 1 record.)

Then the first voice you hear on *One of These Nights* is the same guy. Only this time, he's singing the title track, which has a bit of bite to it, and the vocal work is pretty amazing, both by Henley and the band. All of a sudden, Henley changed the band by revealing a voice that could do as many positive things as bandmate Glenn Frey. And maybe, just maybe, Henley had the capability to add enough hits to Eagles' catalog and maybe bury "Tequila Sunrise" in the graveyard it deserved to go.

That set the stage for Eagles' greatest moments and Henley's first steps toward being bigger than big. Because the next release was *Hotel California.*

It's not a surprise that *Hotel California* is an album that divides Eagles fans. It's whiny, entitled, celebratory of excess and misogyny, and it's arrogant. The story had played out that way before and would again. It was Eagles' turn. You loved them or hated them.

Or you did both, like I did. The missing word in the series above is "smug." Smug is when you're arrogant about your talents and contemptuous of those who don't recognize those talents. Don Henley gave the interviews to put those traits on display. Liberal politics? Environmental protection and conservation? We were on the same side. But given the way he was preaching, I knew he was going to be pinned against the wall by people arguing the other side.

But for the life of me, I can't find any of the quotes that so inflamed my passions in the 1970s and early 1980s. And therein lies some of the complexity of the relationship. Is it possible that Don Henley was so wise beyond his years that 20 or 30 years later, as I read things he'd written and said, I realized he'd been right all along?

Nah.

But it's certainly a case of things that once meant a great deal grew to mean significantly less.

Besides, I could and can forgive a lot when I listen to some of those songs. He has four tour de forces on *Hotel California:* the title track, "Life in the Fast Lane" (even though that song makes every complaint about the band accurate -- they were living this life while pretending to be above it), "Victim of Love" and "Wasted Time." The next studio piece they released after *Hotel California* was "Please Come Home for Christmas," a holiday recording clearly designed to show they still existed as an entity. Henley's singing of it is my favorite version. He brings some true sadness to his delivery, setting it either off or perfectly with the picture sleeve on the single, with the band sitting poolside in all their weedy 70s shirtless splendor.

See, there's part of the problem. Their communication with us came via interviews and song lyrics and photographs. They chose to allow the image that went out with the "Please Come Home for Christmas" single, shirtless guys sitting around an opulent pool, with a handful of "chicks" around for decoration. They also chose to allow the image of the allegedly Satanic inner photo on the *Hotel California* album. (That was stuff I didn't hear about until long after the fact.) How we were supposed to evaluate this in a way other than what I did?

Then again, when Elton John released *Goodbye Yellow Brick Road,* I took the lyrics literally enough that I assume he was retiring from the business. (In retrospect, boy -- talk about going out at the very very top, if he had …) I'm only going to mention The Dude from *The Big Lebowski* to acknowledge a whole movement of Eagles hate in the universe. I get every complaint critics make about the band. I also think most of those complaints apply to a lot of music acts, and Eagles are only a lightning rod because of how high they climbed the mountain. The biggest target draws the most fire.

Henley was an artist who thought the standard contract in the recording industry was unjust, and he fought to change that. He wanted to protect Walden Woods, and established an organization that would do just that. Why would I be bothered by an artist and human following their heart?

I don't know. But Henley sure annoyed me. But at the same time, no matter what artistic or societally corrective path he was taking, I was paying close attention.

His second solo single was "Dirty Laundry," my favorite from his solo career, depending on what day it is. I thought maybe his split from Frey and the rest of the band might be a beneficial idea.

In 1984, he put out *Building the Perfect Beast.* It was an album I liked more than I wanted to (my suspicions of Henley were already growing), but not enough to even ponder it as among the best of the year. I could easily think of a dozen better. It had that song in whose video he rode around in the back of a truck for a night, lip-synced a song, and MTV lost its mind. I was more impressed by the next single, "All She Wants To Do Is Dance," and its video was even more clever.

But that "Boys of Summer" song just hung around. And maybe I was reacting a bit intensely to the lyrics. He sings about seeing a Deadhead sticker on a Cadillac, and I thought, "Oh, and I'll bet that was a fucking *tragedy*, wasn't it, Don? Was it on somebody else's Cadillac? Or on yours, and you finally noticed because you walked up from behind it when someone was opening the back door for you?"

The album sold 3 million copies, but it topped out on the Billboard album charts at No. 13. That's the kind of year 1984 was.

He always managed to surprise me. "Sunset Grill" was near the end of *Building the Perfect Beast.* It ranked with the best of his moderately-paced epics. I was disinterested in *The End of the Innocence* until I heard "The Heart of the Matter." A couple of years later, I was sitting in the theater watching *Leap of Faith* and heard a strange, slow and haunting version of "Sit Down, You're Rocking the Boat" from *Guys and Dolls.* That was done by Henley, and prompted me to buy the soundtrack album.

(Although it also had Patti LaBelle's "Are You Ready For a Miracle," which has to be played with the volume set at "11.")

Then came the true and triumphant tour de force, thanks to Randy Newman.

Newman's apparent respect for the skills of Eagles always threw me for a bit of a loop. Newman's sarcastic disdain for the respectable midstream of rock seemed designed to hold the band in contempt. Yet he had them singing on *Little Criminals.* I chose to ignore that they were singing on "Rider in the Rain," itself a kind of parody of Eagles' style. I caught on more quickly when Newman had Paul Simon make fun of Paul Simon on "The Blues" on *Trouble in Paradise.* It would have been like Newman managing to get members of Electric Light Orchestra to play on the mocking "The Story of a Rock and Roll Band" on *Born Again.*

I wasn't sure what to make of *Randy Newman's 'Faust'* as I looked at the cover. Newman was no stranger to broad concept pieces (exhibit A: *Good Old Boys*). But I looked at the names of the other featured singers -- Bonnie Raitt, Linda Ronstadt, James Taylor, Don Henley -- and thought, "Wait, what exactly is going on here?"

I delved in and was taken with the package. Newman writing himself the best lines as the devil and using James Taylor as a smug God delivering biting sarcasm, that was extra delicious.

Critic Robert Christgau observed, "Newman's Devil is a midlife whiner, James Taylor's God a palavering politician, Don Henley's Faust a bigger creep than both of them put together."

Calling Henley's Faust a creep would be criticizing the least of his sins. But Henley delivers as he blindly follows the devil's lead. Because of course he does.

Every large city has a couple of bands that regularly reunite and eventually give farewell shows, farewell shows that eventually turn into annual farewell shows. The Who are rock's masters of the farewell tour. (Although I once made that assertion in a blog, and was immediately beset upon by Who fans claiming there was only one farewell tour, and there was a reunion tour and an archive tour and another reunion tour and a "Quadrophenia" tour and ... Let's face it: No matter how much you love The Who -- and I do -- their last 40 years or so have been an ongoing pretense that they are doing anything more than giving you a chance to see the museum pieces one more time at arena prices.)

Eagles were and are in danger of becoming precisely that, particularly when the only original member of the band left is the old cranky guy who sings and plays drums once in a while and then makes a pronouncement that he and the band are never doing this again.

If you wanted to write an alternative narrative about Eagles, it could say this was a band that never realized its peak. With the release of *Hotel California,* they were on top. They took their time making the follow-up album, in their own way, anticipating a trend that would dominate the latter half of the next decade. Although I wouldn't suggest they did this deliberately, the release of the greatest hits album ahead of *Hotel California* -- introducing a whole audience to some of their ignored or forgotten early work -- and the "Please Come Home for Christmas" single masked the fact that they weren't matching the output of their peers.

That follow-up album (*The Long Run*) is disappointing, because how can it not be? It still sells a ton. Then they put out a live album, and then they go away.

So you have *One of These Nights* and *Hotel California* and *The Long Run* and a greatest hits and a double-live. And that's how they become on of the biggest selling artists ever -- popping at the right time with only enough pre-*One of These Nights* songs to round out one side of an album.

The excellent execution of the concept of *Hotel California* can not, should not and does not elevate *Desperado*.

Hmmmm. And I wonder why people get so worked up about the band, and why I get so worked up about Henley. I guess it's pretty easy, really. But remember, I was their demographic. They're all older, sure, but their peers weren't buying their early albums and waiting for them to even approach matching that first album like their younger early fans did. They were albums you could bring home to mom. The worst she was going to say was those boys needed haircuts.

**

(This ran somewhere late in 2011. It's a review of Ben Fong-Torres' Eagles book *Taking it to the Limit*. It somehow turned into a review of Don Henley's psyche. In either case, I never saw this quoted anywhere, so it might as well be here again. By this time, I'd given up on my fight against the use of the article, so they became The Eagles.)

I love a lot of Don Henley's music. His voice is most appealing to me of The Eagles' singers (he sang "Hotel California," "One of These Nights," "Best of My Love," "Desperado" and more), and I enjoy his solo work more than anyone else in the band.

And if I lived in a world where I only listened to his music, I'd probably be a huge Don Henley fan.

Unfortunately, I've been reading the guy's interviews and pronouncements for close to 40 years, and I find him to be one of the most insufferable human beings ever. To me, he's the kind of insufferable where even if you

269

share beliefs (and with Henley, I agree politically more often that not), the way the other person presents their views makes you reconsider your positions.

That feeling intensified as I read Ben Fong-Torres' book *Taking It To the Limit,* billed as "unofficial and unauthorized." The 192-page book fills in some blanks on The Eagles' early years, takes a fair amount from Don Felder's tell-all memoirs, features a bunch of great pictures (trust me on this one - I've been looking at photos of this band most of my life, and this book has a bunch I've never seen before) and makes Henley's serious and strident nature more annoying than ever.

This isn't the first 'behind the scenes' Eagles book, and others may have more dirt. Fong-Torres, a long-time *Rolling Stone* writer and confessed Eagles fan, at times takes it lightly on his subjects. And as great as the photos are, some of them are a pointless mess. (Why is there a full-page photo of Jethro Tull's Ian Anderson in a book about The Eagles?)

The way the band goes from a democracy to the domain of Henley and Glenn Frey is documented, but not explained as well as I'd like. Even a theory would be something new. Their cruelty toward the rest of the band's members - booted out one by one - is unbelievably ruthless. And their hypocrisy in adamantly insisting they'd never become an oldies act while ultimately doing that for longer than they were originally a group is ignored by Fong-Torres.

But the worst is reading about Henley's continual whines about being disrespected. Having the best-selling album of the 20th century (*Eagles: Their Greatest Hits 1971-1975*) and the decent reviews they always received should have been enough to counter any negativity they think has been directed at them. (I can easily find reviews trashing every Beatles or Led Zeppelin album without looking too hard. Finding negative Eagles reviews is more difficult.) Henley continues to come off as a complaining entitled crybaby who can't understand why everyone in the world doesn't operate on his mindset.

**

(When Glenn Frey died in 2006, I published this. A couple of days later, a writer for the New York Daily News wrote a piece headlined "Glenn

270

Frey's death is sad, but the Eagles were a horrific band." I mean, aim high if you're going to shoot up, but try to do so with a little panache. I wrote a blog in response, which the writer re-tweeted, apparently wanting to start some social media nonsense. I look, and he -- a New York-based writer -- only had about triple the Twitter followers I had, and I wasn't in four figures. Aim high, but don't waste your time.)

I always saw Glenn Frey as Eagles' David Gilmour to Don Henley's Roger Waters, comparing the power duo from the Frey/Henley band with Pink Floyd.

The roles band members play during the length of a career of a band as productive as Eagles (or as long as Pink Floyd) varies from year to year and album to album. But Frey and Gilmour seemed, in a general way, to be focused on making the music more commercial, more palatable to a larger audience.

Henley and Waters, meanwhile, were political lefties interested in big ideas and big entertainment concepts.

My immediate interest while observing their careers in real time was to follow Henley ahead of Frey. While he was occasionally insufferable, Henley's music was also more challenging as less obvious to my ear.

It seemed fitting to me that Frey was the one who ended up on *Miami Vice* and doing Pepsi commercials. Those were the easy, obvious steps, the ones that required less work.

At least that's how I saw it at the time. Removed from the emotions of MTV drawing lines in the musical sands, Frey's skills and his importance to Eagles became more and more clear.

It's likely fewer of us would know Don Henley without the sweetening and polish Frey brought to the music. Even as someone who disliked Frey's work the more easily he was able to identify it, I recognized and respected his skills. There was nothing easy or obvious about what he was doing. It's just that for a time, Glenn Frey was tied deeply into the sounds a large section of the music-listening public wanted to hear.

It's what made Eagles songs still sound great four decades after the fact, and it's why we mourn the passing of yet another high-level entertainer.

271

No. 77. *Graceland*, Paul Simon (1986) – By this time, Simon had spent a decade drifting away from commercial success and public interest. The video for "You Can Call Me Al" seemed to run 24/7, but that was fine, because it was something fresh, different and fun. Favorite songs: "The Boy in the Bubble," "Diamonds on the Soles of Her Shoes," "You Can Call Me Al"

I love Paul Simon's *Graceland* album. Always have.

It was my pick for album of the year in 1986. I remember hearing it before a concert at the Greek Theatre in Los Angeles – somebody there had landed an advance copy of the album, and we arrived at the show early enough to hear the whole thing.

I adored it. It combined everything I liked about Simon's solo career – the offbeat sounds of songs like "50 Ways to Leave Your Lover," the unlikely takes by a white New Yorker on traditionally black sounds (as on "Mother and Child Reunion" and "Loves Me Like a Rock") – and combined them with some really amazing lyrics. ("The Mississippi delta was shining like a National guitar" – wow. What a way to start a song.)

Now, in 1986, I wasn't completely ignorant about apartheid, the legal and enforced minority rule of whites in South Africa, which lasted from 1948 to 1994. If you want to be amazed at how horrible humans can be to one another, that's one bit of history that's not too far in our past – and post-Nazi Germany to boot – that will make you shake your head and question whether humanity is by nature good or evil.

But I'll also admit that a lot of what I knew about apartheid came from a whole bunch of people I recognized singing "I ain't going to play Sun City" on MTV.

That, by the way, is a pretty crazy list of folks put together. Steven Van Zandt wrote the song. The producer wrangled in Bruce Springsteen. Some of the other faces you see include Miles Davis, Grandmaster Melle Mel, Ruben Blades, Bob Dylan, Herbie Hancock, Ringo Starr, Lou Reed, Run DMC, Peter Gabriel, David Ruffin, Eddie Kendricks, Darlene Love, Bobby

Womack, Afrika Bambaataa, Kurtis Blow, Jackson Browne and then-girlfriend Darryl Hannah, Peter Wolf, U2, George Clinton, Keith Richards, Ronnie Wood, Bonnie Raitt, Hall and Oates, Jimmy Cliff, Stiv Bators, Gil-Scott Heron, Nona Hendryx, Pat Benatar and Joey Ramone.

Simon's *Graceland* came out to much uproar. He'd violated a United Nations sanction against performances in South Africa, said sanctions aimed at eliminating apartheid. South Africa faced sanctions and boycotts in many areas – economic, academic, cultural and sporting (the country was not invited to participate in the Olympics for years), among others.

Simon protested he was an artist, and besides, his efforts to expose the world to music from South Africa certainly helped the cause, raising more awareness of the wonderful art that was based in the country.

I bought into that. I had seen the name Ladysmith Black Mambazo, for example, but had no idea who they were. I probably never would have heard the multiple-member vocal group sing if not for the *Graceland* album, and I guarantee I never would have bought any of their albums. (And I did buy their albums for a while post-*Graceland.*)

I understood the protests. By the letter of the sanctions, Simon was guilty of a violation. But the United Nations didn't think so. And plenty of South African artists backed Simon, who employed musicians from the country on his subsequent tours (and one musician remains a Simon sideman to this day). I remember in particular being touched by the support of Hugh Masakela, a trumpet player who was one South African musician I knew.

(And a lot of you know at least one of his songs – he wrote "Grazing in the Grass." Go look that one up. You're likely to recognize it.)

The controversies circling *Graceland* weren't just about the cultural boycott. There were claims that Simon was stealing songs outright. Los Lobos was the loudest about this, and remain so.

Until I read a piece on the recording of the album in *Uncut* magazine, I had no idea how many studio tricks were involved. My favorite fun fact: The "bass solo" on "You Can Call Me Al" is in two pieces – the start is played forward, and the end is the same thing with the tape reversed. The bass player says it was a bit of a task learning how to play the piece live.

The *Uncut* story essentially hints that Simon *was* doing cultural and musical thievery. Musicians accustomed to recording dozens of songs in a day were baffled to be playing the same riffs (at this point, they weren't even really songs) over and over as Simon searched for inspiration.

There's a fine line between inspiration and stealing. Depending on how charitable you're being, Simon might have crossed it. The story indicates he at least borrowed heavily for some pieces from native musicians who wouldn't have known better.

(And to be fair, Simon did share some songwriting credits on the album.)

It seems to always be something with Simon. Either he's accused of thievery with Simon and Garfunkel's "El Condor Pasa" (on which he shared a writing credit) or of front-running with the rock instrumentation added to "The Sound(s) of Silence" (done without Simon's knowledge).

I've looked for years, and can't find any trace of this allegation. However, I distinctly remember reading this in the 1980s: A friend of Simon's broke a leg playing softball. The two were riding together in an ambulance, and Simon asked the friend to listen to a new Simon song and give his opinion.

It's probably not true, but it says something that I have to write "probably."

The between-the-lines and behind-the-scenes news from the *Uncut* story haven't changed my opinion about *Graceland*. I've listened to it through three times while writing this, and still think it's a brilliant album, far and away the best thing with which Simon has ever been associated. And that covers a lot of ground.

But it also makes me think of this moment. I saw Simon perform in Peoria in 1991. It was a fantastic show, relying heavily on *Graceland* and his recently released *Rhythm of the Saints*. (He also did a great version of "Bridge Over Troubled Water," which he originally wrote for partner Art Garfunkel.)

Near the end of the show, Simon played "You Can Call Me Al," to the audience's delight. When it was done, basking in the ovation, he said, "You liked that one? We can play it again."

And they did.

I turned to one of the people with whom I attended the show, and remembering the decades of fussy and intense Simon stories, said, "That's the most spontaneous thing Paul Simon's ever done in his life!"

I repeated the remark a couple of weeks later to a friend in Minnesota.

"Yeah, I saw him a few days ago," my friend said. "He did the same thing at the show here."

Which means something.

***

No. 76. *The Who By Numbers*, The Who (1975) – I didn't realize how personal these songs were to and about Pete Townshend. They just felt honest, touching, and hit me somewhere deep in my soul. Favorite songs: "Slip Kid," "Blue, Red and Grey," "In a Hand or a Face"

***

No. 75. *Ram*, Paul and Linda McCartney (1971) – It can be easy to lose sight of the fact that he wasn't Rock Senior Statesman at the time. He was the struggling Paul McCartney, who had less commercial success than his fellow ex-Beatles. This didn't help much with his chart success, but it's his most delightfully wacky efforts. No two songs are the same style, and "Monkberry Moon Delight" is his most brilliant non sequitur. Favorite songs: "Too Many People," "Smile Away," "Monkberry Moon Delight"

The great under-recognized part of Paul McCartney's history comes shortly after the breakup of The Beatles.

Nowhere is this better seen than in any collection of bootleg recordings, live recordings, unreleased recording and alternate takes from an incredibly fertile and yet relatively un-mined stretch between Wings' *Wildlife* album (his first chart "failure," it barely scraped Billboard's top 10 album chart in early 1972) and *Red Rose Speedway*. That album's summer 1973 ascendancy to No. 1 was the middle of a bizarre chart stretch where The Beatles "*1967-1970*" compilation topped the charts for a week, followed by *Red Rose Speedway* for three weeks and then fellow ex-Beatle George Harrison's *Living in the Material World* for five weeks.

(Other No. 1s from 1973 include Pink Floyd's *The Dark Side of the Moon, Don't Shoot Me, I'm Only the Piano Player* AND *Goodbye Yellow Brick Road* by Elton John, and Led Zeppelin's *Houses of the Holy*. What an odd and captivating year.)

What the 13-year-old me didn't realize as he was listening to *Red Rose Speedway* (and thinking, "Yeah, this has some good stuff on it, but it's really not as good as *Ram*, is it?") was McCartney had recorded close to another album and a half of songs that he trimmed from a planned two-album release. And some of those songs remain unreleased to this day.

You don't know McCartney songs like "1882," "Tragedy," "Best Friend," "Jazz Street" and "Night Out." Unless you're a trawler and collector in the music underground, where these tracks have been available for some time.

I was listening to a two-CD set, *The Complete Alternate Red Rose Speedway*. The original album runs 42 minutes. The *Alternate* collection runs about 150, with alternate takes, mixes and versions of the officially released tracks. Especially around this period, McCartney was a master at monkeying with arrangements and mixes, and many of these takes are just a little polish short of being releasable. (Similarly, some of the released tracks suffer from too much polish.)

I mentioned how 1973 was an odd and captivating year. Let me expand it a bit and consider this:

The Beatles' breakup announcement came in spring 1970. From that point through the end of 1973 – a four-year stretch - the three songwriting Beatles were particularly prolific. McCartney released 52 songs on five albums (and an addition eight songs on singles only). John Lennon released

49 songs on four albums (including one double album). Lennon also released seven non-album single cuts. And George Harrison released 34 songs on two albums (one was a triple-album) and four singles-only songs.

That's how crazy prolific and talented these guys were. And I hold McCartney up as the shining example of their talent and prolific nature because not only did he release all of those songs, there are literally dozens of other finished pieces that have only been heard by adventurous collectors of the offbeat.

I trash Paul McCartney for a number of offenses. I think sometimes he's lazy as an artist. Sometimes I find him to be a huckster who just happens to remember a story about The Beatles and uses that story as an entry point to make a sales pitch for his new album. Sometimes his music is just mediocre.

Then I have an experience like sitting and listening to 2½ hours of great Paul McCartney music, and I remember he's got a lifetime pass from me, and has had it for decades.

***

No. 74. *Dreamboat Annie*, Heart (1976) – Hearing the album in total for the first time 20 years after its release, a young friend said, "This is just like a greatest hits album, isn't it?" I didn't argue. Favorite songs: "Crazy on You," "Dreamboat Annie," "How Deep It Goes"

No. 73. *The List*, Rosanne Cash (2009) – A great tribute to her father, who provided her a list of songs vital for her to know as a performer. She twists up enough songs to make them hers. Favorite songs: "Motherless Children," "I'm Movin' On," "Long Black Veil"

No. 72. *Zoot Allures*, Frank Zappa (1976) – Features a trio of songs that figured heavily in performances the rest of his career. But honestly, if this only had "Black Napkins," it would still be pretty close to this high on the list. Favorite songs: "Black Napkins," "The Torture Never Stops," "Disco Boy"

No. 71. *Don't Shoot Me, I'm Only the Piano Player*, Elton John (1973) –

This was in the midst of a six-year Elton John stretch (1970-1976) that I'll stack up against any other performer's six-year period. It's as though each of the 10 songs fits a specific period genre. Perfectly. Favorite songs: "Daniel," "Teacher I Need You," "Crocodile Rock"

No. 70. *Toys in the Attic*, Aerosmith (1975) – They could have gone either way after the challenging *Get Your Wings*. This is merely the template for what was to come. (This is the first of three Aerosmith albums on this list.) We thought this was the grand slam, but it was just setting the table for *Rocks*. Favorite songs: "Sweet Emotion," "No More No More," "You See Me Crying"

No. 69. *A New World Record*, Electric Light Orchestra (1976) – They finally synthesized their perfect pop capability. With shorter songs and infectious melodies, they were set to rule. For at least a little bit. Favorite songs: "Tightrope," "So Fine," "Rockaria!"

No. 68. *Physical Graffiti,* Led Zeppelin (1975) – The longest wait endured (up to that time) for a Led Zeppelin album, or for an album by any major act. But they tossed us a double-album set with some rock-n-roll, some blues, and a couple of things that reminded us of "Stairway to Heaven." I should allow myself more than three favorite songs because it's a double, But so are eight other albums still to come on this list. I'll sadly lop off "Custard Pie." Favorite songs: "In My Time of Dying," "Kashmir," "Sick Again"

No. 67. *Peggy Suicide,* Julian Cope (1991) – The greatest album title ever. Kind of an ecology and human rights concept piece, he mixed plenty of melody and rock with the preaching, which is just the right amount of not overt. The mixture of musical styles is as effortless as it is surprising. Favorite songs: "Hanging Out & Hung Up on the Line," "Safesurfer," "Drive, She Said"

No. 66. *Treasure*, Cocteau Twins (1984) – An ambitious record store clerk challenged my preference for the "different" when he played this, not expecting that it would fire a three-year obsession with the band that played along with pre-recorded drum tracks and sang (beautifully) in a language they defied anyone to understand. Favorite songs: "Ivo," "Lorelei,"

"Persephone"

No. 65. *Magical Mystery Tour,* The Beatles (1967) – An album that isn't really an album. The U.S. release gathered up the six-song double-EP and 1967 singles that hadn't appeared on albums yet. The production strains in an effort to move beyond *Sgt. Pepper*, but the songs here are better. Favorite songs: "I Am the Walrus," "Hello, Goodbye," "Strawberry Fields Forever"

No. 64. *Cosmo's Factory,* Creedence Clearwater Revival (1970) – The perfect peak for a close-to-perfect band. It's fascinating to note how little "swamp rock" is here. These are just clean, well-crafted pop songs, impossible to not enjoy. Favorite songs: "Travelin' Band," "Up Around the Bend," "Who'll Stop the Rain"

No. 63. *Pump*, Aerosmith (1989) – Proving *Permanent Vacation* wasn't a fluke, and cementing them at the top of their genre almost permanently from this point forward, regardless of this being their last gasp of greatness. "Janie's Got a Gun" may be both the best and most important song they ever created. Favorite songs: "Young Lust," "Love in an Elevator," "Janie's Got a Gun"

No. 62. *Decade*, Neil Young (1977) – For me, Young's most important album (although not my favorite – there are still four more to come on this list). Even though it features five new songs (which I never would have realized), it gave a superb overview of Young's numerous faces and styles. Favorite songs: "Sugar Mountain," "Soldier," "Campaigner"

No. 61. *Breakfast in America*, Supertramp (1979) – I didn't really grasp the *Abbey Road* comparisons until I started to understand they were referencing the production. All I heard was wall-to-wall good songs, the peak for a band I'd been following for a few years. Now, I call it "the greatest offspring of *Abbey Road*." Favorite songs: "Gone Hollywood," "Goodbye Stranger," "Take the Long Way Home"

***

No. 60. *Moondance*, Van Morrison (1970) – The first side may be the most perfect album side ever. As I have observed more than once, "Crazy Love" makes Al Jarreau's entire career redundant. Favorite songs: "Moondance," "Caravan," "Into the Mystic"

The conversation was innocent enough as I sent a message to a generation-younger friend while listening to a classic rock album.

"The first side is about as close to perfection as you can get," I typed.

"Side?" my friend responded.

Literal tears of laughter clouded my eyes before my friend sent an additional (and unnecessary) message.

"I've only ever heard that album on CD."

It took a message that comical and that literal for me to realize something I should have realized years ago: My way of listening to music, if not dead already, is slowly dying.

I regard the recorded album the most significant art form created in the 20th century. In less than an hour (in most cases), you could be transported to another place and land back safely in your home. If you were lucky, you came back with a greater appreciation of something, be it lyrical, musical or some concept that had never occurred to you.

If you were unlucky, you were probably listening to a Uriah Heep album.

But one key point to listening to albums as I grew up was flipping them over. Vinyl albums were generally limited to 20 minutes a side, less for performers who programmed dynamic extremes in their music, extremes that required more sensitivity in the cutting of vinyl masters.

That limitation shaped the expectations of listeners from the 1950s through the early 1990s, when the longer format of compact discs, which would hold 70 to 80 minutes of information, became the accepted form of delivery. (And briefly before that, audio cassettes were holding more information and sometimes additional, otherwise unavailable songs.)

Some artists chose to stay with 40-minute album tradition, while others crammed every second possible into those new silver discs. (One of the most effective efforts I remember from my early CD days is Julian Cope's 1991 release *Peggy Suicide*, which ran 75 minutes. I could never satisfactorily put it on a 90-minute cassette. It was too much of a complete whole. It couldn't be split without losing its impact.)

Those limitations led to the development of certain styles and artistic statements on vinyl, and some of those became either cliches or definitive, depending on your point of view.

The Beatles would conclude their albums with experimental or forward-looking pieces ("Tomorrow Never Knows," "A Day in the Life"), leaving the listener even more excited about what was to come. The quiet or mellow conclusion to the first side of an album ("The Song Is Over" on The Who's *Who's Next*, "Thank You" on *Led Zeppelin II*) became a subconscious signal to flip the album over.

Even more clever was the use of moods assigned to sides on double-album sets. In general terms (and in the best of those double-disc sets):

* The first side set the mood.

* The second side was quiet, reflective and almost "unplugged" (before we came up with that term).

* The third side was experimental (or drove the story full forward on concept albums).

* The fourth side was ambitious, and almost inevitably a letdown.

(These are very general observations, of course, but they fit solidly with most of my favorite double albums: The Who's *Tommy*, *The Wall* by Pink Floyd, The Beatles' *White Album* and *Jesus Christ Superstar*, to name the first four that come to mind. After advancing this theory, a co-worker and I went through a couple dozen double albums and found, with a little creativity, the theory held true with almost every album. Except Led Zeppelin's *Physical Graffiti*, which flipped the second and third sides.)

But those probably are to be expected. I first experienced them all via vinyl. But the feeling carried over. One specific instance was Marty Stuart's 1999 concept album *The Pilgrim.* The quiet finality of the song "The Observations of a Crow" (admittedly coupled with Stuart immediately following that song with a 30-second instrumental "Intermission") made it FEEL like "The Pilgrim" had two "sides," even though what felt like the first "half" of the 48-minute disc ran 28 minutes.

It's fascinating to me that millions of people know exactly what I'm talking about in this case, and millions of others - like my friend - never have and never will.

(And the album we were discussing, just for the record, was Van Morrison's *Moondance*.)

***

No. 59. *I'm With Stupid,* Aimee Mann (1995) – There are so many delightful things hidden in this album. Solos sneak in from other songs, sounds bounce across the spectrum, and it sounds like the boys from Squeeze who are guesting are having the time of their lives. Brutally sharp lyrics. Favorite songs: "Superball," "That's Just What You Are," "It's Not Safe"

Concept albums can be subtle. They don't have to be sledgehammer-to-the-head heavy concepts like The Who's *Tommy* or Pink Floyd's *The Wall.*

In fact, my favorites among the genre are the ones that take the less-connected thematic route, like XTC's *Skylarking* and *Dog Problems* by The Format.

I've been revisiting some old favorite albums, and finding concepts in them and in new works. Specifically, Aimee Mann's *I'm With Stupid* is a fantastic concept album, hands down higher quality than her boxing story *The Forgotten Arm* (2005).

I'm With Stupid was my 1996 album of the year. Back then, I wrote:

"Held up for a year thanks to record company problems, Til Tuesday's lead singer's second solo effort was worth the wait. Want some subtle fun? The guitar solo on 'Superball' is repeated at the end of 'It's Not Safe.' 'That's Just What You Are' has one of the some simple yet beautiful verse music ever written. This woman is so full of hooks, she puts them in those verses. Wow."

Now, it's not exactly news that Aimee Mann writes some great heartbreak songs, and some of her oeuvre is filled with recrimination, guilt and anger. There's a reason she and Elvis Costello have exchanged mutual admiration. But *I'm With Stupid* strikes me as a piece about one relationship, and the trek of one person dealing (not so well) with its conclusion.

There's no song called "I'm With Stupid" on the album. Instead, there's "You're With Stupid Now," a nice relationship kiss-off in which the subject tries to take satisfaction in the previous paramour's new love. But we're not exactly feeling it as true, and neither does Mann, based on her resigned tone.

I'm With Stupid is a heartache album just past the heartache's deepest burn. Now, along with the resignation of loss, there's the resentment and anger and things that should have been said. And even a point of a soft bittersweet longing for romance's return.

The nice thing about me stamping that soft "concept" template on the album is if another listener approaches *I'm With Stupid,* they could easily enjoy it without picking up on the general idea.

***

No. 58. *I Often Dream of Trains,* Robyn Hitchcock (1984) – All acoustic, largely bleak, and fully memorable. Hitchcock sets autumn (the season and the time of life) perfectly to music. And there are jokes, too. Favorite songs: "Uncorrected Personality Traits," "Flavour of Night," "I Often Dream of Trains"

***

No. 57. *Goodbye Yellow Brick Road,* Elton John (1973) – He started the year with the *Don't Shoot Me...* album and ended it with this. Not many performers have had a more impressive 12-month stretch. Favorite songs: "I've Seen That Movie Too," "All the Girls Love Alice," "Harmony"

(NOTE: Clearly, "Your Sister Can't Twist (But She Can Rock 'n Roll)" fell in favor with me between writing this and compiling The Big List.)

I've never understood the plain fanaticism about Elton John's "Bennie and the Jets."

That may tell you all you need to know about how I feel about Elton John's work.

Based on the first 10 years of his career alone, Elton John is one of the greatest composers and performers in rock music history. I have no qualms about mentioning him in the same breath as Paul McCartney. Both write inspiringly addictive earworms. With the exception of the occasional horrifying effort (the previously mentioned "Benny and the Jets," McCartney's "Ebony and Ivory"), the earworms are fascinating and pleasant to me.

But "Bennie and the Jets"? It was John's second No. 1 in America. ("Crocodile Rock," one of his best songs, was the first.)

Nevertheless, I fought through the song on a regular basis as I consumed the *Goodbye Yellow Brick Road.*

My parents bought me the 17-track double album for Christmas 1973, and I marveled at all of the new music from the man who earlier in the year had released *Don't Shoot Me, I'm Only the Piano Player,* which was among my favorites. *Goodbye Yellow Brick Road* cemented John as one of my favorite performers ever. And as disappointed I've been off and on since, I've never abandoned hope for him, primarily because he had a better 1973 than most musicians have careers.

I've always considered *Goodbye Yellow Brick Road* far and away John's best album, even when I go back and listen to *Don't Shoot Me ...* and find it to be 10 perfect or close-to-perfect tracks. The depth of ambition and style in the *Goodbye Yellow Brick Road* album makes it as stunning in its own way as *The Beatles/The White Album.* (And fitting with his fantastically prolific abilities, he released another double three years later, *Blue Moves,* whose dark attitude made it a proper parallel to *The Beatles.*)

Now, at the time, hipsters looked down their nose at my preference for the 1973 albums. Most preferred *Honky Chateau* and its trademark "Rocket Man." There were also those convinced that *Tumbleweed Connection* was one of the greatest albums ever, and while my appreciation for that has grown in the last 15 years or so, I still don't know what the people who consider it a great album are talking about.

For the third time in the digital area, the album has been released. The new "40th Anniversary deluxe edition" boasts one of those remixes where I can't hear any difference, but adds a live London show from 1973 and the bizarre *Goodbye Yellow Brick Road: Revisited & Beyond.*

The live set shows a band just beginning to discover the way it can stretch within John's songs. The best parts are the way they fill in gaps occupied on the studio recordings by strings, and their enthusiasm over reworking solid deep album cuts from earlier. The nine-minute "Hercules" is fantastic.

The *Revisited*, meanwhile, is an assortment of covers by current acts. I've heard of some, am just learning about others, and find all nine recordings deathly dull. I couldn't get through most of them. Attempts at mimicry were embarrassing, and new arrangements bristled.

Is the new content worth the cost of the package? Not really, especially if you can find the two-disc reissue (all John, all studio), or even the CD that crams the entire double album on to one disc. (The original ran just shy of 77 minutes.)

(If it takes The Band Perry doing "Grey Seal" to get you interested, I'm not sure how much of his catalog you'll dig. But if that's what ends up working for you, welcome aboard.)

In advance of the release of the 40th anniversary edition, the All Music website conducted a user survey of favorite songs on the album It prompted me to list mine, even as I was troubled that my favorite song on the album was least-mentioned by those taking part. Probably all lovers of *Tumbleweed Connection*, too.

My top-to-bottom *Goodbye Yellow Brick Road* preference list.

"Your Sister Can't Twist (But She Can Rock 'n Roll)"
"All the Girls Love Alice"
"Harmony"
"I've Seen That Movie Too"
"The Ballad of Danny Bailey (1909–34)"

"Grey Seal"
"Saturday Night's Alright for Fighting"
"Funeral for a Friend/Love Lies Bleeding"
"Candle in the Wind"
"Roy Rogers"
"Social Disease"
"Jamaica Jerk-Off"
"This Song Has No Title"
"Dirty Little Girl"
"Goodbye Yellow Brick Road"
"Bennie and the Jets"

***

No. 56. *Singles '96-'06*, Hooverphonic (2006) – I found this band via a friend listening to trip-hop on Pandora, a superb endorsement for that service. The chance to discover a decade of stunning music via binge listening was a delight. Favorite songs: "Mad About You," "Vinegar & Salt," "You Hurt Me"

No. 55. *Rust Never Sleeps,* Neil Young (1979) – A remarkable combination: An arena show well worth the experience, featuring an album's worth of new songs the audience largely loved after one album. As he did years later when grunge deemed many rock veterans irrelevant, Young fired a shot back at punk, and hit. Favorite songs: "My My, Hey Hey (Out of the Blue)," "Thrasher," "Powderfinger"

No. 54. *Pretty Little Lonely*, Michael Petak (1994) – The album begins with an angry acoustic guitar riff and a man scream/singing "INSANE!" It immediately grabbed and held my attention. I was ready for much more. Favorite songs: "Wrecking Ball," "Careless," "Medicinal Purposes"

No. 53. *Hooverphonic Presents Jackie Cane,* Hooverphonic (2002) – A stunning pastiche of style and content. Beautifully layered songs, and a superbly gifted vocalist holding the whole thing together. I haven't stopped listening to it for two years. Favorite songs: "The World Is Mine", "Sometimes," "One"

No. 52. *Aqualung*, Jethro Tull (1971) – Songwriter Ian Anderson always said this wasn't a concept album. Everyone who listened to it knew otherwise. This is really all the Jethro Tull you need. But you should definitely have it. Favorite songs: "Aqualung," "Hymn 43," "Locomotive Breath"

No. 51. *After the Gold Rush*, Neil Young (1970) – Often overlooked in evaluating this album is how simply beautiful the songs are. The quieter songs show the depth of his composing capabilities. Favorite songs: "Only Love Can Break Your Heart," "Southern Man," "Birds"

No. 50. *The Right to be Italian*, Holly and the Italians (1981) – A kind of cross between New Wave and melodic rock that seemed to slip through the cracks more during the 1980s than any other time. Favorite songs: "I Wanna Go Home," "Just For Tonight," "Means to a Den"

***

No. 49. *100 cc*, 10cc (1975) – My introduction to the band, enough to make me think they would rule the 1970s, if only people got a chance to hear them. I now realize they're a little too odd for the mainstream, even though they sound like that's where they ought to be. Favorite songs: "Somewhere in Hollywood," "Fresh Air for My Momma," "Silly Love"

I'm pretty sure I liked 10cc's music before I ever heard it. I know I was eager to be a fan.

I first read about them in late 1972 or early 1973, in those pre-Internet days where my knowledge of music came from magazines like *Rolling Stone, Circus, Hit Parader* and *Creem.*

I was reading about a track called "Rubber Bullets," and how it combined The Beach Boys, the plot of "Jailhouse Rock," a prison riot, and criticism of the United States all into a rollicking little four-minute track.

I never heard it until I bought their first album a couple of years later. We of course didn't have the chance to sample tracks then - we had to wait for our local radio stations to play them.

When I was growing up, I didn't have a decent FM radio. I had tiny transistor radios that picked up nearby AM stations. The hippest of all was KAUS, based in Austin, Minn. Formats were much freer in those days, so while technically KAUS would have been considered a top 40 station, they allowed their disc jockeys some free rein, especially in the evening hours. I mean, honestly - one DJ used to play the full 11 1/2-minute version of Traffic's "The Low Spark of High Heeled Boys." Now, he may have been playing it to take a smoke or bathroom break, but he played it a lot.

I used to lay awake nights in the dark with a tiny microphone attached to a $30 cassette player and record songs off the radio, laying the microphone on top of the radio speaker. How much did I love "The Low Spark of High Heeled Boys"? I taped it off KAUS and listened to that tape continuously. There was even a skip in it - the record skipped every time the DJ played it - that I memorized.

How hip was this station? I remember hearing Styx's "Lady" for the first time on it on Christmas Eve 1973. If the DJ was playing it off the album, that was pretty cool. I had no idea who the band was - my note on the cassette referred to them as "The Sticks." The single charted a year later, to my confusion. Just like the chart success of Aerosmith's "Dream On," which charted low in late 1973 and higher in early 1976.

I digress.

That station played 10cc's "The Wall Street Shuffle" one of those nights. The band's sound was much tougher than I expected, both vocally and musically. (The Beach Boys' guitars never sounded like 10cc's do on that track.) But I was immediately smitten.

But I couldn't find their records anywhere. I wasn't even sure what I was looking for, since (a) I didn't know what the covers looked like and (b) I was never sure whether record stores would list them under numbers, or under "T." And I even by that time was accustomed to record store clerks reacting to my special requests as though I was speaking in a language they didn't understand.

In 1975, when 10cc's "I'm Not In Love" became a hit single, I was more fascinated by the process than by the song. I think it's far from their best work, although I admit the vocal tracking is simply amazing. And the idea behind the song - a six-minute screed in which the narrator is clearly in love but denies it - was typical 10cc. But something was missing.

My memory is I picked up the compilation *100cc* (I had the U.S. version, which has a similar but less horrific-looking cover than the U.K. version.) before buying *The Original Soundtrack*, the latter being the album that featured "I'm Not In Love."

And I developed a deep and abiding love for the band. I eventually went back and found their first two pre-"I'm Not in Love" albums, and stuck with them until the band kind of dissolved. *Look Hear?* in 1980 was the last album of theirs I bought.

But I've continued to go back to their work and be amazed.

Sometimes you think you understand a musical performer and its fans and critics. And sometimes, it takes stepping back to listen to things in a new light to successfully make that analysis.

Tenology, the four-CD anthology of the band, accomplishes just that for me.

It only took one pass through *Tenology* for me to recall listening to those albums repeatedly, memorizing every musical and lyrical nuance. For me, they were a superb combination of The Beach Boys and The Beatles and the Marx Brothers. They made me sing along, they made me marvel at their harmonies, they made me laugh out loud.

But that's exactly the kind of thing that irritated the band's critics back in the day. They were called "smart aleck" and "college rock." As though intelligent lyrics and thoughtful compositions are something to be mocked, something of which to be suspicious.

Village Voice's Robert Christgau, one of the country's most respected reviewers, went from saying about their first album, "A calculated, devilishly clever version of what the Beach Boys ought to be doing" to about its follow-up, "too-too apollonian (cerebral? professional? glib?) endeavor." By the time of *The Original Soundtrack*, he wrote, "stretching your only decent melody (a nonsatirical love song) over six tedious minutes, is that a joke?"

It got worse. The *100cc* pre-*Soundtrack* compilation received this drubbing: "It can't be easy to put together a compilation album that's less listenable than either of the two regular-issue LPs to which you have access." By 1976, a mere three years after the debut, Christgau dismissed an album with "they don't know whether they're supposed to be funny or pretty, and so nine times out of then they're neither."

All of that, in retrospect, is probably fair if you were expecting the 50s parodies and uptempo rockers. I liked that stuff, but I also adored something like "Somewhere in Hollywood," which features a two-minute wordless outro of which The Beach Boys would have been proud.

"Silly Love" - a song that predates Wings' "Silly Love Songs," and had Paul McCartney briefly reconsidering naming or even releasing his song - includes what remains one of my favorite couplets ever: "Ooh, you know the art of conversation must be dying/Ooh, when a romance depends on cliches and toupees and three-pes." "Sand in My Face" shows a fascination with Charles Atlas and his "dynamic tension" workout. I was amused that Monty Python had made some similar jokes. It made the world a bit smaller - the Brits were seeing the same ads I saw in my comics books. Later, "Blackmail" was extra clever, telling the tale of a man who follows a woman for the purposes of blackmail, but when he sends her husband the photos, he likes them so much, he orders copies.

But good things come to an end. The band split in half near the end of the 1970s, and nothing any of them have done since has moved me the way the original quartet's albums did. (Although you might know Godley and Creme's "Cry" from its innovative video, and Graham Gouldman's *Love and Work* album is top notch.)

What a set like *Tenology* does is make it clear how much good music 10cc released in a short time. Their greatest hits packages would comfortably fill one CD (stretching the definition of "hit," but the songs were always good), and could be padded to two discs, and normally that would be quite enough for anyone. But for people like me, the format of the box is what I've always thought box sets should be: Two CDs of "hits," a disc of prime album cuts, and a disc of "rarities" - B-sides and other oddities, from the time when that was a thing to do.

Spending some time with this set was a pleasure. It revived for me a band I love a great deal, and made me realize while some of the criticism of the band was justified, it doesn't matter much to me. 10cc gave me a foundation for bands and performers I would appreciate later on when they appeared - XTC, Robyn Hitchcock, Moxy Fruvous. I see straight lines from one to the next.

***

No. 48. *The Pilgrim*, Marty Stuart (1999) – A concept album that not only spans the history of country music and has an interesting story, it has magnificent songs as well. The one country album I think every music fan should hear. Favorite songs: "Hobo's Prayer," "Goin' Nowhere Fast," "The Observations Of A Crow"

He was country when country wasn't cool. But Marty Stuart missed out on the credit and the sales.

The sad fact is if everyone attending a Marty Stuart show purchased a copy of Stuart's 1999 album *The Pilgrim,* sales of that disc would jump almost 50 percent.

According to one trade publication, *The Pilgrim* sold 25,000 copies. (By comparison, the Grammy-winning soundtrack to *O Brother, Where Art Thou?* sold double that in an average *week,* and almost 10 times that the week after it won its four Grammys.)

The Pilgrim deserves better. And that's not a statement from a raving Marty

Stuart fan.

In 1993, Stuart performed at Nashville North USA in Taylorville, Illinois. Those anticipating a performance from a true link between bluegrass music's origins and country music's present - as would have befitted Stuart's talent and pedigree - received a disappointment.

Between songs, a handful of women in the hall exhorted Stuart , "Turn around!" Initially, he at least pretended not to realize they wanted photographs of his rear end. Then he teased the women from the stage, with some fans thinking the whole time, "Please, Marty, don't turn around."

There's no question the appeal Stuart has for certain members of his audience isn't his history as a bluegrass prodigy, nor his apprenticeship with country pioneers like Johnny Cash, Doc Watson and Lester Flatt. Some of them were looking at his tight jeans or his foot-high hair.

And as someone who thinks the Beatles' hair in the 1960s is the essential definition of cool, it's easy to understand that image sometimes is as much a part of popular music as the music itself.

Like Stuart 's *The Pilgrim,* this story is one of fall and redemption. The fall? When Stuart obliged the requests and turned around. The music took a seat behind his seat, and my exit off the Marty Party train was slowed only by the rush of people scrambling to get on.

And Stuart did quite well. Gold records, a TV show, a growing reputation as a superb performer. But for a handful of us, he still hadn't fulfilled his potential.

Then came *The Pilgrim.*

Perhaps Stuart is just a victim of poor timing. Remember those Grammys won by *O Brother, Where Art Thou?* "That album was where many discovered the voice of Ralph Stanley. But two years earlier, Stanley sang "Harlan County" on *The Pilgrim.*

Emmylou Harris reached a wider audience with her *O Brother* performance with Gillian Welch and Decatur native Allison Krauss. But much earlier - in 1996 - Stuart stood side-by-side with Harris and Krauss singing at the memorial service for bluegrass music creator Bill Monroe.

And Harris also sang on *The Pilgrim.*

A concept album that tells the story of love lost and subsequent redemption, *The Pilgrim* has drawn comparisons with Willie Nelson's classic concept piece, *Red Headed Stranger.*

A key difference, though, is while Nelson relied on outside sources for about half of the material on his record, Stuart wrote or co-wrote everything on *The Pilgrim* (with the exception of Johnny Cash reading a Tennyson poem that caps off the whole album not with hubris or laughability, but a fitting amount of finality).

Somehow, some way, Stuart assembled everything in his past and present - bluegrass, country, rock, virtuosity, storytelling - in an album frighteningly head and shoulders above almost everything released in the decade.

(Unfortunately, of the three albums that top my list for the best of the 1990s - *World So Bright* by Champaign-Urbana's Adam Schmitt, *Whitechocolatespaceegg* by Liz Phair and *The Pilgrim* - only Phair managed to put out additional records on the same label.)

With *The Pilgrim,* you don't even have to buy into the concept. Just listen to the 11 or 12 songs without the story links, and you've got a fine album.

Add in the links, though, and you have a piece of art, something you can and should listen to in one sitting to have the emotion wrung out of you.

While the album starts with the driving country tune "Sometimes the Pleasure's Worth the Pain," and that's quickly followed by "Reasons," a classic 1960s-style male-female duet, the highlights come in the middle of the album, where one great song follows another and leaves you thinking, "This *can't* get any better."

"Hobo's Prayer" is his musical rewrite of "The Boxer," with a nice moral besides:

"Face the fact that you're a circle in a world full of squares/ Trading sorrows for tomorrows, now that's the hobo's prayer."

Back in the 1970s, the last great golden age of popular music on AM radio, you could hear the Spinners followed by Grand Funk Railroad followed by Charlie Rich. At that time, Stuart 's "Goin' Nowhere Fast" would have been a Top-40 smash.

Imagine a fast Tom Petty song with a little bit of steel guitar.

The next cut is Stuart 's tour de force, the 5 1/2-minute "The Observations of a Crow." Written while flying to Hawaii, the song actually hearkens back to Stuart's youthful home in Mississippi. The song cries "swamp." There's a frightening amount of foreboding in it.

And if that's not cool enough, how about these lines:

"Hey quarter moon, well how was your night/Yeah well, any minute now God's gonna hit them brights/... And if he looks at you, well try not to look so afraid."

Isn't that amazing?

And a little later, in slides "Draggin' Around These Chains of Love," another sure hit single.

Not enough? How about a couple more instrumentals that should take your breath away? A nice package? A nice story?

It's not out of line to suggest this is a country music *Pet Sounds* - that is, an ambitious concept piece that didn't find the audience it should have. A rare piece of beauty, honesty and unexpected maturity.

It deserved much better, but it will certainly live on in the hearts of its fans.

***

No. 47. *whitechocolatespaceegg*, Liz Phair (1998) – With its combination of indie edginess, pop sensibility and weird chords and sounds, this seems like the album that best represents all of what Liz Phair is. Favorite songs: "Polyester Bride," "Baby Got Going," "Girls' Room"

No. 46. *Love Junk*, The Pursuit of Happiness (1988) – If I wasn't the precise target for Moe Berg's songs of anger, disappointment, misogyny and regret, I can't imagine who was. His ability to wrap them all up in tasty and extra-powerful power pop was a bonus. Favorite songs: "Hard to Laugh," "I'm an Adult Now," "Killed by Love"

***

No. 45. *The Bis-Quits* (1993) – An interesting collection of folk, rock and country, with a little Bach thrown in on their "Johnny B. Goode"-alike track "Yo Yo Ma." Comic, touching and repeatable. Favorite songs: "Yo Yo Ma," "Anal All Day," "Walking on a Wire"

There should always be room in rock music for the clever. And by clever I don't mean Sting showing you how much smarter than you he is. Or, no matter how much I love the guy, "Weird Al" Yankovic doesn't fit the bill of what I'm talking about.

What I mean is the smirk you have to get on your face when you think about Chuck Berry inventing the word "motorvating" for use in "Maybellene." Of course, Elvis Presley practically invented clever parody in his prime. Think about the clips of him gyrating wildly, then grabbing his leg and putting it back in place. Or the way he mocked his own "lip thing" in the 1969 TV comeback special.

For all their other failings, some of the hair-metal bands of the 80s used video to make themselves appear clever and intelligent, particularly Twisted Sister, who were pretty funny.

The Presidents of the United States of America appear primed to make a career out of being intelligently clever, and they have a respect for the history of music as well. PUSA was preceded by a band out of Tennessee called The Bis-Quits.

295

If you love clever and fun rock and roll, this had better be in your collection. And the best part is they don't stick to one style of music -- there's blues, pop, rock, folk and even classical in a top-to-bottom 12-song delight.

Maybe these guys would still be together if I'd been around to write copy for them in 1993.

At work one day, a friend excitedly charged in to tell me about this song called "Anal All Day," which he swore was the biography of one of our co-workers. Truth to tell, everybody's got an "Anal All Day" person in their life:

>>Every task you undertake becomes a mountain that you make from molehills you pass along the way<<

Imagine a songwriter so good that you sing along with a line like that when it comes up. A true toe-tapper. And not only that, at the end of the song (it took me weeks to catch this) is a steal/tribute from Mott the Hoople's "All the Young Dudes" which, if you're in on the joke, is thrilling to hear.

(In the early days of the web, I had a site which was essentially a blog before I knew they called it that. A few months after I posted this, I received an email from one of the members of the band who thanked me and congratulated me on hearing the Mott the Hoople reference. I choose to believe he was sincere.)

When I finally heard the disk, "Anal All Day" wasn't even my favorite song. That was reserved for "Yo Yo Ma," a song so wonderfully clever that I never stop wishing that I'd written it. It starts with a chunking Chuck Berry rhythm, then suddenly laid over the top is a distorted electric guitar playing Bach's "Jesu Joy of Man's Desiring." (Remember when I wrote "classical?" You thought I was kidding.)

Then the lyrics start to tell the life story of famed classical cellist Yo Yo Ma, in a virtual re-write of "Johnny B. Goode."

>>He's got the long-legged groupies of the classical kind Got the sole intention of blowin Yo Yo's mind<<

The Bach line comes back in for another solo after two verses, then the two guitars meld into some kind of bizarre universe all their own, playing dual solos like Derek and the Dominos on a three-day bender. Then it's a final verse and out.

And that's not all. "Cyberpop" takes some shots at unnamed bands, but I prefer to think they're talking about the 80s synth bands. I always picture A Flock of Nimrods (thanks for the reference, Bobcat Goldthwait) when I hear "dancers start to prance and the poseurs to preen." "76 Bis-Quits" is an instrumental that acts as a song -- through its two minutes, they build on 32-bar structures without repeating, which is probably just a fancy way of saying I dislike most instrumentals but this isn't boring.

Then there's "Tennessee Valley Girl," which mentions John Hughes and Tears for Fears and paints a melancholy picture of early adult life for people born in the late 60s. It also features a wonderful line I wish I'd written, but won't repeat for fear of spoiling the ending.

The Bis-Quits spent a lot of time in my CD player after I found the disc. I waited patiently for them to come out with another record.

When my patience finally wore out, I called the record company, and was promptly told that the band had broken up. Heartbroken, I kept returning to the CD and still got my joy from it.

So it was worthwhile in late 1996 to find Tommy Womack's area on the Web (Tommy was one of the Bis-Quits guitar players) and find out that they didn't break up because they hated each other -- they broke up for the right reasons. In what I thought was a great phrase (that probably didn't originate with Womack, but that's OK), he said they grew weary of playing for the door (ticket sales) and sleeping on the floor (which is pretty self-explanatory).

That made me love them even more.

(It didn't hurt that I found a couple of Womack solo songs that I found as important as the Bis-Quits disc -- "Skinny and Small" and "Sweet Hitch-Hiker" [not the Creedence song -- better, if you can imagine], both on his

Positively Na Na album. Joe Bob says check it out.)

***

No. 44. *SMiLE*, Brian Wilson (2004)/*Smile*, The Beach Boys (1966-1967, 2011) – The strangest journey of any release on this list. Rather than speculate about how its release would have been received in 1967, we should let the beauty of these odd songs settle in our skulls. Favorite songs: "Heroes and Villains," "Roll Plymouth Rock," "Good Vibrations"

(August 2005)

I went to church last night.

At least that's what I told anyone who asked. I actually went to St. Louis to see Brian Wilson in concert.

I didn't go to see a Beach Boys show, even though Wilson had at least a hand in composing most of their most memorable works and acted as producer for some of the most amazing music performed by an American group.

What I went to see was popular music's most unlikely third act, and pay some small tribute to the man for sharing that gift.

The list of pop musicians who do their best work after they reach age 40 is a short one. Frank Zappa released the three *Joe's Garage* albums and the double set *You Are What You Is* in a two-year stretch when he was 39; Willie Nelson's *Red Headed Stranger* came out when he was 42; and Aerosmith members were in their late 30s (and Steven Tyler was 41) when *Pump* came out.

(If you really want to tick off Velvet Underground fans, suggest [as I once did] that *New York* is Lou Reed's best work. He was 47 at the time.)

So here's Brian Wilson at 63, sitting on stage and singing songs he wrote and conceptualized as a piece almost 40 years ago, and after years of rumors, speculation, bootlegs, ruminations, criticisms, mental damage and physical abuse, we have the chance to experience *SMiLE*.

It's amazing.

Some overviews on the tortured history of the Beach Boys album leave out details about Wilson's prodigious drug use at the time, and Mike Love's irritation that Wilson was messing with the formula that had made The Beach Boys so popular.

And they leave out that Wilson apparently couldn't get the sounds that were in his head onto tape. So recordings from sessions from The Beach Boys' *Smile* circulated among collectors, and we discussed and argued about what was to go where and in what order. (I even planned out my own version that I hoped to circulate among friends back before CDs, using "sophisticated" cassette deck-to-cassette deck technology.)

A couple of years ago, Wilson began to re-visit *Smile*, and even as the reports came out, the cynical among Beach Boys and Wilson fans found themselves smirking. We'd heard this so many times, there was no reason to believe it again now.

But last June, I found myself in disbelief standing in line at Circuit City, holding a copy of the new Brian Wilson CD, now christened *SMiLE*. The clerk smiled herself, saying, "All right -- Brian Wilson, musical genius."

"I've been waiting 40 years to hear this," I replied, which wasn't exactly true, given that it came out 38 years after original recording began, and I wasn't really aware of it until the mid-1970s. But 30 years, 40 years - after a while, what's the difference?

Listening to *SMiLE*, I found it perfect. I couldn't imagine that I'd ever thought of it any other way. And I also couldn't imagine that these sounds could be reproduced in concert.

Yet there I sat.

It was like two shows -- The Beach Boys opening for the Brian Wilson show I really wanted to see.

Don't get me wrong. I love The Beach Boys. I stayed away from later period shows because to me, Mike Love is not The Beach Boys. Brian and Carl and Dennis Wilson are.

But my love for Brian Wilson's *SMiLE* has nothing to do with The Beach Boys. They're two completely different entities. (Which may explain why The Beach Boys can play state fairs and stadiums and Brian Wilson plays theaters. Frankly, for what I wanted to hear, I'd rather be in the theater.)

So Wilson and the 17 (!) other musicians on stage played a bunch of Beach Boys songs as a kind of prelude to *SMiLE*. And while a couple of the *Pet Sounds"*songs were painful to hear (Wilson's voice got ragged toward the end of the first set), he also threw in a couple of unexpected tunes that kept me wondering what would come next.

But the main reason for my presence was to hear *SMiLE*, which the troupe pulled off amazingly and (to my ears, anyway) flawlessly.

The piece has three movements, and I've described it as a symphony. In a book I've been reading about The Beach Boys, someone refers to it as "a funny oratorio," which may be an even better description. At any rate, it's not a collection of three-minute straight-forward pop songs.

Not that there's anything wrong with three-minute straight-forward pop songs. But I don't want to eat steak for every meal, either.

"You sure make listening to something like this sound like a lot of work," a friend said.

That wasn't my intention. To me, it's not work -- it's a joy. (And that's what the tears on my face a couple of times at the concert said as well.) If music is just background in your life, *SMiLE* is probably not for you. If music is a passion in your life, I'd suggest *SMiLE* is a must.

***

No. 43. *Rough Mix,* Pete Townshend and Ronnie Lane (1977) – In the midst of a period where Townshend was creatively on fire. This is folk-based, and still allows Townshend plenty of room for experimentation. This includes some of his best songs. Favorite songs: "Keep Me Turning,"

"Annie," "Heart to Hang Onto"

No. 42. *Pet Sounds*, Beach Boys (1966) – Essentially of one piece with the long-delayed *SMiLE*. You can't understand this album until your heart has been crushed by someone you loved. Favorite songs: "Wouldn't It Be Nice," "I Just Wasn't Made for These Times," "Caroline, No"

No. 41. *Bridge of Sighs*, Robin Trower (1974) – The spot where he came into his own and came closest to matching the work of his hero, Jimi Hendrix. One of the first of the second wave of great classic rock. Favorite songs: "Bridge of Sighs," "Too Rolling Stoned," "Lady Love"

No. 40. *Oil and Gold*, Shriekback (1985) – When people talked about "dance music," I didn't realize this was what they were talking about. I just thought this was solid rock with a bit of rhythmic beat. Not only are they the only band to fit the word "parthenogenesis" into a pop song, they use it right, and it fits the song's story. Favorite songs: "Malaria," "Nemesis," "Hammerheads"

No. 39. *Venus and Mars*, Wings (1975) – I always liked McCartney's 70s work more than anyone around me. This gave credence to my claim that he'd fully come back. This is a band album in theory, but as usual, McCartney's handprints are everywhere. Favorite songs: "Rock Show," "Letting Go," "Medicine Jar"

No. 38. *We're Only in it for the Money*, Frank Zappa/Mothers of Invention (1968) – When I was finally able to dig into this, years after its release, I was stunned to listen as he essentially predicted two years in advance what would happen at Kent State. This may not be the place to start with Zappa, but it's a place that will nevertheless open your eyes. Favorite songs: "Mom & Dad," "Flower Punk," "What's the Ugliest Part of Your Body?"

No. 37. *Jam Science*, Shriekback (1984) – It really felt as though they were pushing a new area of pop. They were, as it turned out, just not a very popular area. There are two versions of this. Both are good. The Arista release is better, and considered "official" by the band. Favorite songs: "Hand on My Heart," "Mercy Dash," "Suck"

No. 36. *Message from the Country*, The Move (1971) – As they transitioned into becoming Electric Light Orchestra, they recorded this, a last shot at offbeat and improbable rock. It's better than any ELO album. It rocks, it pops, it even countrys once, and it's endlessly entertaining. Favorite songs: "Message from the Country," "Don't Mess Me Up," "The Words of Aaron"

No. 35. *Ringo*, Ringo Starr (1973) – There were Beatles and good feelings all over this album. In retrospect, it's a soft-ish melodic effort, Boomer easy listening. It's hard to complain about people clearly enjoying themselves. Favorite songs: "Hold On (Have You Seen My Baby)," "You're Sixteen," "Six O'Clock"

No. 34. *Band on the Run*, Paul McCartney and Wings (1973) – The uneven nature of his previous post-Beatles releases made this feel like a rocket exploding. "Here's another good song. And another good song." How confident he was, in the midst of a period of lows. Make sure your version has "Helen Wheels" on it. Favorite songs: "Jet," "Let Me Roll It," "Nineteen Hundred and Eighty-Five"

***

No. 33. *Billion Dollar Babies*, Alice Cooper (1973) – Either the most successful melodic rock album ever, or the most successful parody album. Or maybe both. Alice and band could do no wrong at this point. Every song mocks a style or individual, but still works as a straight listen. Favorite songs: "Unfinished Sweet," "No More Mr. Nice Guy," "Generation Landslide"

In my teens, Alice Cooper was one of my favorite acts.

Did I like Alice the singer or Alice the group? Both. I continue to buy Alice Cooper albums, and I bought some of the side projects from band members, specifically Billion Dollar Babies. And I've had personal interaction with both guitar player Mike Bruce and drummer Neil Smith, long after they parted ways with the singer.

At his height, Cooper was kind of considered a heavy metal act. A heavy metal act that got on Top 40 AM radio, sure, but the loud guitars, his runny black makeup and his menacing lyrics had parents scared. (This is the guy who had a song about blowing up a school, and it made the top 10.)

What I liked about what Cooper did was largely his vocals. I rarely took the lyrics seriously - usually, I laughed. (I asked Bruce once whether *Billion Dollar Babies* was a parody album, because it was one of the funniest records I ever listened to. Like Fee Waybill of The Tubes when I asked whether their *The Completion Backward Principle* album was a parody, Bruce said no. But then, again like Waybill, he went on to explain what they'd meant to do with the album, and he essentially made my point for me.)

But Cooper's vocal strength - especially his sneer - was and is pure rock and roll. And he still maintains the sense of humor that amused me 40 years ago. He covered Lady Gaga's "Born This Way" on one tour, and he appeared in the *Dark Shadows* movie. (At least I hope that was a show of his sense of humor.)

The early 1970s were golden for Alice Cooper. I'll start with 1971 and a pair of albums from Cooper, *Love It To Death* (with his still-brilliant anthem "I'm Eighteen") and *Killer* (the one with the snake on the cover, and the scandalous "Dead Babies"). 1972's *School's Out* was a top 10 single and the album peaked at No. 2. A year later, *Billion Dollar Babies* topped the album charts.

As an aside, the Cooper box set *Old School* features outtakes from the recording of the kid choir section of "School's Out," and is a riot.

I found Cooper's attempts at an intimidating scowl and his "shocking" makeup entertaining and amusing, I can probably credit him with helping me realize the difference between a performer's real life and their stage persona.

But as much as I link Cooper with his distinct appearance (which he maintains to this day), for me the music is the key. That melodic metal was in vogue when I was in high school (Bachman-Turner Overdrive, Deep Purple, Thin Lizzy), and to this day, its combination of melody, menace and cool guitar solos appeals to me.

No. 32. *Revolver*, The Beatles (1966) – The certain sign they were on to something else. *Rubber Soul* was a huge step forward, but the work here left that album in the dust. A perfect opener, a perfect closer, and "Yellow Submarine" and "Good Day Sunshine" for feel-good good measure. And, one of the greatest album covers ever. Favorite songs: "Here, There and Everywhere," "Good Day Sunshine," "Tomorrow Never Knows"

No. 31. *Energized*, Foghat (1974) – Each classic rock band had in them one album where every cut was perfect. This was Foghat's. It's made more fascinating with the revelation that it was recorded soft. The recording was mostly live in the studio, and they all heard each other all the way through. Favorite songs: "Honey Hush," "Wild Cherry," "Nothing I Won't Do"

There was a time in my life when Foghat was the coolest band in the world. I'd guess my pick for favorite Foghat album would be different from most of their fans, because by the time they got to *Fool For the City,* I thought they might have reached their sell-by date.

There remains a theory about 1970s pop-metal bands that they had at best four good albums in them, and after that it was all downhill. KISS didn't fit that, and neither did Lynyrd Skynyrd. But Molly Hatchet didn't even make it that far, and Bachman-Turner Overdrive and Bad Company were the epitome of the argument.

But I was crazy about *Energized*, which came out in early 1974.

Billboard doesn't list their version of Buddy Holly's "That'll Be the Day" as a charting single, but I remember hearing it on the radio a lot. (Let's blame a rogue DJ.) A funkified version with loud guitars, a horn section and female backing vocals, it was probably presented in a way Buddy Holly never heard in his head, but that's part of what made it enjoyable.

And the rest of the album was solid. Rock and roll. Solos, catchy arrangements, a nice combination of thievery from pop, rock, heavy metal and R&B, all strung together into a palatable chunk for a teenager with both metal and pop tastes.

And that neon-styled cover was just plain cool.

Talking with drummer Roger Earl 40 years after the album was released, he pulled back the curtain a bit. He said his memories of the album consisted of the band sitting in a circle facing one another and recording the tracks. I replied I found that difficult to believe. There was so much volume on the record that I'd have figured everyone would go deaf facing one another. And I also couldn't imagine anyone sitting and playing those songs.

Foghat was a boogie band. How did they record their best album and not – well, boogie?

Speaking of cool covers, the cover for 1977's *Live* (their best-selling album) was really neat. The *Live* letters were cut out, so you could see the photos of the band members from the inner sleeve. They weren't the first band to do that. I still treasure my original issue of The Who's *Odds and Sods,* and I spent hours monkeying with the windows on Led Zeppelin's *Physical Graffiti* and the spinning *Led Zeppelin III* cover.

Foghat Live might not have been in that league, but it was nevertheless a piece of cardboard that scored me points with fellow teens.

A friend in high school called Foghat's second album *Stone and Biscuit,* and since that's what was on the cover, that's what I called it as well. I have no idea how long it was before I realized they were giving a visual pun of "Rock and Roll." It was a long time.

I feel pretty foolish about that to this day. But I still call it *Stone and Biscuit.* I think that's more clever.

And finally, in college, a friend was entering a photography contest. The theme was "The Environment." My friend was convinced he was going to win. I was to be his model. We went to a dead-end street in Rochester, Minn., lifted the manhole cover off a sewer grate, and he shot dozens of photos of me recreating the album cover of *Fool for the City*.

He didn't win. It was still pretty funny.

***

No. 30. *Psonic Psunspot*, XTC/Dukes of Stratosphear (1987) – XTC dons the guises of any number of 1960s bands and styles: Procol Harum, The Hollies, The Beach Boys, The Byrds. It's decidedly psychedelic, clued-in, and intelligent and catchy pop, both as parody and especially as form. Favorite songs: "Vanishing Girl," "Pale and Precious," "You're My Drug"

No. 29. *A Night at the Opera*, Queen (1975) – As much of a step forward as "Sheer Heart Attack" was, this was that step forward tenfold. This is everything that's great about Queen, with a minimal amount of those things that are annoying. Favorite songs: " '39," "Sweet Lady," Bohemian Rhapsody"

No. 28. *You Are What You Is*, Frank Zappa (1981) – He either skewers (listeners think) or reports (his version) on excesses of the late 70s and early 80s. He reserves his most intense venom for organized religion and televangelists. Favorite songs: "Doreen," "Dumb All Over," "Drafted Again"

No. 27. *Sound Affects,* The Jam (1980) – They peaked in New Wave's most brilliant albums year. You can almost see the passion charging out of the speakers when you listen. Favorite songs: "But I'm Different Now," "That's Entertainment," "Boy About Town"

No. 26. *Rocks*, Aerosmith (1976) – Their 1980s comeback didn't approach this, because it couldn't. They were the greatest American band at the time and they knew it. That almost made this effortless in its brilliance. Their best cover too. Favorite songs: "Back in the Saddle," "Sick as a Dog," "Home Tonight"

No. 25. *Fragile*, Yes (1971) – What an amazing stretch of albums these guys had. Fantastic that this has four "group" songs and how the linking pieces expand the band's personality. This made prog as easy for me as bubblegum. Eventually. Favorite songs: "Roundabout," "South Side of the

Sky," "We Have Heaven"

No. 24. *Abbey Road,* The Beatles (1969) – What a testament, even as their professional relationship was in tatters. This contains Harrison's beautiful songs, Lennon's craziest dark ideas, and McCartney acts as the glue to tie it all together. Favorite songs: "I Want You (She's So Heavy)," "Come Together," "Here Comes the Sun"

***

No. 23. *This Year's Model,* Elvis Costello (1978) – The way he spits out the lyrics of "Radio Radio" was the sound in my head at the time. He said his songs were about "revenge and guilt." That was and remains wildly satisfying. Favorite songs: "Radio Radio," "Pump It Up," "This Year's Girl"

Saturday Night Live marked its 40th anniversary with a three-hour prime-time special.

I definitely watched the show more in its early years, when it was truly one of the few intelligent things on television aimed at my age group. To be honest, the earliest episodes were really targeted at people three or four years older than me. It took me some time to catch on.

But the show, nevertheless, was appointment viewing, and in those pre-VCR days, the most valuable skill I had was a keen ear and a capability of remembering lines. *Saturday Night Live, SCTV* and *Monty Python's Flying Circus* were new to all of us. Comedy ground was being seriously broken.

With *Saturday Night Live,* musical grounds were also being broken. Not only were we seeing some of these acts for the first time, we were also hearing some of them for the first time.

In the third season, The Sex Pistols were scheduled to appear as musical guests. In those times, when music was less a corporate concern than it became, the English punk bad boys (about whom we'd read much but only seen bits) were unable to secure visas in time for the show. Elvis Costello and The Attractions replaced them.

I returned home from a miserable date that Saturday evening earlier than I expected. I dejectedly slumped into my room in front of a 13-inch, 13-channel black-and-white television with rabbit ear antennae. I turned to NBC and heard Costello sing "Watching the Detectives." Costello was another performer about whom I'd read much, but heard nothing.

"Watching the Detectives" was interesting. But it was the second song that turned into one of my life-changing musical moments.

Costello started playing one song, then stopped and played another.

The other song was intense, accusatory, filled with blind rage. Much like I felt at the time. Through the TV's two-inch mono speaker, I couldn't make out many lyrics, but words stuck me like darts: "fools." "Muzak." "Radio radio." He wasn't singing about how much he loved his radio and how much good stuff was coming out of it.

It was electrifying.

And he was angry. I've told people since that part of my initial Costello fascination was he was so much angrier than I was. I grew to appreciate his depth as he showed it in the ensuing decade. I bought *My Aim is True* at the next opportunity, and grabbed every subsequent Costello album the instant it came out. The 20-song *Get Happy!!* appeared so quickly and had such a cheesy-looking cover, I assumed it was a bootleg of some sort. It wasn't.

If I made a list of my favorite Costello songs, "Radio Radio" would easily be in the top five. And the history the song and that *Saturday Night Live* performance left a mark with many more people than just me. (I really wish I'd had a chance to see "Weird Al" Yankovic have to break into "Radio Radio." He'd do so it concert anytime there were technical difficulties.)

And imagine how blown my mind was 10 months later, the first time I saw Devo.

***

No. 22. *Mistakes*, Gruppo Sportivo (1979) – An unbelievable concoction of perfect pop, as satirically seen through the eyes of a Dutch band with a delightfully warped sense of humor and satire. Favorite songs: "Blah Blah Magazines," "Beep Beep Love," "Disco Really Made It"

***

No. 21. *Who's Next,* The Who (1971) – More brilliance borne out of band troubles. Pete Townshend wrote even more amazing songs, and the synthesizer work was groundbreaking and standard-setting. Favorite songs: "Baba O'Riley," "Won't Get Fooled Again," "Behind Blue Eyes"

Here's to shining a light on some mysteries.

Consider The Beach Boys' *Smile.* The unreleased 1966-67 Brian Wilson effort that might have been majestically game-changing, but it being unfinished turned it to just mythical. But the album was updated and released by Wilson in 2004, so at least we have some kind of idea what he might have been thinking.

An even longer-lasting mystery is that of what was going on with Pete Townshend and The Who in the early 1970s, following the release of the rock opera *Tommy.*

Richie Unterberger's book *Won't Get Fooled Again* delves deep into the era. And while it doesn't give all the answers, and while it ends with a severe and disappointing anti-climax, fans have a better picture of what was going on at the time.

Let's step back in time. *Tommy* is released, moving the band forward by leaps and bounds artistically and commercially. Years of trudging across Europe and America as a support act on multi-show concert bills have built them a solid cult core following, and *Tommy* explodes them into headlining, and their starring role at Woodstock (the concert and the film) raises their profile even higher.

Songwriter Townshend is unquestionably at the peak of his talent. He is writing songs that will prove timeless, as meaningful 40 years down the line as they are when they're written. He's dropping throwaway lines into songs that could launch careers for other writers.

He's pioneering use of synthesizers in rock music. He's producing dozens of songs at his home studio, providing frameworks for Who classics. Many of these could be released in their own right (and eventually many of them will be). But the talents of the other members of The Who take the songs to an even higher plane.

And Townshend has a concept that's going to make the rock opera of *Tommy* look like a nursery rhyme.

Lifehouse was the original project Pete Townshend conceived. Many of its songs became the *Who's Next* album.

Lifehouse was to be a concert experience. It was to be filmed and released as a movie, and also an album. It was a concept piece.

This is as much as I've ever been able to figure out about what he was trying to do:

Using the then-nascent synthesizers, Townshend was literally turning *people* into music. He fed "vital statistics" (I assumed birthdate, eye color, height and weight) of Meher Baba (Townshend's "spiritual avatar") into a synthesizer, and what came out was the opening notes of "Baba O'Riley." Townshend theorized he could do this at a concert and feed the "vital statistics" of the audience into the synthesizer and create a song for and actually BY them.

Lifehouse was to be set in a future where people lived in hazmat suits and were tied into what Townshend called "The Grid." William Gibson be damned - Townshend visualized the Internet WAAAY before Gibson. The plot was to be driven by characters who wanted to live "outside The Grid." Those living outside are drawn somehow to a huge concert, and during the concert, the music builds to a fever pitch, and the audience disappears.

Roll credits.

I loved some of the thoughts in the lyrics Townshend wrote at the time:

"There once was a note pure and easy, playing so free like a breath rippling by ... the note is eternal, I hear it, it sees me, forever we blend and forever we die."

But he couldn't get the totality of his idea across. Maybe it was half-baked, or maybe he only had framework. Maybe they asked too much of the audience, maybe they didn't ask enough. Maybe it was business concerns. But it's become this whole *thing* that never was completed, even though its fragments include a ton of great songs and, in *Who's Next,* one of the 25 or 30 greatest albums ever made.

In some ways, the book confirms that. Unterberger details people complaining that what Townshend was saying didn't make any sense to them. The band members who trusted him on the troubling trek through the creation of *Tommy* seem to suddenly lose faith in what he was doing. And producer Glyn Johns is described as listening to Townshend describe the idea for 90 minutes and after that time saying, "I have no idea what you're talking about."

Townshend's *Lifehouse* concept may have been heady, especially for people uninterested in some of its more technical or science fiction concepts.

On the other hand, these guys managed to make sense of *Tommy,* which always seemed to me to have been much more convoluted that the concepts of *Lifehouse.*

An interesting theory that emerges in the book is the description of Townshend as the artist with no sense of constraint or reality. Some theorize that's why he really needed singer Roger Daltrey. Townshend would say, "This can change the world!" And Daltrey would say, "Why don't we start with Shepherd's Bush?" (referring to the band's London neighborhood).

Lifehouse eventually disintegrated, more in a slow fade (as is later the case with another effort detailed in the book) than a fast burn. Townshend said he suffered a nervous breakdown and pondered suicide. The band cherry-picked some of the better songs from the project, added bass player John Entwistle's "My Wife," and produced *Who's Next.* (Even *Who's Next,* as great as it is, had its own troubled birthing process, detailed well in the book along with the extra songs on the 2003 "deluxe edition" release of *Who's Next.)*

Townshend has never fully abandoned *Lifehouse.* As detailed in the book and in events since, every once in a while, he returns to it. Songs on 1978's *Who Are You* fit into the concept. Townshend released a box set, *The Lifehouse Chronicles,* in 2000, and in 2007 launched a website using the concept of turning people into music. None of these felt complete, either to Townshend or those interested in the project, but as technology expands, the possibility of the full realization of the project remains a possibility.

Townshend stepped back and internalized after *Lifehouse/Who's Next,* producing *Quadrophenia.* It's the only Who album for which Townshend wrote every song.

Unterberger spends an amount of time discussing how the very British concept of the album - focusing on a "Mod" named Jimmy - may have alienated the large American audience the band had developed.

But as an American kid who bought the album, I have to say that was never a problem for me. The package made it pretty clear what the album was about. Maybe I was aided by my understanding of the time period because of my passion for the music produced during it, and additionally by my treating Townshend's interviews accompanying the album's release as scripture. But the idea that *Quadrophenia* was high concept - higher concept than *Tommy* or *Lifehouse* - was and is confusing to me.

A THOUGHT OR TWO ABOUT *QUADROPHENIA*

Quadrophenia was released in 1973, when I was 14, and it may have been the first Who album I bought when it came out. (I vividly remember buying *The Who By Numbers* upon its release two years later. My mother told me, "If you want that album, you're going to have to buy it yourself.")

One of the great things about The Who's two major concept pieces was the packaging. You could get lost in the cover of *Tommy*. (I love the scene from *Almost Famous* that involves *Tommy*.)

Quadrophenia was a fantastic package as well, with a centerpiece of 42-page booklet illustrating the story. And it had a beautiful and iconic cover.

Here's the thing about the cover. (And consider these thoughts came from a 14-year-old.)

Today, I can look at it and not be sure whether it's a photograph, a line drawing, or a hybrid. But in 1973, I was certain it was a photograph. And I was astonished - ASTONISHED, I tell you - at how beautifully the four members of The Who lined up in the motorcycle's mirrors.

"What a tremendous amount of work," I thought, "must have gone into making sure those guys were standing in the exact right spots so their pictures could show up where they do."

Yeah. And if *Star Wars* had come out in 1973, I probably would have believed Wookies really existed.

THAT'S THAT.

Less confusing are the issues The Who had with performing the material. They needed to use tapes to reproduce the sounds the audience would expect. They declined to add any additional onstage players, sneering at The Rolling Stones adding a keyboard player and a horn section. (Of course, The Who got over this later.)

Playing to tracks was trickier in 1973 than it is today, and the band grew frustrated with tapes out of kilter and being cued at the wrong time and the limitations presented on improvisation as a result of their needed use.

They gradually pared *Quadrophenia* songs out of the set, and even though they eventually revisited the album and toured behind it 1996, they essentially ignored it for 20-plus years. (Although they played four cuts from it the one time I saw them - on the 1978 "Farewell Tour." The people with whom I went stopped paying attention after *Who's Next,* and as a result were asking me to place every post-1971 song the band played.)

Unterberger doesn't make the point, but it's difficult to avoid the conclusion: *Quadrophenia* and its lack of success - either as considered artistically by the band, or their perception of how the audience received it - was the point at which The Who became an arena rock band. From that point forward, they relied on the bombast of the *Who's Next* material (even as they had derided it in the months after its release), and they pulled back from challenging themselves and their audiences to that degree again.

Still, "Baba O'Riley" and "Won't Get Fooled Again" kind of kick ass, don't they?

***

No. 20. *Marshall Crenshaw* (1982) – New Wave music was a pleasant shower that washed away a lot of dreck and replaced it with stuff like this, melodic pop delivered sincerely. It's a treasure Favorite songs: "She Can't Dance," "Mary Anne," "Cynical Girl"

No. 19. *Animals*, Pink Floyd (1977) – It's almost comic that this release was sort of a forced afterthought after the tracks were left off *Wish You Were Here*. Their most brutally cynical and depressing album. Favorite songs: "Dogs," "Pigs," "Sheep (Three Different Ones)"

***

No. 18. *English Settlement,* XTC (1982) – They moved further into exotic rhythms and odd song subjects. It was their creative peak. The British double-album version was the one to have. Favorite songs: "Runaways," "Snowman," "No Thugs in Our House"

It seems many of the 1980s musical acts whose work amazed me weren't that different from those from the 1970s. They have at best five years of excellence. They might stay good, or make the occasional surprising comeback effort, but the true treasures of many of those acts I love had a stretch of five infallible years.

XTC is a British band which started as almost a prog-rock/New Wave hybrid, and grew into (I'll argue) New Wave's version of The Beatles, at least for a stretch.

That stretch would include *Skylarking* (1986), the brilliant love-and-death cycle concept album, which came from an unholy alliance between the band and producer Todd Rundgren; *Psonic Psunspot* (1987), a full album recorded as the band's alter-egos, The Dukes of Stratosphear; and my personal favorite, *English Settlement* (1982). (That evaluation applies to the original British 15-cut, two-album set, not the U.S. version which eviscerated five songs and turned it into a single disc.)

Skylarking is probably their most well-known and celebrated album on these shores, thanks to the inclusion of the atheist anthem "Dear God." That song wasn't on the original British release, which came out before the U.S. version. The original is actually a better album, with the concept holding together much better without "Dear God." But both versions are still superb albums.

And *Psonic Psunspot* is nearly the equal of both *Skylarking* and *English Settlement*. *English Settlement* is rich with melodies, thoughtful lyrics and an ongoing nod to reggae, ska, and rhythms non-traditional in classic Western pop. But *Psonic Psunspot* is almost a history of late 1960s popular music. (Much like The Beatles' *White Album* is essentially a history of popular Western music from the first 60-plus years of the 20th century.)

XTC masquerades as The Dukes of Stratosphear on *Psonic Psunspot*. The band created alter-egos for themselves (Sir John Johns, The Red Curtain, Lord Cornelius Plum and E.I.E.I. Owen) and created songs in the styles of The Byrds, The Hollies and The Beach Boys, and wrapped it with a kind of Small Faces' *Ogden's Nut Gone Flake*-style narration by a young girl. In the midst of XTC's serious work, it was fantastic to learn they had a sense of history, style and humor, and made me love them even more.

Following *Skylarking* proved to be as difficult for the band as progress seems to be for many artists who reach a peak of some sort. I kept listening, and liked at least one subsequent release enough to put it on my year-end list, but a peak was reached in the late 1980s. For a five-year stretch, though, they did little wrong, including close to an album's worth of non-LP cuts.

There's a depressing part of the story, though, one I've only come to learn recently. The band's lack of extreme chart success and the original contract it signed with a label meant they eventually got to the point where they were better off not releasing anything, because their releases put members deeper into financial holes. They seem to have emerged relatively safely now (finally), but they're not afraid to talk about where they were.

I assumed enough of the rest of the world was listening as intently as I was. I've come to realize recently that not only did these men whose success I longed to mirror in my own artistic life not live in huge houses and have all the material accoutrements I thought they did, the simple fact was I was living much more luxuriously.

That remains sobering and just a little depressing.

***

No. 17. *Every Picture Tells a Story,* Rod Stewart (1971) – I wore out (literally) three vinyl copies of this album. A beautiful combination of folk and rock, and Stewart sings like he means it for close to the last time. Favorite songs: "Every Picture Tells a Story," "Mandolin Wind," "Tomorrow Is a Long Time"

No. 16. *Machine Head*, Deep Purple (1972) – They completed their transition from a cover-infatuated heavy pop group to the prototype working British band. "Smoke on the Water" is a cliche now. It was revolutionary then. Favorite songs: "Highway Star," "Space Truckin'," "Never Before"

No. 15. *Everybody Knows This Is Nowhere*, Neil Young (1969) – Its lack of interest in what it was is part of its genius. There's a mournful violin, roaming harmonies, and a song whose guitar solo features the same note 38 times. If you didn't understand what was brilliant about that, you never could. Favorite songs: "Cowgirl in the Sand," "Cinnamon Girl," "Down By the River"

No. 14. *Odessey and Oracle,* The Zombies (1968) – An album that might as well have been dropped in from the 19th century. There's little here to identify its time, despite "Time of the Season" becoming an anthem. They chose the misspelling in the title. Favorite songs: "A Rose for Emily," "This Will Be Our Year," "Friends of Mine"

No. 13. *The Dark Side of the Moon,* Pink Floyd (1973) – Of all the popular rock bands, Pink Floyd's success baffles me most. This doesn't seem to be the kind of package that would engage millions of listeners. But it does, and because of that engagement, I'd guess the majority of people reading have heard the album, like it or not. Favorite songs: "Time," "The Great Gig in the Sky," "Us and Them"

No. 12. *The Wall,* Pink Floyd (1979) – Creator Roger Waters has evolved the piece from whiny rock star biography to the tale of a war-weary world. The pure opera style of repeated themes and the disparate pieces (especially on side three) show the effort in the construction. Favorite songs: "Comfortably Numb," "Nobody Home," "Another Brick in the Wall"

No. 11. *Led Zeppelin IV* (1971) – Many albums in the upper reaches have that one iconic song. Some of them are iconic because they can't not be. Each song here is iconic in a way equal to "Stairway to Heaven." Favorite songs: "When the Levee Breaks," "Rock and Roll," "Black Dog"

No. 10. *The Records,* The Records (1979) – My favorite sub-genre of music is power pop, and for years this was power pop's crowning achievement. To critics, these songs all sound the same. I can easily identify the differences between mixes on the American and U.K. editions. They're still both good. Favorite songs: "Starry Eyes," "All Messed Up and Ready," "Another Star"

No. 9. *Joe's Garage (Acts I, II and III),* Frank Zappa (1979) – It's not about the story, although it could be. "Act I" is solid, but by the time we get to "Act III," the songs are epic, complex, and constructed breathtakingly. Favorite songs: "Catholic Girls," "Packard Goose," "Watermelon in Easter Hay"

***

No. 8. *Get Happy!!,* Elvis Costello (1980) – After this plateau, he slowed down the breakneck speed of the music and the frequency of the releases. But this foray into soul and R&B showed there was more to the man than the New Wave efforts he'd presented. Favorite songs: "Love for Tender," "Clowntime Is Over," "Riot Act"

317

Elvis Costello saved rock music twice for me. Before I turned 21.

As was the case with a lot of music in my youth and young adulthood, I was aware of Costello before I actually heard his music. I wanted to write "long before," but I don't remember how long it was between reading about Costello and seeing him appear on *Saturday Night Live* on Dec. 17, 1977.

I was having a difficult time with the transition between high school and college. Most of my longtime friends had found their way to colleges and living away from home. I had no aspirations. I wanted to be a newspaper reporter, but the extent of pursuing it was just me wishing really really hard. I only ended up in college because one day at school, the student counselor (there was just one – it was a small school) asked me where I was going after graduation, and I shrugged.

"Didn't we get you accepted in college?"

Nope.

That's the way things worked in Dodge Center, Minnesota, in 1976.

I was living at home. It's the modern cliché – I was in my parents' basement. It didn't bother me a bit. I was barely 18, and didn't have many reasons or means to be anywhere else. But in retrospect, I think I was probably foundering.

I came home from a miserable date that evening of Dec. 17. I retreated in the dark of my house to my room, and flipped on the television. Do you want an even more cliched picture of the college freshman living in his parents' basement? This was pre-cable. It was a 13-inch black and white TV with rabbit ears. Volume was adjusted with a sliding knob.

Saturday Night Live by that time was a perfectly reasonable option to rescue a weekend night that had ended early or gone badly.
Then everything changed.

The video of Costello's stop-and-start performance of "Less Than Zero" into "Radio Radio" was only available to see again whenever NBC deigned to show it, if they ever did. Of course, we all realized that at the time. That's why the viewing experiences were so vital, and why my ability to lock down words and music was so invaluable (even though I wasn't always laser-accurate).

In the mythology of the moment as the years built on it and my story became more idealized than actual, time stopped and I stared at the screen in a trance as I saw a musical performance unlike any I'd ever seen on TV.

There's a part of my mind that thinks it actually saw *Saturday Night Live* producer Lorne Michaels stomping around and giving Costello the finger after the singer started "Less Than Zero," stopped, then went into a furious "Radio Radio." But I also know I only got that detail long after the fact.

So what I'm left with is the image of this skinny, pigeon-toed, bespectacled geek staring into the camera and spitting out lyrics like "the radio is in the hands of such a lot of fools" and I couldn't understand the rest but that was OK because I agreed 100 percent with the evaluation.

I thought, "Wow, this guy is even angrier than I am." Suddenly, I was interested in music I thought I could call my own. If this guy was angrier than me, maybe we had some other things in common.

As it happened -- and it took me years of experiencing Elvis Costello good, mediocre and indifferent -- we were at once far more similar and far more different than I could ever have imagined.

Two days later, I was at my new favorite record store – Headquarters, in Rochester, Minn. – buying Costello's *My Aim Is True* album.

Headquarters was a place that saw the transition in my musical taste and in my life. A few months earlier, I'd been there buying a copy of Lynyrd Skynyrd's *Street Survivors* with the original flames cover, and negotiating to purchase a used copy of an album by Felix Pappalardi and Creation. Hey, I was casting about. I never claimed any of the places I landed would be places I stayed, or even places that gave me reasons to stay.

That was also the place I bought what I guess the kids these days call a "smoker's stone." It's still around here someplace. Mine was white and had a ink drawing of Betty Boop on it.

Just a few months after buying *My Aim Is True,* I went back to Headquarters and picked up Costello's second album, *This Year's Model.* It seemed like he was putting out music at a record pace. Imagine how I felt in 1980, when he put out two 20-song albums in nine months time.

And around the same time, I bought Cheap Trick's *Heaven Tonight*, based on hearing "Surrender" played in the store. It always amazed me how susceptible I was to music played in a store while I was in a good mood and shopping for records.

My Aim is True had 13 songs at a time when I was accustomed to new albums housing six or eight songs tops. It didn't have a song longer than four minutes, and the one that grabbed my attention first, "Mystery Dance," ran under 100 seconds. But all 13 songs grew on me, and the 11 songs on *This Year's Model* did the same.

The intensity of my passion for Costello's music became either legend or joke among my peer group. As a gift for my fall 1981 wedding, a talented friend painted a recreation of the *This Year's Model* album cover.

But that was after the second time he saved rock music for me.

The night John Lennon was murdered is among the 10 worst days of my life. (I readily acknowledge that having that death high on a list of worst days really only means I haven't had that many really horrible days in my life.) That murder also occurred a few weeks after my father's death in a construction accident.

I felt overwhelmed and under way too much pressure to become an adult long before I wanted and long before I was capable.

I'd given up going to concerts a couple of years earlier. We sat and waited a half-hour for Player ("Baby Come Back") to open the show, and they played 40 minutes. Another half-hour, and Heart went onstage and performed for exactly 90 minutes. (The Met Center in Bloomington, Minn., left the digital clocks lit during concerts.) I thought if concerts were timed that tightly, I wasn't interested. I wanted to be surprised.)

I'd considered returning to concerts for Queen's 1980 tour, but they arrived in Minnesota shortly after my father's death, and I didn't feel very joyful. But Elvis Costello in a January 1981 show in a theater? This after every concert I'd attended previously was in an arena. I had friends who claimed to have connections. I was in. I was aware of Costello's prickly performance nature. The idea of the excitement of a live performance returned.

And this was after Costello's "Ray Charles incident." In what he later explained was a drunken effort to disengage himself from a conversation he'd been cornered into, Costello decided to refer to Charles and to James Brown in a fashion that was unacceptable in 1979, and is even more so now.

Something rang odd about the accusations of racism against Costello, and that was the album *Get Happy!!* (which came out after the scandalous incident). Costello and the Attractions were re-writing Motown and Stax, they lifted from Booker T. and The M.G.s, they covered Sam and Dave and The Merseybeats. I was in so early on *Get Happy!!* that my first copy did not have the designed "ring wear" that other editions have. When I got my first import copy of *Get Happy!!* (which I want to say was in the mail, but I'm not certain), I thought I'd been given a bad deal. If the cover looked like that, what was the vinyl going to be like?

Halfway through the first time I saw Coatello in concwet, after playing my anthem "Radio Radio," the lighting changed. Costello then led the band through an almost tentative version of "He's Got You," his regenderized reworking of Patsy Cline's "She's Got You." The audience was oddly quiet, and it amused me to think that I was probably one of the few people apart from those on stage who'd actually heard the original version. Whether I was or not.

He worked Stevie Wonder's "Master Blaster" into the middle of "Watching the Detectives." From that point forward, whether I was hearing it in person or via an audience recording of some sort, every time that breakdown came in the song, I was both thrilled and amused.

And I do remember "Help Me," the Sonny Boy Williamson song they covered. It became a personal favorite. While Costello never released a recorded version of it, I treasured the live recordings it popped up on and sang along regularly, mimicking Costello's inflection on the line "and when you talk, you talk to me."

That was the first of about a dozen Costello shows for me. Curiously, none of them rank among the best shows I've seen. They've all been good at the very least. There are memorable moments from most, specifically the moment on the *Punch the Clock* tour where he stomped off the stage to apparently yell at someone about the non-functionality of onstage monitors. But he never lashed in the audience's direction. All in all, I'd categorize every Costello performance as "charming."

And I'd also categorize every Elvis Costello album released on Columbia Records as must-listen. They're vital to my music mountain. And they saved rock music for me before I turned 21.

***

No. 7. *Squeezing Out Sparks,* Graham Parker (1979) – For a brief time, I thought everything I liked sounded like Elvis Costello, and it probably did. Parker's lyrics were never better, and his recordings never more urgent. Favorite songs: "Discovering Japan," "Local Girls," "Protection"

One of the best albums I've ever heard is Graham Parker's *Squeezing Out Sparks.* (If you go looking for a CD of the 1979 release, be sure to pick up the version that includes *Live Sparks,* which includes Parker's great, great live recording of the Jackson Five's ""I Want You Back."")

A few decades back, an Internet mailing list was discussing great lyrics. *Squeezing Out Sparks* contains many memorable lines, but my favorite came from "Protection," in which Parker sings:

"Your love letters are confetti
I ripped them up, my hands were steady"

Wow! What a magnificently bitter kiss-off to a paramour. In essence, he's saying he's so confident in his decision to end the relationship - or destroy what's left of it by throwing away love letters - that he didn't blink before doing it. It's the metaphorically obscene gesture every one of us has wanted to give (or had to receive) at least once.

Only that's not what he sang.

Once I posted my note, I was set upon by people on the mailing list who said I had the lyric wrong. Parker, they said, sang "my hands were *sweaty*," drastically changing my interpretation of the line.

I listened. To the CD. With headphones. OK, he probably *wasn't* singing "steady," but it sure sounds like it might be "schteaty," like he didn't really know what he wanted to sing.

I like my version better.

***

No. 6. *Katy Lied,* Steely Dan (1975) – Oh, the world of miscreants, degenerates and misanthropes to which Steely Dan introduced us to here. And you could sing along without realizing that, for example, you were singing a song about a Nazi rally. This didn't exactly hammer the Top 40. Favorite songs: "Rose Darling," "Chain Lightning," "Any World (That I'm Welcome To)"

No. 5. *Underwater Moonlight,* The Soft Boys (1980) – Robyn Hitchcock was a Syd Barrett acolyte who loved 1960s psychedelia. He and his band ran their offbeat songs through that filter, and came up with something altogether new. Favorite songs: "I Wanna Destroy You," "Insanely Jealous," "Underwater Moonlight"

No. 4. *Tonight's the Night*, Neil Young (1975) – A friend introducing me to Young's earlier work refused me access to this one, fearing my reaction. He was more frightened when the bleak songs, focusing on dying and death, were so much to my liking. Favorite songs: "Tonight's the Night," "New Mama," "Lookout Joe"

No. 3. *Blood on the Tracks,* Bob Dylan (1975) – Dylan says he doesn't understand people getting pleasure from his pain, as detailed on this divorce and departure album. It's not pleasure. It's more wallowing in the depression with him, and realizing there are opportunities to escape through to the other side. Favorite songs: "Simple Twist of Fate," "Idiot Wind," "Shelter from the Storm"

(2001)

A long time ago, before Michael Bolton started singing advertisements for beer, before Beatles songs were used to sell electronics equipment and when Bob Dylan was in his mid-30s, some FM radio stations made a huge point of playing albums in their entirety.

One far-reaching Minnesota station used to do six albums on a Friday night – "The Friday Six-Pack." The program started at midnight and was designed for taping. Many Fridays were spent shoveling blank Maxell audio tapes into my cassette deck so these albums could be added to my collection.

To this date, my recording of Pete Townshend's *Empty Glass,* taped a few days before its official release, remains a favorite and a great reminder of my generation's early version of Napster.

One night, a couple of years after its 1975 release, the station played Bob Dylan's *Blood on the Tracks* in full. Since Dylan had become largely irrelevant in my life – Led Zeppelin's first five albums came out in the early-'70s time it took Dylan to put out a couple of mediocre studio albums and a soundtrack – this was my first exposure to the total package.

Wow.

Song after song of broken hearts, disappointments, world-weariness - this was a gold mine. Especially for someone whose favorite Neil Young album was - and is - the terminally depressing *Tonight's the Night.* That album focuses on a pair of drug deaths. One was one overdose of which came shortly after Young sent guitar player Danny Whitten home on a plane with a bit of cash. Addict that he was, Whitten is believed to have bought the fatal dose with the cash Young gave him. Essentially, Young fired him and indirectly provided the fatal bullet.

Blood on the Tracks immediately moved into heavy rotation. Its humor and warmth became apparent on subsequent listens. "Idiot Wind" ("We are idiots, babe, it's a wonder we can even feed ourselves") starts out with one of Dylan's best jokes. He shoots a man, marries his wife, she inherits her husband's million dollars.

"And when she died it came to me. I can't help it if I'm lucky."

Yes, he originated it, and Hootie and The Blowfish had to pay him after they stole it. Maybe Dylan even predicted that in an earlier version of the song. He sang in complaint about the "imitators (who) steal me blind."

"You're Gonna Make Me Lonesome When You Go" is an upbeat song about an offbeat topic - an anticipated breakup. "Lily, Rosemary and the Jack of Hearts" is a movie condensed to nine minutes.

So much of the album is simply Dylan, his guitar, his voice and a handful of slight garnishes that the words leap out. And what words! If lyrics are at all important in your consideration of music, Dylan has always offered thousands. The 10 songs on *Blood on the Tracks* provide some of his most potent.

At the time *Blood on the Tracks* was filling my ears on a regular basis, my college roommate was singing the praises of Rush. Their progressive rock was always too busy for these ears, and Geddy Lee's vocals were as grating to me as Bob Dylan's are to others. It's impossible to deny Rush's musical skills, they just weren't very appealing.

For my roommate, meanwhile, Rush's *Permanent Waves* album was a masterpiece. It sounded to me like a rip-off of the Police, and "The Spirit of Radio" haunted my sleep. His mood turned as foul during Dylan as mine did during Rush.

After a couple of weeks, we reached a truce. The Rush album was hidden, except in my absence. The *Blood on the Tracks* eight-track (yes! which tells you how old this story is) remained threateningly dangling in the deck but was ejected whenever my roommate appeared.

Flash-forward 20 years. We stayed in touch, and an annual visit was paid to that college roommate. His music collection was and is wildly eclectic, and it's always fun to see what recent surprises have been added.

While idly thumbing through his CDs, my fingers stopped on one disc, and a smile came across my lips.

Dylan. *Blood on the Tracks.*

My roommate listened. He learned.

There are no Rush CDs in my collection.

***

No. 2. *World So Bright*, Adam Schmitt (1991) – The songs were up-tempo, the guitars rung and rocked, and the lyrics were deceptively deep. The best power pop album ever made. Favorite songs: "Can't Get You on My Mind," "My Killer," "Elizabeth Einstein"

No. 1. *The Beatles (The White Album)*, The Beatles (1968) – For years, I have said this is the most significant artistic achievement of my lifetime, and possibly the most significant of the 20th century. Favorite songs: "Dear Prudence," "Helter Skelter," "Cry Baby Cry"

APPENDIX

ROBYN HITCHCOCK

I thought I might help newcomers through the best of what this eccentric psychedelic pop folk master has to offer. This list includes albums Hitchcock recorded with his first band, The Soft Boys. Those albums are marked with an asterisk (*).

15. *Tromsø, Kaptein,* 2011

14. *Eye,* 1990

13. *Invisible Hitchcock (Outtakes and rarities, 1980–1986),* 1986

12. *Gotta Let This Hen Out!,* 1985 (with the Egyptians)

11. **Invisible Hits,* 1983
Three of these are compilations, the others kind of quiet acoustic works. Only *Eye* really holds together as a solid album front-to-back, even though *Gotta Let This Hen Out!* wants to pretend it's a live show from the band. It's also includes the best song from these five albums, "Listening to the Higsons."

10. **A Can of Bees,* 1979
The first long-player with which Hitchcock was involved. "Human Music" was done better on a later release (listed below), but it's still a standout track here.

9. **Two Halves for the Price of One,* 1981 (Studio rarities and live tracks)
A Soft Boys compilation, notable for a couple of breathtaking live tracks, a version of "Underwater Moonlight" (see more below) and the definitive version of "Only the Stones Remain," the coolest Stonehenge song ever written.

8. *Love From London,* 2013
Hitchcock produces a wonderful blend of his eccentric lyric and instrument choices with some heartwarming folk and pop. This is a perfect album for a

60-year-old to have made in 2013.

7. *Groovy Decay*, 1982
Hitchcock comes into his own with his weirdness, stretching out to create a world where travel and rain mean as much as footwear meant to an early Bob Dylan. "Fifty Two Stations" is a distinct songwriting style.

6. *Queen Elvis*, 1989 (with the Egyptians)
In a song about love ("Freeze"), Hitchcock sings: "I know who wrote the book of love. It was an idiot. It was a fool. A slobbering fool with a speech defect and a shakin' hand." You have to love that. In another piece, the beautifully abstract "One Long Pair of Eyes," features my favorite Hitchcock couplet ever: "She falls on you like rain/When will she fall again?"

5. *Element of Light,* 1986 (with the Egyptians)
"Somewhere Apart" is his most comically John Lennon-esque track, and "Raymond Chandler Evening" is a ballad that creates a film in your head. It's an album that feels as though it's living in a minor key.

4. **Live at the Portland Arms* (cassette, 1983; LP, 1988)
One of the most anarchic live albums ever, it was years before we vinyl-starved Yanks could hear the album. The performance is largely unplugged (with a beautiful "Human Music" at its center). Hitchcock's lyrical crushing of "That's When Your Heartaches Begin" (including a spoken interlude that could compete with Elvis Presley at his Vegas weirdest) and "All Shook Up" are priceless and memorable.

3. *Fegmania!*, 1985 (with the Egyptians)
Probably the most oddly pop album of all of Hitchcock's efforts. It has pretty and lyrically odd pieces like "Egyptian Cream" and "Strawberry Mind," as well as the Hitchcock song title that most makes people look askance: "My Wife and My Dead Wife." And yes, that's exactly what the song is about.

2. *I Often Dream of Trains,* 1984
That this album – one of the most beautiful acoustic packages to come out of the 1980s – is only second on this list is a huge tribute to Hitchcock's

skills. A couple of instrumentals, a couple of strange but fitting a capella pieces, and an album that sounds as though it could have been recorded in the Middle Ages.

1. *Underwater Moonlight,* 1980
Not just Hitchcock's best album but one of the greatest albums ever released. (It is right now No. 5 on my list of all-time favorite albums.) A loud, raw album the exploits the energy and volume of punk, but the melodicism of New Wave. The title cut, "Insanely Jealous" and "I Wanna Destroy You" are all worth the price of admission.

THANK YOU

There likely should be hundreds if not thousands of people I list here. As people who are bad at writing these parts always say, if I've left you out, it's likely more an oversight than a snub.

The Lovely Mrs. Cain has tolerated this for decades. She's listened to a lot of the songs and a lot of the thoughts. She's the person who convinces me that I'm fascinating.

Michelle Stephens and Jim Thielman, who have done this book thing many times. I stand in awe of their skills and in appreciation of their counsel.

Greg Gilman and Tom Weber, my musical brothers who have traveled many of these roads with me.

My mother, my sister, and their family. I have two goddaughters who, as a gift for me, created and choreographed a presentation of "Yellow Submarine." I wasn't crying. You were crying.

My high school friends, who have always encouraged me more than they realize.

The whole Illinois crew: Amy, Shelby, Andy, Stacy, the other Amy, Mike, Todd, Mark, Scott, Erin, Allison, Allyson, Amanda, Stephanie, Ralf, Shelby, Doug, Austin, Jim, Hugh, Justin and Coco. (I expect this is where I have forgotten someone.)

To anyone who has ever given me the gift of music.

And to the musicians who make it all possible, Some have been more than generous with their personal time, and I have been honored to spend time with them: Mike Jarvis, Brian Curtis, Frank Huston, Brian Cutright, Brad Elvis, Chloe Orwell, Barbara Bailey Hutchison, Julie Rust, Jill Sobule and way too many more.

ABOUT THE AUTHOR

Tim Cain's life changed from black-and-white to color about the same time The Beatles changed his life, when he was about 5. He started getting paid to write at age 13, and has been employed at daily newspapers since 1978. He lives in Illinois with his wife, their cats and thousands of pieces of vinyl and aluminum and billions of bytes of music.

Made in the USA
Monee, IL
05 May 2020